D1587846

CHANGING TIMES
Ireland since 1898

Irish Eclogues (1915)

Sir Horace Plunkett and his place in the Irish Nation (1916)

Self-Government and Business Interests (1918)

The Gael (1919, reprinted 1920, 1929, 1939)

Irish Eclogues and Relationships (1922)

Cúrsai Thomáis: shíos seal a's shuas seal (1927)

Short Study of a Transplanted Family (1935)

Toil Dé (1936)

Irish Life in the Seventeenth Century: after Cromwell (1939, revised and enlarged 1950, reprinted 1969)

An Aifric Theas (1947)

Irish Families, their names, arms and origins (1957, revised 1972)

More Irish Families (1960)

Supplement to Irish Families (1964)

The Surnames of Ireland (1969, revised and enlarged in 1973 and 1978)

'Forth the Banners Go' reminiscences of William O'Brien as told to Edward MacLysaght (1969)

S. R. Lysaght. The Author and the Man (1974)

Leathanaigh óm' Dhialann (1978)

Edited for the Irish Manuscripts Commission

Calendar of the Orrery Papers (1941)

The Kenmare Manuscripts (1942)

CHANGING TIMES
Ireland since 1898

as seen by
Edward MacLysaght

COLIN SMYTHE
Gerrards Cross 1978

Copyright © 1978 Colin Smythe Ltd.

First published in 1978 by Colin Smythe Ltd.
Gerrards Cross, Bucks. SL9 7AE

Distributed in N. America by Humanities Press Inc.
171 First Avenue, Atlantic Highlands, N.J. 07716

ISBN 0-901072-88-5

British Library Cataloguing in Publication Data

MacLysaght, Edward
    Changing times.
    1. Ireland — History — 20th century
    I. Title
    941.5082′092′4   DA959

    ISBN 0–901072–88–5

Printed in Great Britain
Set by Watford Typesetters Ltd., and
printed and bound by Billing & Sons Ltd.
Guildford, Worcester and London

Contents

CHAPTER I

Background

This book is not intended to be an autobiography in the ordinary
sense of the word but rather an autobiographical commentary, as
exemplified by my own varied experiences, on the Ireland I have
known during one of the most interesting and eventful periods in
our history.

I must explain that I have kept a diary (if I can so describe
entries seldom made daily and often at quite long intervals)
since I left school. At first I thought of making this book consist
mainly of extracts from the diaries with some necessary explanatory interpolations. Two considerations caused me to abandon
that plan. One is that many of the entries are in Irish – nearly
all of those from 1919 to 1930. The second is that diary entries
tend to be scrappy and incomplete when dealing with events or
people who occur frequently, so these would have to be combined
and to some extent re-written. A straightforward narrative with
selections from the diaries at appropriate places seems to be the
best method to adopt.

I have divided the book into three parts which I can fairly
aptly label as Rural, Political and Academic.

The rural part, filled as it is with episodes of my youth, with
farming and everyday life west of the Shannon in those far off
Edwardian days, is the part I have most enjoyed writing. It is of
less general interest than the other sections, but I think that, as
well as showing the background of the narrator, which in a
book of this kind is almost essential, it does help to give a
picture of the Ireland of that time. To most people of today
that must seem to be almost a different world, untroubled by
major wars or inflation, and with motor traffic, television, central
heating, social services and all the rest of the modern world still
to come; as different from the present day as it was itself from
the eighteenth – I might even say the seventeenth – century.

As I have said the background of the narrator is essential and
in my case I think it can best be shown by giving some account
of my father.

The liveliest of my boyhood memories is of him. If I were asked what is the most vivid recollection I have of him it would be of him sitting at the piano playing Irish airs; my earliest childhood memory of him is just that and my last before his final departure is the same. I can hear him playing my favourite 'Cailín deas crúidte na mbó' and then the whole family of us singing 'Cockles and Mussels' as if it were yesterday, not nearly forty years ago that silence fell on that cherished custom.

His outlook on religious matters also had a lasting effect on me. Though he was agnostic for most of his life – he died a Catholic – from the worldly standpoint his attitude was pro-Catholic. He would sometimes talk about religion in the sense in which the word is ordinarily used. I remember when I was about fifteen years old we were talking together one night and he reminded me of the traditional Catholic background of our family and how it had only become Protestant as the result of a mixed marriage after the Penal Laws had expired. 'So,' he said, 'you can be a Catholic or a Protestant, whichever you wish: I rather hope you will be a Papist like our forebears.' I had no hesitation in accepting his and my mother's advice.

Though family history can be boring to people not closely concerned I must briefly explain this remark of his. Our family (in Irish Mac Giolla Iasachta, whence MacGillysacht, MacLysaght and Lysaght) is an offshoot of the O'Briens of Thomond (Co. Clare) where near Kilfenora they lived till in the late sixteenth century our ancestor moved to Limerick. His descendant married the heiress of a landed family in that county only to be dispossessed a few years later under the Cromwellian régime and transplanted as an Irish Papist. Though transplantees from Co. Limerick were ordered to be resettled in Co. Galway, with definite instructions that it should not be Co. Clare, this William MacLysaght had in fact to go no further than east Clare and got a good farm at Ballymarkahan near Quin. His son, however, wasted his substance in gambling and foolishness and was reduced to penury. He evidently turned over a new leaf for he got a job as estate manager to a Protestant relative in Co. Cork. Our branch was thus established near Mallow in the parish of Doneraile in mid-eighteenth century and in due course became what were called 'gentleman farmers' and as such ranked as minor gentry. My father was the son of a younger son, one Thomas Lysaght a brilliant but feckless Cork architect, and so could not expect to inherit his uncle William's place (Hazelwood) where he was reared and where his heart was. He thus became one of the countless Irish emigrants of the nineteenth century, but one who never lost touch with his own country.

Soon after the turn of the century he found himself in a position to return permanently to Ireland and he bought Raheen, our present home in Co. Clare, which is not far from where the family lived before migrating to County Cork. Some ten years later, old William died; his eldest son was by then an American citizen having no desire to return to Ireland and by a family arrangement, S. R. Lysaght, my father, got possession of Hazelwood, where he lived till he died there in 1941.

Notwithstanding the close association with County Clare, he always regarded himself as a Corkman, or, more particularly, a Doneraile man. He was a friend of Canon P. A. Sheehan, who was parish priest there, so much so that when he died in 1913 his brother presented S.R. with a manuscript commonplace-book compiled by the canon, remarking that no one had a better right to it than S. R. Lysaght. That book is in this room as I write.

I have heard him described not inaptly as a dual personality. The one best known to his friends and neighbours was an old-style country gentleman in cap and Norfolk jacket and knickerbockers, fond of a day's rough shooting, or overseeing the building of walls and outhouses (he often said he 'must have been bitten by a mad mason'), keen on golf, too, (he was, in my young days, captain of Lahinch Golf Club).

That however is a one-sided picture, as it ignores his practical patriotism. I will have occasion later on to mention some of his plans for the promotion of the economic and social life of the community in our part of Co. Clare.

The other S.R. entity was a poet and novelist. His literary output was small, a mere nine books in the forty-three years between 1893 and 1936. His poetry enjoyed a *succès d'estime* but he was best known for his last two novels, *Her Majesty's Rebels* and *My Tower in Desmond*, both mainly based on the impact on his characters of the politics of the period – Parnell and 1916.

To some extent the central figure in *My Tower in Desmond*, Nick Quin, is autobiographical. As one reads one visualizes S.R. himself. He was known by everyone locally as 'S.R.' The R stands for Royse, the name of his Co. Limerick grandmother. He was given the Christian name of Sidney which was quite out of line with family usage, William, Patrick and Edward being the traditional names. In passing I should mention his attitude to my action*, in company with ten other families of Lysaght, in

*This was initiated by William MacLysaght of Doon, Co. Limerick.

resuming the prefix Mac, discarded like so many other O's and Mac's, in the period of Gaelic submergence. He approved of this but felt that because he had made his name as Lysaght so it should remain. My mother, however, did use the Mac on suitable occasions.

My mother would not have been described as a beautiful young woman but her face had a charm of expression which I think must have made it more attractive than mere perfection of feature. I was fond of her, but perhaps my principal feeling for her was one of admiration. She had two main characteristics which do not always go together, saintliness and determination. As for the first I doubt if she ever committed a serious sin in her long life (she was a hale woman except for her sight when she died in Cork at the age of ninety-two). For the second, learning Irish, as she did in order to be able to join the rest of us in speaking Irish only to her grandchildren, required determination. She showed this quality even more in her constant part in the resistance to the Auxiliaries and Black & Tans: more about this at the appropriate place. Yet in a sense she was not technically Irish, that is to say her ancestors (Clarke and Moore of Laois) had been in England a long time. As often happens in such cases the Irish blood in her must have come to the surface.

My father had attained a good position in the export side of a steel works in Wales which his uncle John (another emigrant from Hazelwood) had founded and his work as overseas salesman frequently took him to South Africa, Australia, South America and other far off places causing him to spend months of each year abroad. My mother often accompanied him so that I had no place which I could regard as a permanent home. In the first twelve years of my life we moved house no less than five times. My father was able to arrange that his long absences abroad did not occur during the summer and from 1899 the family regularly spent the long school summer holidays at Lahinch, where in due course I felt I could call myself a resident rather than a visitor. I will revert to this later. My shorter Christmas and Easter holidays were often spent with relatives or friends in Ireland, though only occasionally at Hazelwood. Of these the one I remember most vividly and liked best was Roxborough near Limerick.

Apropos of Roxborough my first attempt, at the age of sixteen, to keep a diary was a failure as, apart from some jottings, the following entry was the only one for that year. I regret that it does not present a picture of a nineteenth century

10

country house and surroundings or of the people 'upstairs and downstairs' who inhabited it, yet even as it is it may help to convey the atmosphere of that time.

Jan. 2, 1904.

I got this diary as a Christmas present from Aunt Eleanor, as I call Tom's aunt (Lady Shaw). I hadn't time to start it yesterday (New Year's Day) so I'm beginning now. I suppose I should note down where I am, etc. Well, I'm at Roxborough staying with the Shaws (Dad and Mother being in Australia) for the long Christmas holidays – nearly six weeks, unusually long for some reason this year. It's a big house about four miles south of Limerick. Why here? For three reasons I'd say 1/ The Shaws are friends of ours; 2/ Tom [Gubbins] and I are school pals as well as Lahinch ones – he lives here; and 3/ Dad's rule says it must be in Ireland (good rule). I was here last year too.

Lady Shaw, if you please. Yes, she's a good old Co. Limerick Gubbins, but Sir Alec is only a 'bacon' knight.

Not much to report today. Got soaked wet 'navigating' the raft we've made for the stream, water not so cold for this time of year. Had an interesting talk with Eric S. mainly about John Redmond – Eric is more of a Home Ruler than the rest of the family. That's all for tonight, it's more than bedtime. PS or afterthought: I'm rather keen on Cecil even though she's nearly two years older than me. Cecil: what a ghastly name for a girl.

The date of my birth is of no importance, but as it has appeared in some publications, such as *Who's Who*, as 1889 perhaps I should correct that. It was 1887, as stated in some more recent books of reference. The day, November 6th, is the best day an Irishman could wish for: it is the Feast of all the Saints of Ireland, as distinct from All Saints a few days earlier. The only birth certificate I could produce when taking out insurance or joining the staff of the National Library was an affidavit sworn by my mother stating that no certificate was available: birth at sea somewhere in the Indian Ocean was the reason given. In such cases a person's official nationality is presumably that of his father. I would like to have been born in my own country. Many good Irishmen were not: James Connolly in Scotland, Clarke and Davitt in England, de Valera in America – I could list dozens. Horace Plunkett used to say that being born in England was his 'first mistake'. Similarly Lord Kitchener was not an Irishman because he happened to be born in Co. Kerry when his father was stationed there as a soldier. Since the practice of going to hospital for childbirth has become widespread actual birthplace means little. Take my five grandchildren who have lived continuously at their home in Co. Clare all their lives: some of them were born in Limerick, some in Dublin, but that doesn't make the latter Dubliners.

Apart from my father and mother I have few memories of my childhood as distinct from boyhood; my first recollection in life is the waves of the Atlantic seen at the age of four from a seat on the deck of the old Cork packet seamer – I think she was called 'Juno' but possibly it was 'Argo'. I do clearly remember learning to swim on a holiday in Co. Donegal when I was ten years old, perhaps because the method adopted by my instructors (two young business men from Belfast), after I had got to the point of swimming a few strokes, was to drop me in deep water at the end of the pier at Port Salon and then dive in after me.

It is sometimes difficult to be sure whether one's childhood 'recollections' are actually things remembered or just imaginative reconstructions of incidents related by one's parents. For instance my recollections include an occasion when we were travelling to Lahinch on the old West Clare Railway. I think it was about the year 1899. The engine broke down and left us stationary on the steep incline near Corofin. Now my father often said that Percy French was a passenger on that very train and that he wrote his famous song 'Are you right there, Michael, are you right' as a result. That incident would surely have faded from my mind had not my father afterwards told us about Percy French.

At the age of fourteen I was sent to school at Rugby. I have no recollections of any interest of that school beyond the fact that Rupert Brooke, an athletic Adonis, later well known as a poet, was head of my house, which meant a very unusual state of affairs because his rather ridiculous pot-bellied old father, bawdily nicknamed 'the tooler', was the housemaster; but I do not remember that the troubles latent in such a situation ever occurred. The boys, whose rigid conventions I was inclined to flout, seem to have tolerated me as a 'mad Irishman'. Going to school in England may have an anglicizing effect on Irish boys with a Unionist background, but it certainly tends to strengthen the Nationalist outlook of those who, like myself, were brought up to think of themselves as Irish, not 'West Britons'.

Background

At the time I left school the National University, where at University College Cork I finally took my degree, was barely established. I was anxious to go to Trinity, so my father consulted a great friend of his, whose advice he thought should be followed. This was Professor Francis Ysodor Edgeworth of the famous Edgeworthstown family. He was a 'character' who became something of a legend in his lifetime. I remember him when I was a boy as a friendly old gentleman with a beard and a quaint way of speaking. When my father asked Edgeworth's advice – he was a graduate of Trinity College Dublin but became an Oxford don – he said in his drawling voice: 'Don't send Ned to Trinity, my dear man'. And when my father asked him why he replied 'Vice stalks the streets in Dublin'. I knew nothing about Dublin at that time but there is no doubt that his advice was ill-considered if not ridiculous. When as a consequence I went to Corpus Christi College, Oxford, he did not fail to ask his friend's son to dinner at his college – All Souls – but the invitation was not repeated for on that occasion I drank too much of the famous All Souls strong ale and treated the assembled greybeards to a dogmatic disquisition on Irish nationalism. His relatives, anxious not to see the distinguished family of Edgeworth die out, did their best to get F.Y.E. to marry and even succeeded in getting him engaged for a while: if my father were alive he could enliven this page by recalling some of the professor's delightful comments on the embarrassments of being alone with his fiancée and the difficulties of finding an honourable way out of the frightening prospect of marriage, from which I need hardly add he escaped in due course.

I was at Oxford for only two terms. I did no good there and left the place abruptly in a disreputable atmosphere of whiskey and horses.

I have a diary entry which shows how I dealt with the situation in the absence of my father – by going to work on a farm. I will quote it later on; but before I come to my life on the land I am tempted to devote a few pages to what was possibly the happiest and certainly the most carefree time of my life – the three summers I spent in Co. Clare living in a converted ambulance wagon near O'Brien's Bridge in a quiet hollow of the sandhills between Liscannor and Lahinch. (This O'Brien's Bridge in north Clare is not to be confused with the village of that name on the other side of the county). The first two summers I was still a senior schoolboy, the next I was a first year University student, absent from college the whole summer following an operation for hernia which I had in April of that year.

It is a wild coastline that of north Clare. It is to me the most fascinating part of Ireland, perhaps because it is the 'cradle of my race'. Standing on the sandhill above my shack I could see to the west beyond the point of Liscannor, with its old square tower silhouetted against the red glow of the sunset, the breakers foaming on the 'undiscovered shore' of the legendary island of Cillstifiann. Near at hand, the wide mouth of the river cleaved its way between the sand-dunes meeting the Atlantic in the bay. Behind me a strange almost barren-looking landscape rising beyond the marsh through which the two rivers – Inagh and Lickeen – run to their union at the old O'Connor castle of Duagh, away to low treeless hills; yet not barren, as the white walls of the dotted homesteads shining in the evening sun or the multitude of twinkling lights at Samhain could show. And Duagh Castle itself, man's work, is here more striking than nature. What builders they were in the days when Ireland is alleged to have been less than half civilized. This old block – and Clare, and indeed Ireland, is full of castles, towers and abbeys like it – is built almost as if of one piece. Wars swept away three of the four walls. The other remains standing at its full height defying the Atlantic storms, indifferent to the disintegrating tendency of the centuries. Five storeys are there, each with its naked window, scarce buttressed by any piece of the other walls. And where these have fallen they still remain, enormous blocks of masonry not breaking to pieces into individual stones but like great granite boulders, their mortar harder than the rock itself.

(Lahinch)
8 July, 1907.

I have made great friends with an old man named Andrew Lysaght, who lives at Kilshanny near Kilfenora, not far from here. I have only been to his house a couple of times but he often comes to see me and spends hours telling me story after story about the people of west – or rather north-west – Clare, and particularly about the Lysaghts who numbered among them the notorious 'Seoirse an Óir' and of course the only member of the family who ever attained any real fame, Edward Lysaght ('Pleasant Ned', who, by the way, I was named after): he was bi-lingual like almost all Claremen of his time (Andrew says he was born in 1782) and one of his best known poems

14

'Garnavilla' was first written in Irish. Andrew says our name is given as Macgillysaght (if I've got the spelling right) on an old map and that we should be MacLysaght not Lysaght.

There are still some families of Lysaght and MacLysaght living in the baronies of Burren and Corcomroe but I regret to say that the name has now become quite rare in the area which is its original homeland; but as recently as 1855 there were 42 families of the name living in west Clare, 31 of them in Corcomroe. The way a numerous family can die out is exemplified by the Kilfenora MacLysaghts. A generation ago there were no less than six young boys in the home. Patrick the eldest in due course inherited the farm. He married and their first-born was a girl. Some mishap in that birth resulted in his wife being unable to have any more children, so in due course the place fell into the hands of people who did not bear the surname Lysaght. The other boys had all emigrated. One time, fifty or more years ago, when my father chanced to be staying in a New York hotel he noticed that the lift-man spoke with an Irish accent and he asked him where he came from. 'County Clare', was the answer, and, on being asked his name he turned out to be one of those emigrant brothers. There is little chance of the likes of him returning to Ireland.

I have to confess that I actually do not know whether Andrew was a fluent native speaker of Irish or not. He must surely have known Irish for it was still the native language of much of that part of north Clare. Clare Irish had been badly neglected, though something was done to revive it by the college at Carrigaholt, soon after the time of which I am writing, and an Irish-speaking priest was sent to Liscannor, which is in the diocese of Kilfenora, attached to that of Galway whose Bishop – Dr O'Dea – was sympathetic to the language movement. A parish priest could give new dignity to the despised native language of the people by using it from the altar. At that time, apart from Latin, English was the language of the Church as much as of the State and in west Clare no value was then set on Irish. It was regarded as a mark of social inferiority spoken only by the fisherfolk and the very poor. I heard it, of course, frequently and while I absorbed it unconsciously I never dreamed in those days of making a serious study of it, any more than I studied the cries of the various sea birds that frequent the estuary.

My home, as I used to call my shack, lay at the far end of the famous Lahinch golf links. I learned the game there in my early teens but, though I was fairly good at it, I did not play golf regularly when I was living there. Every year in September the South of Ireland championship is held at Lahinch. A later entry in my diary recalls an amusing incident in this connexion which I quote here.

12 September, 1909

The English upper classes are supposed to be very conventional. Everyone knows the old joke about pukka sahibs dressing for dinner when camping in the central African jungle. I came across one of this type in amusing circumstances the other day at Lahinch. Like all locals with a reasonably low handicap – mine is now 5 – I entered for the South of Ireland championship. Dad and Mother and Pat were staying at the Golf Links Hotel and I joined them there. The night before the championship began I was going along the corridor (wearing dinner jacket and boiled shirt like everyone else) when a voice called out – 'Waitah, bring me two w'iskeys and sodahs'. As there was no one else there except the man the voice was talking to, I twigged at once that it was addressing me, so said in a good Clare accent: 'To be sure I will, sir. Is it Irish or Scotch ye'll have?' Off I went to the bar and returned with the glasses, etc., on a tray. He paid and tipped me 3d. (I must keep the threepenny bit as a memento). Well next morning being scheduled to play a Major So & So of some Londonish club at 10.5 I turned up at the first tee to see in my opponent the very man who had tipped me the night before. I thought he did not recognize me as he was affable enough though stiff; but having walloped me in the match by 5 and 4 and stood me a drink according to custom (the winner pays) he joined a friend and in a voice he probably did not mean to be audible to me he remarked: 'This is a damn queer countrah, wat, waitahs play goff heah.'

Before passing from my care-free days I will add a short diary entry, written fifty years after the event, recalling an incident well suited to a book entitled *Changing Times*.

23 October, 1955

Pat and Mamie both had teeth extracted yesterday morning and were in poor shape when I came back, but thank God both are better now. How times are changed. I could hardly face now what as a boy of fifteen I cheerfully – resignedly

would be a better word – accepted, e.g. the time I went to
Limerick and the dentist, Mr Coogan, pulled out a bad tooth
without giving me gas or cocaine or palliative of any kind.
How well I remember that day. On the way back I had of
course to change at Ennis. For some reason it so happened
that both the G.S.W.R. and the West Clare trains moved off
at almost the same moment, ours just ahead, with the result
that there ensued what we pretended was a race side by side,
until our narrow gauge train branched off at Cushnahowna. All
the young people in both trains leaned out of the windows
cheering and urging on our respective engine-drivers, mar
dheadh. It was a cold day and I got a blast in my lacerated
jaw and had to lie up for a couple of days afterwards. . . .

But enough of my carefree days in west Clare: Back to the diary
entry by that disgraced undergraduate.

Tunley [Somerset]
21 June, 1908
  I wonder will Dad be mad with me when he comes back
from Australia. Of course he knows already that I left Oxford
three months ago without adding any lustre to the laurels of
Corpus [Christi College] but he doesn't know yet that I am
working for a farmer under the name of Jim Hogan – not that
he need know that part any way. I really don't know myself
why I'm not sailing under my own colours at present.
  I'm a long time without making any entry in this diary (so
called): this is the first since I came to work for old Mr
Gibbons here at Tunley; and if this afternoon wasn't wet and
a Sunday I suppose I wouldn't be doing it now. I may as well
give some account of myself or rather of life here.
  As an apprentice I don't get proper wages but I get plenty
to eat of good food (unlike Albert, the permanent hand who
sleeps out in a loft, I have my meals with the family), the only
thing I don't like about that is their habit of having a regular
solid meal every night before going to bed but I don't take
much of that. We make cheese here and eat a lot of it –
Cheddar cheese. Sometimes I have to help in the dairy but
not often. I get up every morning before six; Albert has the
cows in by six when we start milking. He milks eight, I do
six and young Collins about eight more. Collins takes the milk
into Bath. A regular quantity is sold in the town every day
and all the surplus in the summer is made into cheese. Bert

Collins can't work in the coal mine for some reason, dizzy head or something. His wage is 12s. a week. Everyone works in coalmines here and farming is only a secondary employment. There are two coal mines, one of which – the shaft I mean – is actually on this farm. Albert is *sui generis* (I put that in to show that I haven't forgotten all my Latin). He sleeps in a loft over the stables and as far as I can see has only one shirt. When he washes it I think he stays in bed on a fine Sunday afternoon while it dries. He does all the regular work around the yard, with my help. Apart from milking the real day's work begins at 2 o'clock when the shift of miners who come up at 1 o'clock have finished dinner. Then lots of them come to us. That's how we save the hay for instance. I find it easy enough to work hard for Mr Gibbons at saving hay, but at jobs like picking stones off a meadow, which we had to do with a láte clover field, I'm not so energetic. We're right into haymaking now and up to today the weather has been good for that. Albert and I and Mr Gibbons get everything ready before dinner like raking the hay into rows, so that when the mining chaps come along we can get straight to work 'ricking' it. It's so different from Ireland. The hay goes straight into mows, as they call the ricks here; no wynds or trams. If that was done in Co. Cork or Co. Clare the hay would heat – almost go on fire.

The people are bovine. I sometimes go to a pub at night but as far as I can hear from their talk, beer and fornication are the only subjects of conversation that interest them. The semi-public copulation of a dwarf man and a giant woman (locals) has given great food for talk for the past four weeks.

I expect I'll stay on here till the harvest is saved, and after that what?

When my father returned from Australia he evidently realized that my humiliating departure from Oxford and subsequent experiences had taught me a severe lesson and changed me from a callow idler to a young man who had resolved to be a worker. I was thankful for the chance he then gave me to show him that his judgement was well founded and I gladly accepted the opportunity of starting life as a farmer, though I was not too confident of my ability to make good as such.

It was to be in Co. Clare, not far from the former home of our family, for there seemed at the time no prospect of my father ever being the master of his old home in Co. Cork.

18

Actually, as I have mentioned, he did get the place a few years later; but, for my part, though it was the family headquarters and I lived there with my parents at one period for several years when I was at University College Cork, I never really felt there the sense of traditionally belonging to the place which I have always felt in Co. Clare.

CHAPTER II

On and off the farm

Clonboy, O'Brien's Bridge
3 July, 1909

It's past 12 o'clock; I've only just come up to bed in this strange room and it's too late to write much tonight especially as the candle is flickering a lot wherever the draught is coming from. I must just record our visit to Raheen today or, more to the point perhaps, the fact that it's up to me to make the most important decision of my life tomorrow morning, namely will I take on the job of going to live there – all by myself, for a while at any rate – and running the place for my father.

Mr Crofton and Morgan came with us from Lahinch. We travelled in Ernest Brown's motor car which accomplished the journey of more than forty miles without mishap. I enjoyed it but the weather is warm: these yokes must be fierce cold not to speak of wet in the winter. The Croftons are very keen on our getting the place rather than some stranger. Moreland doesn't care a dàmn of course. Ernest (or to give him his familiar moniker, Jimmy) says the first Moreland there was a lawyer who managed to get the old Brady property under the Encumbered Estates Act, I think he called it. It is in a frightful state of neglect and half the 600 acres is old woods or waste, but it attracts me somehow and if I feel the same way tomorrow, or I should say this morning, I'll surely say yes. After all the price is small, only £1,500 plus the annuity of £108 as Land Commission tenant; and another thing I will have Jimmy Brown to give me advice. All the same it's the hell of a responsibility with little more than my year's experience; but I wish it was part of the Clare property we lost long ago: it's not far from it anyway.

When I decided that summer morning in 1909 to tackle the job of working a farm in Co. Clare, I did not stop to consider fully what was before me, nor indeed would I have had any accurate idea of it had I spent days in careful consideration.

The day I saw Raheen first the place gave me the impression of a wild and derelict waste, profuse in furze and tall bracken; straggling woods of rugged trees of great antiquity set among rocks; below these a long stretch – a mile or more – of rushy meadows skirting first a pleasant sluggish river and then the shores of Lough Derg, both used by some kind of cargo-boats, I observed; these and some poor grass fields near the house, struggling to defy the swarming rabbits which had all but the centre of these eaten bare. A confused idea of a big range of half-ruined farm buildings adjoining a large decayed dwelling house of the castellated type with a square tower, somewhere in the middle of an avenue more than two miles long, completed my meagre recollection. The great lake, stretching away till lost to sight to the north-east, alone touched in me a responsive chord that first day. For the rest I felt a sinking of the heart when I recalled that hulk of a splendid place with the poverty-stricken looking village of Tuamgraney, at its gates. Though it is clear from my diary entry at the time that I felt the attraction of the place it was not a case of love at first sight; I accepted it because it offered me the chance I wanted and was in that county of Clare which I regarded as my homeland.

Today historic Tuamgraney presents a very different picture. I remember one day nearly seventy years ago my father referring to the village of Tuamgraney at our gate, said 'This must be one of the most depressed and poverty-stricken places in Ireland: let's do something to give at least one place west of the Shannon a better life'. Within a year or two we established the nursery industry at Raheen; and this, under the management of one of his grandsons, William MacLysaght (whom S.R. only knew as a little child) has now become one of the largest concerns of its kind in the country. Its establishment actually changed the appearance of the country for miles around us, for by 1923 the farmers had got from the nursery more than a million young trees to plant shelter belts and groves, and a few years later the Department of Lands, starting at Raheen, began an extensive programme of afforestation in east Clare. Timber being the requisite raw material, the selection of our parish as the site of the large chipboard factory was the final stage in this development. Since then our area has been less troubled by the problems of unemployment and emigration than most places. It cannot be said that S.R. foresaw all this expansion but, in fact, it did result from his action in those far-off days before the first World War.*

To revert to the year 1909, an arrangement was made with a friend of ours; Ernest (alias Jimmy) Brown of Clonboy, a few miles from Killaloe, that I should live with him for a time until I got things going; and I owe it to him that I did get things going at all.

At the time of our taking over Raheen any hay worth cutting had been sold in meadowing and the rough furze-covered portions carried a few cattle, put on by local people who took the grazing of one or more at so much a head from May to November. So I spent a couple of months at Clonboy without doing much at Raheen.

Very pleasant months they were, working with Ernest Brown on his farm, going with him to fairs and travelling with him to many farms, chiefly in Co. Limerick, which he had to inspect in his capacity of land-valuer. Non-purchased tenants were at that time going into court to get their first and second term rents reduced; and in these cases two valuers were usually employed, one by the landlord and one by the tenant, each of whom acted in the capacity of chief witness for his client when the case was being heard by the Land Commissioner. I learned a lot about local conditions in this way and in the evenings we had many interesting discussions. These turned chiefly on farming, for at that time Irish politics were not the absorbing subject they were to become a few years later. The Councils Bill, acceptance of which I may recall was favoured by Pádraic Pearse, had been rejected at the convention in Dublin and while hopes centred in the great Liberal majority of that date were still high, no immediate outcome was expected.

Brown had but very recently taken up Clonboy, which had been let by his father to one of the numerous families of Studdert some fifty years before. They had changed the Irish name of Clonboy into 'Keeper View', though the real name of that fine mountain is not Keeper but Slieve Ciamalta. After the manner of that section of the ascendancy of which they were typical,

*I showed this paragraph to Denis MacMahon of Scariff, my contemporary and life-long friend, and he remarked that, while he agreed with everything in it, I should have added that S.R. took a leading part in the promotion of the social as well as the economic life of Tuamgraney, notably in building the ball-alley which has become a major venue for handball matches and has produced in Pat Kirby of Tuamgraney an international champion of the game.

while abusing the tenant farmers whom their class had bullied into a subservient ignorance, they had treated the farm in which they were themselves tenants deplorably, running it out till the pastures were but moss and Yorkshire fog, and by way of tillage, if they did any, taking more than one crop of oats from the same field without manure. Brown was always a man of terrific energy and enthusiasm and all this he was just then putting into the restoration of the fertility of his impoverished land; so I could not have fallen in with a man who was doing work more suited to my needs. He had been a boxer of some note and in his youth an all-round athlete. He still kept himself so fit that I found to my surprise that though I had worked as a farm-hand he could beat me at labouring work at which I fancied I was fairly proficient.

Jimmy's enthusiasm was to draw him into a very different field of activity later in his life. I will say something of this now, though it means anticipating a good many years; for although he was what is called a 'character' it is unlikely that I shall have occasion to mention him again. His one-time friends of the County and Junior Clubs in Limerick thought he had gone 'dotty' or at least had become unbalanced. His actions did show a certain eccentricity and gave some excuse to his uncharitable critics. During the first World War he astonished everyone by, at the age of fifty-one, joining Driscoll's Scouts, as tough an outfit as fought in any campaign of that war. I have in my possession his manuscript description of his experiences with them. On returning, this ex-land-agent and ex-soldier of fortune became a Sinn Féiner, but he hit no headlines for, though he propounded a number of schemes to the party, chiefly relating to farming, they never came to anything and he suffered many disappointments. In the end, he was reduced to near poverty. I remember not long before his death he asked me to help him out when he was in more than usual financial difficulties. He said he'd never be able to repay a loan and in return for the cash I produced he gave me the deeds of the headrent of the police barracks at Castleisland now occupied by the Garda Síochána. I still get a few pounds a year rent out of it. He contracted an excruciatingly painful disease and died in 1925 quite alone at Clonboy – a gaunt shadow of the well-kept bright house of my memories – where one faithful ploughman, Thady Keane by name, careless of arrears of wages, found him dead one morning when he came in to prepare some kind of meal for his miserable master. I had never lost touch with him altogether and I went to see him shortly before his death – one of the most harrowing visits of my life.

To return, however, to the year 1909 when thoughts of the distant future were far from our minds; that autumn we set about starting operations at Raheen. Up to this there were but two men employed by us there. One of these was an old game-keeper with an enormous white beard, Dave Flannery by name, who exhibited doglike devotion for Mr Crofton, our friend and immediate predecessor in the place, and at whose instance Dave entered our employment at the very beginning; the other was William Morrissey an ex police sergeant who was living in the so-called steward's house near the yard and who automatically became our general factotum. Of his memory I have nothing but the deepest affection. I will have more to say of him later on in connexion with the Irish language of which he was an enthusiastic native speaker from Ring.

A certain uneasiness was growing up in me with regard to Raheen. Soon after it became known that we meant to farm the place I received a threatening letter of the usual illiterate type, with a crudely drawn sketch of a figure in a coffin. Lest the identity of the corpse should be in doubt it was labelled with my or my father's name and our crime the 'grabbing'* of Raheen. It came to me as he was abroad at the time. I did not take it very seriously until two or three weeks later we prepared to start work in earnest.

When, therefore, Brown announced to me, on the eve of our going over to Raheen for that purpose, that there might be trouble, this statement seemed not unreasonable and it gained colour from the contrast between the pleasant life I was leading with him at Clonboy and the unknown which was before me. 'We must make sure of the labourers', he told me. 'If we have them on our side no one else will put up any fight against us. There's no constant employment in the district and if the labour-ing men are not frightened off coming in they'll be too glad of regular wages, especially coming on the winter, to stand any nonsense from a few blackguards'. I assented and went to bed in an uneasy frame of mind.

The next morning before we started off in Brown's motor car – it was a Peugeot and one of the very few cars then in

*The word 'grabbing' in this connexion was commonly used to denote the acquisition by one person of land which it was claimed locally should have been divided among neighbouring small-holders. The Land Com-mission considered Raheen quite unsuitable for that purpose.

Clare – he said to me quite casually in the hall:

'Have you your revolver?'

'Revolver!' I repeated. 'Why, I've hardly ever fired one, much less possessed one.'

'Well you'd better take this so', he said, handing me a terrific looking weapon.

I had already learnt to use a twelve bore gun tolerably well, but that morning I felt the same distrust of this new and somewhat melodramatic weapon which I used to feel as a boy towards my gun when I first went out after snipe with my cousin Bob Lysaght in Co. Cork.

Morrissey had been told to let it be known the Sunday before that we wanted workmen and to have such applicants as he should get to meet us at the house on the appointed morning. We covered the fourteen miles between Clonboy and Raheen without a puncture – in those days punctures were a commonplace of motoring. I was to get to know every inch of the ten miles from Killaloe later from slogging them with bicycle or horse, but the lovely scenery through which we passed made no appeal to me that morning. I was nervous. However to my immense relief we found waiting for us at the Raheen hall-door a motley crowd of men whom Morrissey had gathered in. I was quite inexperienced in dealing with any situation outside the ordinary even course of my life and my normal self-consciousness in meeting new people in new places was now intensified as I realized that I had to deal with and give orders to these wild-looking mountainy men. It was not that any danger threatened us: I might possibly have met that coolly. In fact the presence of these dozen or so ragged strangers, who showed neither hostility nor enthusiasm at our arrival, was something of an anti-climax after the vague forebodings which had filled my mind during our drive. I felt that morning, in a way I never did before or since, that I was undertaking a task I was entirely incompetent to cope with. No one, however, seemed to notice that I was experiencing a most uncomfortable sensation, or indeed to notice my presence at all, for Brown, after a few words with Morrissey, immediately proceeded to get down to business and, after secreting his cumbersome revolver in the car, I was only too glad to let him do everything for me that day.

In a very short time he had four of them hired as day labourers at the current rate of nine shillings per week without perquisites. Allowing for inflation the current rate earned by their successors, working for my son William seventy years later, represents a rise of at least 300%; and they come to work in their own motor cars. I welcome this great improvement in the standard of living, though I sometimes wonder if the men of the present day are intrinsically much happier than their poverty stricken grandfathers. Their names, for names are always interesting, were James Shaughnessy, James Flynn, Paddy Wilson and Mick Sullivan. Only one of them was for looking for higher pay but he got no support. Afterwards I was not long finding out that he was the .only lazy man of the bunch. Actually only one of these four, Mick Sullivan, was a 'mountainy' man. Paddy Wilson came from the village. As a rule these people with English names, however their ancestors came to settle in a remote corner of Celtic Ireland like ours, are as a result of intermarriage with our own people as Irish in appearance and character as any O'Brien, MacMahon or MacNamara; but this man was a real British navvy type quite unlike his brother Martin, a typical Irishman who was until recentl·, our postman. These four were put to rebuilding the fallen boundary wall along the main road; it is a low stone wall, for the high demesne walls, which are so striking a feature of some parts of the country, were uncommon in Co. Clare, perhaps because the demesnes were so large.

Four others (Danny and Michael Coughlan and James and Denis O'Brien, all real mountainy men) were to clear the trenches in the callows, by piece work at one shilling per perch, Irish measure for the wide ones and 6d. for the narrow. Brown told me on the way back that they could not stick it out at that price and that he would not blame them. In the event, however, they proved the hardiest and most industrious set of men I ever met. They remained at their job the whole winter without a complaint, though at this hard piece-work they earned not much more than the other men. They were I remember favoured with exceptional weather, for on the 10th November that autumn we were actually skating at Kilboy and mangold crops rotted wholesale in the fields if not pulled before the 5th when the frost began in earnest.

Paddy O'Brien, too, was at the hall-door that morning: the young burly but pale-faced carpenter who lived nearby in one of those roadside cabins which the present generation have abandoned as unfit for human habitation. He was reserved and had little to say but seemed happy to get an order for a common car, the price of which was then £6.10.0. Thus began one of the closest friendships of my life which only terminated with his lingering and painful death in 1944 after many years in Raheen

26

as my right hand man and in his later years my trusted manager.

Many people came to Raheen later that day in 1909, but I did not know by name half of those who came in to bid me welcome. AE used to say that the Irish people, while democratic in their economics, are aristocratic in their thinking. Certainly race, blood and family mean something to the Clareman. After the first self-consciousness I felt at the beginning I soon recovered myself and made the acquaintance of a number of people who all seemed anxious to welcome me as a Dalcassian returned to his natural home. One man in particular I recall, long since dead. He would be an anachronism now, a kind of chieftain from the mountains on the Galway border, Moloney by name, tall, gaunt, majestic-looking, with long white hair and beard. Brown said that his handshake did more to consolidate our position in wild Clare than anything else. His visit was entirely spontaneous and he knew nothing about us beyond the bare fact that the Mac-Lysaghts really were a Dalcassian sept of Co. Clare, if a very minor one.

It seemed natural to remain living in comfort in Clonboy even though work was already under way at Raheen, for Morrissey was there to superintend it. The house was hardly fit to live in and I had no furniture; nor was it likely that I could get any woman to come out as housekeeper to such a wild place, so far from the railway station – that is how we thought in pre-bus days. Ernest Brown did not have enough time to go to Raheen to inspect progress very often; and even if he had I would soon have taken the bit between my teeth for I was disinclined to accept a subordinate position on my own or rather my father's farm, however young I was and however small my knowledge and experience. For some time I went often, though not daily, to Raheen on a bicycle – a real old boneshaker it was, with no free wheel of course – fourteen miles of mud, ruts and loose stones each way, morning and evening, for steamrolled roads had not yet come our way. The days were occupied chiefly in getting familiar with the geography of a most confused conglomeration of woods, waste and water.

An incident, however, trivial enough in itself, occurred which, more than the rough road and the angular saddle of my bicycle, induced me to take up permanent quarters in the tumble-down manor house without further delay. Thady Anglim, who, as herd, completed our first team of workers, wrote or got his wife to write to Ernest Brown to say that one of the cattle we had bought at O'Brien's Bridge fair was sick. Actually his not writing direct to me was quite understandable but I felt annoyed, and it put me in just that temper which was required to make me willing to commit any mistake rather than be second in our own place to anyone other than my father. So I packed my trunk and off I went one evening on an outside car, bidding goodbye to Clonboy and its pleasant people. That journey and my un-expected arrival on that November evening to take up residence in the almost derelict big house at Raheen, Co. Clare, are des-cribed in my first novel *The Gael* which was published in 1919. The early part of it is mainly autobiographical, being based on my own experiences a decade earlier. P. S. O'Hegarty, in reviewing it, highly commended the book as a true picture of rural Ireland, but thought that the earlier chapters were less true to life than the rest. I chuckle when I reflect that my descrip-tion of that event and many other incidents in the 'not so true to life' part of the book are in fact a record of what actually took place.

At Christmas time I resolved in my father's absence abroad to be sociable and I asked Jimmy Brown, Val Macnamara, Eddy Hunt of Limerick and one or two others whom I now forget to make a party to shoot the woods which, in spite of systematic poaching, were fairly well stocked with pheasants and wood-cock. When Morrissey had reported the activities of the poachers to the previous owner he was ignored so he felt unable to make even a pretence of minding the place. When Dave Flannery was brought back to the job of gamekeeper the poachers faced a different situation, for he had a reputation for toughness which stood him in good stead: had he not shot Jack Donelan and he snaring rabbits and done six weeks for it in the eighties? Dave was an unusual type, taciturn and forbidding in manner and unwont to mix with the neighbours. Yet his family is no intrud-ing breed, for they even have the right of burial on the island of Iniscaltra in Lough Derg (better known as Holy Island).

The party went off successfully, the day was fine and we had an enjoyable day's shooting. The guns came the night before and the sergeant's son Paddy, who was home on holidays (or I seem to remember he was sacked) from a solicitor's office in Dublin, constituted himself master of ceremonies. He was the most comical figure of a man, as round as an egg and short; with a Dublin brogue superimposed on a Clare accent. Val MacNamara was the last to arrive and he was almost overcome at being met at the door by this most remarkable 'butler' who brought him to the great bare room where the rest of us were sitting on chairs and boxes around the fire and, depositing his bag and gun on the floor, he announced in stage accents and Dublin twang 'Mr MacNamara has arrived'. This fellow, losing his job in Dublin, remained at Raheen in the unofficial capacity of public jester until he went to America. Val MacNamara was a very ordinary young man, different from his brother Francis the poet: the epithet used by the latter's daughter Nicolette in the title of her recent book *Two Flamboyant Fathers* is apt, though when I knew him before he left the family home at Ennistymon House he had not yet developed the unconventional exuberance which later characterized him.

Getting together this Christmas shooting party had moved me to buy a few beds and to put some glass in the windows and to stop the worst holes in the roof. In fact I found that it was not so very serious a matter to make the house fairly habitable according to my standards and it was not long before I had the sounder rooms cleaned out and whitewashed. When I had chosen two which were more suitable than the vast apartment I had up to then been using I began to feel really at home.

We seldom had covert-shooting of that type except when my father (who was the 'master' and paid the gamekeeper and beaters) was at Raheen. I did not care much for it: what I really enjoyed was rough shooting, mainly on Lough Derg. The following pages are based on a long diary entry of thirteen pages which I made in Irish some years later.

I learned the finer points of wildfowling which I extol there from a remarkable character Simon Flannery by name. Ex-gamekeeper, ex-soldier, ex-adventurer, there was little this brother of Dave's did not know about fishing and shooting. No country but Ireland could have produced Simon; no other country in the world could have offered him the sporting life he had for the last twenty years of his life.

Looking east from our woods you see a little distance from the shore of the lake a square stone mass rising out of the water, its lichen-covered wall glimmering almost like gold. It is Bealkelly Castle. The rock on which it is built is not more than a hundred yards from the shore and in summer when the reeds are thick it looks from a distance like a little peninsula. At its base the castle is shattered just as a hayrick which cattle have broken into is eaten away at the bottom. This marked the futile attempt of the excise men to blow up the castle when a hundred years or so ago it was used for illicit distilling; but sixteenth century masonry could defy nineteenth century explosives. The southern wall, however, is no longer standing; I do not know when it fell. On its grassy ruins you mount to the first floor where Simon lived. In the open hall he had his kitchen, a wigwam built of sticks and thatch around the great yawning fireplace. For bedroom he used a narrow cell just wide enough to sleep in, ventilated by the stone doorway at his feet as he lay full length in his blankets. There was a rickety ladder by which the more daring of his friends could mount to the top of the building to look out across the lake: the old circular stairway has disappeared. His valuables were stored in a big black trunk in the open hall outside: flies, hooks, lines, Sunday clothes, razor and the rest. The piece of broken looking-glass stood with its face to the wall 'the way that old lad of a blackbird wouldn't be losing his day pecking at himself in the glass'. Small as it is, birds of various kinds – duck, coot, waterhen and his blackbird – used to build on Simon's tiny island, though they must have been constantly disturbed by his passage from his dwelling to his boat and back. The blackbird seemed to be a great pet though I could never see him except at a distance since seemingly he knew me for a stranger.

Simon had an abundance of anecdotes and an astonishingly varied vocabulary. He was the original of Alban O'Brien in my novel *The Gael*. I made old Alban an Irish speaker. The real Simon, however, had no Irish at all beyond the amount which every dweller in the west of Ireland has, often without knowing it. I once asked Dave Flannery had he Irish and he replied somewhat haughtily that he was 'reared among gentry', though he admitted that both his father and mother had used Irish more naturally than English as their language. Now Simon was Dave's brother and we must forgive this deficiency of his by registering it as a grievance against the ascendancy whom Dave meant to extol! Their parents were Irish speakers and most of Dave's children were tolerably good in their turn, the intermediate generation alone being ignorant of the native language; Dave's answer is comment enough on the spirit of their time.

Simon must not die unrecorded in some page of the world's writings. In truth no man ever appeared less likely to die than did Simon at that time. He was about fifty-five years of age; tall, upright and as tough as iron. I suppose he was one of the happiest men in the world – had he not congenial occupation, independence, the best of health and complete freedom from worry, four of the essentials of happiness. To most people the shelter he contrived for himself in the castle would appear intoler-

ably bare and exposed even in summer, and Simon, though he
cared nothing for such discomforts, seemed conscious that they
were obvious to the sophisticated.

'Amn't I a queer class of a fella to be living in the like of that
place: begor, I'm a wonder,' he was fond of saying; and it was
no bluff, for it sheltered him through twenty winters on the
storm-swept lake.

I remember he used to abuse the poaching community and
also the gentry of Clare (in his knickerbockers and stockings and
tweed coat he looked very much like one of them himself); the
latter as 'beggarly paupers' who were of no use to the country,
the former as spoilers of honest sport, by which he himself
lived – granted, as I think it may be, that the 'otter', if technically illegal, is still honest sport.* Apropos of the contraption
called the otter I once was responsible for making Maurice
Headlam, the King's Remembrancer (in those days the principal
Treasury officer in Ireland) spend a morning engaged in this
illegal sport. He said afterwards, of course, that he did not know
what he was doing, but my half regret was that the water bailiff
did not make a timely appearance and catch us *in flagrante
delicto*.

Simon was in his best form on one occasion when the postman had failed to deliver a parcel of fish-hooks he was expecting.
The man was not supplied with a boat and could not swim even
if he had succeeded in threading his way through the maze of
little fields and furze-covered waste which divides that shore of
the lake from the nearest road.

'There's a bloody woman called Victoria' roared Simon, and
I remembered that he had once been a soldier in India. 'I gave
her ten of the best years of my life and now she'll not as much
as send her amadán of a servant boy to me with what he has
a right to bring.' This sentence had an almost majestic ring
about it when it was uttered in mid lake across the twenty yards
or so separating our boats as naturally as an ordinary voice
crosses a dining table.

Quite unexpectedly he got an army pension a few years after
he had taken to life on the lake. A chance meeting with another
ex-soldier who was an itinerant fiddler led to his applying for it.

---

*The *Oxford English Dictionary* thus describes the otter: 'A tackle
consisting of a float with line and a number of hooks used in freshwater
fishing'. The use of a second boat instead of a float was not illegal. As the
O.E.D. does not mention the question of illegality possibly the use of the
otter is legal in Great Britain.

I was with him when he filled in the War Office application form
and in spite of my advice I remember his reply to a question
regarding his conduct while in the army was the single word
'Bad'.

My final memory of this remarkable man is that romantic
journey of his when his funeral cortège made its way across the
lake in boats to lay him to rest in the family burial place beside
one of the 'seven churches' on the island of Iniscaltra.

For the five years from 1909 to 1914 I led the life of a hard
working farmer and had but little interest in anything unconnected with farming. I will give a few diary entries of that
time, but I have not chosen typical agricultural entries which
tell, for example, of the pleasure I felt as I looked at the first
crop of oats I had ever 'shaken' by hand coming up green and
even in the brown soil of a field which we had reclaimed from
a furze-covered waste; of the exhilaration derived from getting
a field of well saved hay into 'trams' shortly before the threatened
rain fell; or of things like an all-night vigil with a sick cow. I
have picked a few less obvious, even comical, entries to show
what our life was like apart from the daily work of the farm. I
have left them as they were written, colloquialisms and all.

11 October, 1911

S.R. sure has his heart in the right place. He is after arranging with Miko Scanlan to build a full sized ball-alley on the
piece of land belonging to us between the Castle and the
Protestant church. That, by the way, is very ancient – Pre-
Norman doorway – and of course is therefore Catholic in
origin. The graveyard on the other side of it is all for Catholic
burials; the few Protestants around here are put on the north
side as you go in the gate.

I've never played handball myself but it is a very popular
gàme in Clare and this will give our local lads a chance to
get good at it and also of course give them some definite
occupation when not working.

O'Callaghan-Westropp and Hibbert called ere-yesterday
and fairly gave out to me because we raised the men's wages
from 9s. to 10s. (without being asked I may add) and said we
should first have consulted them or other people employing
labour. Hibbert is a stuffed shirt, might be an Englishman;
O'C.-W. is a different type, interested in Irish affairs in his own

way – couldn't be anything but an Irish (should I say an Anglo-Irish) landlord. I don't dislike him. As for their grouse I put the blame (from their point of view) or the credit (from mine) on S.R. I'm sorry he'll hardly be here again before Christmas.

December 19, 1911

Well, I sold the Kyloe heifer for £20.10.0: it will be a long time before any animal from Raheen beats that price. Needless to say I did not get it in Scariff. I had her in Dublin at the R.D.S. Fat Stock Show and though she got no prize I am quite pleased. If you come to reckon up everything, she did not really pay because I took Danny Coughlan to Dublin with me to mind the heifer, and his fare and exes make a hole in the money she fetched. Quite apart from the heifer and business, it was almost worth it because not only had Danny never been in Dublin before, he had never even been in a train. Right from the time we started our rail journey at Killaloe his unsophisticated wonder at all he saw was as good as a play. One of the nights I took him to the Royal. We went to the second house so had to wait outside with a long line of other people till the first audience came out. The usual musicianers were there to entertain the waiting crowd, or rather perhaps I should say to get what pickings they could out of them. Anyway when one fiddler who came along the line holding out his greasy cap reached us, Danny, thinking that his fiddling was part of the show we had come to see, looked at him enquiringly and said to him quite seriously, 'How much, Sir, please?' Then again when we came out and were turning from College Street into College Green, he caught sight of the illuminated Bovril advertisement over Fox's. This is so devised that it flashes on and off, now green, now white. 'Oh, Jazes,' he muttered, 'that's the quickest writin' I ever seen.' If Father O'Dea had been with us, he would probably have commented that here was a typical mountainy man from the remote west expressing himself in rather feeble English whose grandparents probably knew but a smattering of that language and habitually used both grammatical and picturesque Irish. Father John's 'Irish-Ireland' ideas are the right ones. I look forward to my copy of *The Leader* every week now: only for him I'd never have heard of it. I did not take very much interest in such things till lately but I'm already convinced that D. P. Moran is worth more to Ireland than all the John

Redmonds that ever were. Not that I've anything personal against Redmond – my father thinks he's a fine man – it's just that he and the politicians are back numbers, or at least they ought to be.

Signs on, the paper on which I'm writing now is not Irish made. I must rectify that.

15 September, 1911

Last year my father who retains the unprofitable parts of the demesne as a shooting place with a view to taking up residence in the big house when he finally retires, built a new entrance gate and lodge here (on the Killaloe road); and I made with my own hands the piece of road which joins it up with the existing avenue. It has proved a successful bit of work and apart from the insight it has afforded me into this kind of undertaking I give myself a pat on the back every time I walk over it. We planted a row of lime trees beside it. I wonder how they will look fifty years from now. This lodge, together with another one he built at the Nurse's Garden has confirmed his reputation as a 'rich man' for they are solid stone houses well built (by Miko Scanlan) and good to look upon – unnecessarily so in the eyes of a population many of whom are still living in wretched cabins. I have lived in this gate-lodge for the past six months while the inevitable new roof is being put on the big house below and apart from the disadvantage of a water supply which is obtained in buckets from the nearby stream or from rain water off the roof, I have been as comfortable here as I could wish.

I have a wonderful housekeeper, Mrs Clancy. She is fond of whiskey and wedded to the methods of a past generation: she makes her butter, for example, in a bowl with a whisk, an operation requiring a strong and untiring wrist; when we were below she had fowl in the kitchen and encouraged the pet sheep Fan to share the household meals until I banished it to the common flock as a punishment for stealing part of my breakfast one morning when I was going off to an early fair. So great indeed were the liberties Clancy allowed the fowl that Fitz Blood of Ballykilty, who often stayed at the old house overnight for Scariff fair, declared he once found a duck's egg in his bed. But Clancy is a terror to work, if not always at the thing which most needs doing. She is a good cook and we get on well; but occasionally she maddens me to the length of driving me to more than verbal protest as on one day last year when we had been working late to finish off the final day's thrashing before the threatened rain came on. We had lunched in the field at 12 o'clock and at 8.30 we returned famished, to find no meal waiting for us. No doubt we both have our faults. Anyway that's not a typical case; as a rule she's great.

She is in her element since we came up here to the lodge for there's no need to make any pretence that we are living like gentry. But even so she sometimes waits on me with a mock grand manner reminiscent of the many gentlemen's houses she has lived in. Never was she seen to better advantage than last week when a party of us arrived in a motor at 8.30 in the morning having driven from Dublin where I had been to pay my first visit to the Horse Show. In Dublin I happened to come across a Mr Fox, a typical Englishman I had met at Lahinch, and he offered to drive me home. For some absurd reason he chose to leave town at midnight. I was supposed to know the way (I admit we had a few drinks taken) but having never been to Dublin except by train I naturally do not. I slept peacefully at the back of the car and he alleges that when asked the way I answered invariably in a drowsy monotone 'the left'. After some hours the car stopped, the chauffeur got out and looked at the signpost. He came over to me and, touching his hat without a trace of the unusual in his manner, he remarked 'If you please sir we was 'ere an hour agone'. I woke up to find my coat was wet (his car has no hood) and we were near Athy, miles off the correct road. The drive home in the dawn through Nenagh was pleasant in spite of wet clothes. When we arrived at the lodge and took off our overcoats we confronted Mrs Clancy in our overnight dress clothes. She rose to the occasion splendidly. Such garments had never been worn at Raheen in my time, least of all at breakfast in a four room cottage. 'Kindly step this way to the servants' hall, Jeames' said she to the chauffeur in her best mock-English accent as she sat us down to breakfast at the kitchen table.

11 January, 1912

Some months ago Jimmy Brown took me to see his uncle's farm near Moneygall and on his advice I invested in two pedigree Shorthorn cows. As a rule Brown's advice is good but a more foolish purchase I hope I will never make. One of them is not much good but there is nothing remarkable about her. The other has given us many adventures. She was in calf at the time I bought her and in due course she calved unexpectedly in the field. Thady Anglim [the herd] in his usual easy-going way walked with me into the field. With a roar the cow charged at him and knocked him down. Fortunately I had a strong stick and I was able to drive her away from the prostrate figure of Thady who lay writhing on the ground, protesting his immediate death but convincing me by the strength of his cries that there was not much wrong with him. With much extra help and infinite trouble we eventually got cow and calf into a house in the yard. Two hours later the calf, at best a miserable specimen, was dying with one eye hanging out, kicked to death by the cow. The problem then confronted us of milking the raging animal. The bolder spirits among us all made the attempt each failing in turn in spite of the fact that we had her partially tied to a bale. I did succeed in drawing a few ounces from her, but she rewarded me by flattening the pail with one stroke of her hoof leaving me at full length on my back rolling in soft warm dung. By good luck 'Foley' arrived the next day and it was he tamed the shrew. Foley was a calf purchased in the Limerick market. He was thirsty when he reached Raheen and we let him in to 'Mrs Foley' as we afterwards called his foster mother. She was by this time overstocked with milk and her antics were not as vicious as they were the night before. Foley got a few kicks but it was not long before he got between her legs and vanquished her. I sent word to Jimmy Brown's uncle that I must send her back to him. He refused point blank and rather than let her die in a railway truck I had to keep her. Foley was reared on her and when she went dry I sold her at half what I paid for her to a butcher who would only take that mad cow when she had been fastened securely by ropes on his premises.

Foley got his nickname from a famous character, a rabbit trapper from Ballyneety, of whom many strange deeds were reported. All the time John Foley was trapping rabbits at Raheen he never, as far as I know, committed any of the crimes he was supposed to specialize in: he paid his £20 down in advance on the kitchen table, giving me 'Foley' by way of payment for the few extra days by which he extended the time limit appointed in our agreement. One clever move he made, but one which proved him astute not criminal. The idea that Raheen was the poachers' special preserve was not yet quite dead and traps belonging to a man legitimately trapping were not safe if left long unminded. Foley's plan was to trap in the comparatively safe neighbourhood of the house first; then as he began to move his traps out to a wider circle he adopted this ingenious device: he and his son were out one night attending to the traps some distance apart. A shot was discharged (by the son of course); the young man was immediately sent post haste to the barracks to inform the police that they had been fired at and henceforth the Foleys enjoyed police protection for their traps.

6 January, 1914

Even though its a Church Holiday and so no work on the farm except milking, etc., I haven't much time tonight but I must record why I have let several months pass without making an entry in this 'diary'. There are several sub-causes, but the primary reason is the starting of a new industry at Raheen.

Last autumn we added considerably to the staff here for the purpose of planting waste land and renewing the existing extensive woods. We don't touch the 'primeval forest' of course. I do not remember did I mention before that quite a considerable part of the woods here is untouched primeval forest, Raheen being one of the few places where the original timber covering of Ireland still exists, and some of the individual trees, old warriors of oaks, are from 700 to 1,000 years old. My authority for this statement is A. C. Forbes the head of state forestry, an Englishman, who is, by the way, devilish uninteresting outside the subject of trees. (If I have time I must record an amusing incident which occurred when he spent the night here lately, but for the moment I must keep to the point.)

Arising out of a remark of mine in my homecoming speech last September my father, commenting on the fact that Tuamgraney, like so many other places west of the Shannon, is miserably impoverished, made the suggestion that we should start some local industry; prompted by the fact that on his behalf I had already begun afforestation work it occurred to me that all things considered a nursery business would meet the case. Well into this we have gone in partnership, having amalgamated my dairy farming concern with it.

A variety of things connected with this have caused me to work extra hard for the past three months, being now 'managing director' of the new concern at £3.10 per week instead of an independent farmer with from that an uncertain and elusive income. (I'd be stoney broke only for what my

37

father allows me for managing his 'Estate' affairs.) The work is in a way now more interesting because there is more scope and more responsibility, but the fact remains that at present I have not a moment to call my own. One week I may mention as the climax when the foreman of the nursery one Parker, an Englishman – anyone who employs an Englishman is looking for trouble – and I parted company without undue waste of time: we were two months behindhand through his incompetence plus bad weather. I took over as foreman worker in his place and finished nearly every day for a fortnight with as much as two hours of office work right into the night.

However that is not of much interest, but it has made a change in my life which I feel should be chronicled. It is a real change inasmuch as it is now impossible for me, except an odd day such as shaking a field of oats, to go out cheerfully in the morning to do a day's manual work on the farm. Conor Clune – or should I say Conchobhair Mac Clúin for he is an Irish speaker – clicking on his typewriter in the office has become a more familiar sight to me than Thady Anglim with the cows or John Mullins with his plough.

Though I hadn't time to put in the Forbes incident last night I'll add it now before I forget it.

At dinner – we have it at 7 p.m. while S.R. is here instead of my usual 12.30 midday – apropos of something which was said on the subject of pronunciation S.R. told an anecdote I'd heard from him before: about two boys who were arguing as to the right way to say the word phenomena, one holding that it should be pheno*mayn*a and the other replying 'Not at all, 'tis phenomen*aa*'. Though this is of some interest as illustrating the tendency in Hiberno-English to stress the end rather than the beginning of a word it would not have been worth mentioning here had not the sequel reduced me to uncontrollable laughter. Forbes stayed the night and the following morning at breakfast, by way of making conversation, he remarked that he had heard a good story lately and apparently forgetting it was at dinner with us the night before he had heard it, he proceeded to retell it in his unsuitable broad Zummerzet accent. S.R. always the perfect gentleman listened politely as if to something new and made some comment, my mother remained impassive, while I personally nearly rolled under the table with mirth. I think Forbes ascribed this to his skill as a teller of funny stories.

I am surprised to find that I made no entry about the following unusual incident at the time, but many years later I did write an account of it and I quote this here:—

Dick Caunter, who was killed in the War, came to me to learn farming. I was too much of a novice to undertake to teach anyone what I was really only learning myself, but life at Raheen certainly hardened him into a very good specimen of a man. He arrived at Killaloe by the mail one morning in May, 1910, when I had so far advanced in the ways of civilization as to have a housekeeper [Mrs Clancy: see p. 34 supra]. My appearance, however, evidently struck him as uncivilized for he was palpably astonished when I introduced myself to him at the station; he had not expected my rough working clothes and unshaven chin, he told me afterwards when he had himself lapsed into a more cut-throat looking ruffian then ever I was. His appearance surprised me as much as mine astonished him. A pale chubby face under a bowler hat, a black coat with silk facings, spats; among his luggage a tennis racquet and other evidences of intended leisure.

'What's that thing?' I asked him, pointing to it with feigned ignorance.

'Do you mean my racquet?' he asked in turn.

'Whatever it is,' I replied, 'We've no use for afternoon tea parties hereabouts', and with that we piled his copious luggage on the trap.

I am sure he disliked me very much at our first meeting for I played the role of bucolic savage to my heart's delight; and this part I sustained the next day by way of introducing him to farm life. His appearance at breakfast in what he deemed country clothes decided me to take drastic measures with him.

Twelve of our largest bullocks had to be branded with our identifying letters, the very job, I reflected, to soil those immaculate trousers, to obliterate the white clocks on those elegant purple socks, and to take the shine off those shoes. He had to help to catch each of those twelve bullocks and hold him while the horn was branded. The prevailing colour of his clothes at the end was a livid green, for excited cattle fresh off the early summer's grass are inclined to be loose in themselves. In two weeks he had abandoned the use of collars, procured a pair of serviceable breeches and leggings and had learnt to roll up his sleeves. His first night he slept with the door locked and a loaded gun at his side and the following day his idea that Claremen shot strangers at sight gained some colour by the unintelligible jargon of a drunken man whom he happened to meet in the road, words which he interpreted as some kind of threat to an Englishman. This same greenhorn's fists were in a few months the terror of anyone who would chance to cross him and he is reported (though probably by hyperbole) to have driven Jim Flynn from the meadow with a revolver one day when I was away in Limerick and he considered himself in charge. Indeed I never saw a greater change in any man or a tougher nut than he had become when he left me a few years later.

My diary at the time tells how we slept in a tent that summer because the wild deer had to be scared away from the root crops by firing shots in the air. We used a revolver for that purpose because a shot-gun could not be carried around if, as often happened, we wanted to visit a neighbour before going to bed in the field.

It was this that indirectly led to an incident which people to whom I have since related it must tend to believe that I am embroidering, so much does it appear of the Lever-Lover-Somerville and Ross stage-Irish type. Nevertheless this is exactly as it happened. There is no need to exaggerate.

Dick and I used often to play poker with Tim Hurley, the accountant in the National Bank at Scariff. He tended to irk us by playing in such a stereotyped and unimaginative way that we could frequently make a shrewd guess at the value of his hand; and only his luck in consistently holding good cards saved him from losing money. We decided to shake him out of his humdrum equanimity and our chance came when the manager went away on holidays and Hurley was instructed to sleep at the bank during his absence. One night we went over there to play poker with him in the manager's sitting room. I forget what was the pre-arranged signal during the game, but at a certain moment I drew my deer-scarer revolver and told Hurley we had decided to help ourselves to some cash from the safe in the office across the hall; Dick produced a coil of rope and tied the speechless Hurley in his chair. We were just demanding the keys with the intention of course of having a good laugh at what now seems to me a senseless prank when the window of the room was raised a few inches at the bottom and two eyes looked in at the crack. The picture they saw was two desperate looking characters, unshaven and in rough clothes, overpowering the custodian of the bank. The eyes were those of a Miss M., one of the manager's daughters who had not gone away with him on holidays. While Dick released Hurley I went down to the kitchen, absent-mindedly retaining the revolver in my hand, where the maid (there were still 'domestic servants' in those days) went to cover under the table while the other sister, cutting short my attempted explanation, dismissed me in true Edwardian fashion as a 'cad'. After much talk I persuaded them to forget all about it; but it was too good a story for them to keep to themselves and the next day they told the cashier's wife, who passed it on to her husband with the result that in due course Hurley lost his job, dismissed from the bank for consorting with undesirable cornerboys on the bank premises when in charge thereof. I spent much of the next month, including a visit to London in trying to undo the harm our foolish escapade had done. It always seemed odd to me that the National Bank, whose founder was Daniel O'Connell, was the only one of the Irish banks which had its head office in London. Eventually a chief inspector came to Limerick and held an enquiry at which, when I had finally persuaded him to believe my improbable story, I had to listen without retort to a sarcastic and sanctimonious but well deserved lecture. However, it was worth it because Hurley was re-instated at another branch; and the epilogue was that about twenty years later Hurley came back to Scariff as manager. It is due to his memory to add that he felt no resentment but treated the whole affair as a joke and we remained the best of friends.

The infinite trouble and discomfort to which I was put before I finally got out of that absurd scrape turned me to a more serious life again, much as a somewhat similar episode had done earlier in my career. After Caunter left me another young man came to live with me and I subsequently indulged in no more mad sprees.

Though we spent our off time in drinking and cardplaying and dancing we never for a moment failed to work hard by day. Dick Caunter soon became a splendid workman at the less skilled jobs and we continued to pitch hay, fork dung and make roads as hard as ever.

He was succeeded by Harry Orchard, of whom more later. Subsequently I had other 'pupils', three of whom are prominent in Ireland today. John Litton and Stephen Rynne were splendid workers and would have been worth having on the place had no premium been paid for their instruction. Arland Ussher on the other hand had no taste for farming and 'Percy', as he was called then, when not engaged in reading the works of philosophers and modernist poets, was alleged to have spent his evenings trying to persuade our men that they were 'wage-slaves'.

That of course was an exaggeration based no doubt on some casual expression of his mildly radical views. It has the makings of a good joke now if I want to pull his leg in company, for the Usshers keep open house on Sunday nights – the only remaining 'salon' of the old type.

I could continue to recount the occupations and recreations of those five years before the outbreak of the first World War changed almost everything – except the living standards of the workers – for the worse; but I hope I have said enough to give a picture of our life then, an impressionist picture no doubt; if anyone cares to see a full canvas painted by the same hand I may mention that it will be found in my novels *The Gael* and *Cúrsai Thomáis.* I have just re-read these (coming to them almost as to new books by an unknown author, so completely had I forgotten their contents) and I am able to add (though as the saying is 'I say it as shouldn't') that I find them, for all the faults of *The Gael* as a novel, as true to life as I could possibly wish.

Gradually, as all unknowingly we approached the end of our old world in that conclusion of the nineteenth century which lingered on through the first decade of the twentieth, I became conscious of the forces, particularly the Gaelic League and the co-operative movement, which were already revitalizing the country. The Irish language itself was quite familiar to me, having heard it much used around Liscannor in my boyhood and having with me every day William Morrissey, a man who was not only a native speaker but also a lover of the language: he enjoyed imparting it to me, a somewhat unusual enthusiasm for an ex-sergeant of the R.I.C., though in this connexion I may mention that William O'Brien's father, a head constable in that police force, was one of the first members of the Gaelic League. I refer to William O'Brien the Labour leader not to the M.P. So little did I then realize the importance of Irish from a Nationalist, and more particularly a national, point of view that though urged by the sergeant to put myself down in the 1911 census as bilingual I did not do so, thinking that for statistical purposes people like me with little more than a smattering should not be included as Irish speakers.

William Morrissey died in March 1913 and it was at his bedside sometime before that I first really grasped the significance of the Irish language as a factor in the Irish renaissance. Father John O'Dea and I chanced to call to see the sick man at the same hour and the conversation happened to turn to Irish. Somehow though I knew him well – he was the curate of our parish then – we had never had much discussion on this subject and on this occasion I was greatly impressed by his quiet-eloquence. That day in 1912 I determined to become a competent Irish speaker; by 1917 I had the Fáinne; and the extent to which I attained or failed to attain my ambition can be judged by the quality of the three books I subsequently wrote in Irish and by my work as editor of *An Sguab*.

CHAPTER III

An attempt and a failure

Before I get on to topics of wider interest I must devote a few pages to another aspect of our rural life, which, in spite of some pleasant features, is in fact to some extent at least the story of a failure. Instead of quoting isolated and often sketchy diary entries I have combined these into one short chapter.

My ambition was to create at Raheen a community which would provide the answer to the problem of how to keep the people of a once thickly populated western county on the land, for emigration had been a perpetual problem since the time of the Famine, mainly to America for nearly a century but of late years more to Great Britain. (Now net emigration, due partly to the recession in Britain, has ceased). In this I had my father's whole-hearted support. Our dual aim was that our community should be Irish speaking and thus form the nucleus of a nua-ghaeltacht in a district such as ours where Irish as the vernacular had become, within living memory, to all intents and purposes dead.

Johnny O'Brien, Paddy's father, exemplified this. He was quite a fluent Irish speaker when, as usually happened on a fair day, he had a good sup of drink taken and started to give out to his wife and family; when sober, however, he denied being able to speak Irish at all. If Irish as a living tongue was dead it was scarcely cold in the grave.

In 1915 I made a collection of more than 200 Irish words used in everyday speech by people in east Clare who knew no Irish as such, or at least could not construct even the simplest sentence in the language of their forefathers. This collection of words I made partly from my own observation and partly with the co-operation of several school teachers of the locality. The number of these words was remarkable. The majority naturally are essentially rural. The Royal Irish Academy is at the present time making a comprehensive study of this subject and has received a number of such lists from various parts of the country. Three, in addition to mine, have been sent in from Co. Clare, two of them from the Corofin area, considerably more extensive than the 200 words I had in my collection. Only a few of these, e.g. brogue and galore, are used outside Ireland and so have found their way into English dictionaries. When it is remembered that the 'yokels' of a typical rural parish in England were said, at least in pre-radio days, to have a total vocabulary of less than 500 words the comparative richness of the speech of a Clare countryman is the more remarkable.

To revert to our efforts at Raheen the first step was to organize all the local people who had some knowledge of Irish. This they had usually acquired at Gaelic League classes as Irish was not a compulsory subject in schools until the establishment of the Irish Free State. The principal event in this was the monthly 'Tae Gaedhealach', as we called it, at Raheen where some fifty or sixty people came in for a meal followed by an entertainment of some kind. We were still in the experimental stage of that when the activities of the Auxiliaries and Black & Tans put a stop to anything in the nature of social gatherings.

A more constructive move was the recruiting of native speakers to the staff of our firm, then known as the Raheen Rural Industries. Here the personal factor entered into the matter to a large extent. Not all recruits were genuine enthusiasts wholeheartedly devoted to the cause. There was, for example, the man who thought that no matter how little work he did he earned his wages because he was a good Irish speaker. Our selection from the applicants who answered our advertisements was not always as wise as it should have been, as in the case of the native speaker from Co. Kerry whose value was negatived in his home by a wife who was too snobbish to let it be thought that Irish was her native language. In 1932 the following note appears in my diary: 'The only remaining trace of our nua-ghaeltacht is in the O'Neill family – man, wife and six children, who all use Irish habitually in their home in the heart of Raheen.' In 1950 I wrote: 'Since old Pádraig Ó Néill died five of his children have married English speakers; the other lives at home with his mother who had very little English when I first knew her, but now has mainly to use that language.'

In short, alas, it was a failure. And now to consider our other aim. I was at first hopeful of carrying out our ideas for establishing a community rather on the lines of Ralahine* (which I may mention is also in east Clare).

*See AE's Introduction to *An Irish Commune, the History of Ralahine* by E. T. Craig, Dublin 1920; also D. Coffey's notes. The circumstances of the end of that successful experiment when Mr Vandaleur. the enlightened landlord who initiated it, gambled away his property and it passed into other, and unfriendly, hands, provide a sad example of the aloofness and selfishness of many others of that class in the 1830s.

But my hopes were short-lived. What might have been achieved had we enjoyed four years of peace instead of four years of disturbing warfare is guesswork.

Our very radical suggestions, which even envisaged the transfer of the ownership of our land to a commune consisting jointly of ourselves and the workers, did not find favour with the men who felt that a steady certain wage, small though that then was, was preferable to dependence on trading results for their incomes. We had at least got as far as having at Raheen a co-operative society with a store and shop. Its fate will be described in Chapter VIII dealing with our experiences in the Black & Tan years.

Though our somewhat visionary plans came to nothing I have the satisfaction of recalling that my relations with the men who worked for us were consistently harmonious.

In December 1919 *The Irish Monthly* published a very long article by me entitled 'Some thoughts on the rural labour question'. Reading it now reminds me how acute the labour question was about that time, when the fictitious prosperity produced by the first Great War was still an unpricked bubble and our attention had not yet become completely absorbed in our own war at home. For a short time trade unionism succeeded in organizing rural labour and the pay of the farm labourer at least reached a point which was just a little above the bare subsistence level.

I remember with much pleasure that I was probably the only employer in the country who received an illuminated address and a heart-warming welcome from his employees in the very middle of what was commonly then referred to as the 'labour war'.

The long illness referred to in that address was the influenza plague which in 1918 and 1919 killed off almost as many people as did four years of world-wide war. Though I was constantly going from place to place and was surrounded by the disease wherever I went, I completely escaped it until April 1919 when the epidemic was in fact almost over. I then had a comparatively mild attack, but being obliged to go to Dublin on a very urgent matter before I had fully recovered, I had a serious relapse including pneumonia: this kept me in bed in my room in Upper Fitzwilliam Street for over three weeks (for we had not then the benefit of modern treatment) and it took me till the middle of June to recover my normal health and strength. That spring the Irish Transport and General Workers' Union was organizing farm workers and when they came to Raheen they established a branch for our men (30 or so), but two (Donagh O'Regan and Tommy Wilson) refused to join on the grounds that our men had higher wages with better hours and conditions than the Union was demanding. I wanted Donagh and Tommy to join but, when they continued to refuse to do so, I in my turn refused to sack them. The Union therefore decided that a strike must take place. That was the position when I fell ill. I can't remember how much I worried about it as I lay in a fever coughing blood in Dublin, but anyway the men at home took a step which I greatly appreciated and will never forget: they sent me word that they wouldn't think of going on strike and I in the state I was and my father away in Australia. Of all the happy memories I have of my relations with the workers at Raheen that is the one I treasure most. It was two months before I was back at work and by that time the local branch of the Union had ceased to exist.

Of my numerous acquaintances who were carried off by that epidemic the one I knew best was the picturesque Sadhbh Trinseach (*Anglice* Trench) whom Dairmuid Coffey had married only a few months before.

Over the next few years our economic problems became even more pressing. When at length in 1924 I decided that the nettle must be grasped I grasped it firmly. I succeeded in carrying out the drastic economies which were necessary with the least possible hardship to the men employed on the place. Under the new restricted régime I was unable to find work for many myself; but I managed to place them all except two or three who were unmarried and comparatively new members of our staff. These were compensated as well as we were able by being given a month's wages when they were let go.

I always felt that I had a responsibility for all the men who depended on Raheen for their living. I was sometimes told that what I regarded as a sense of duty was mere softness on my part; but I am glad I did not look at it in that light. I never had any doubt that I must do the best I possibly could for every single member of the old Raheen community. I had no sympathy for any man who would be inclined to take advantage of my attitude and play on me – but I must say there was no tendency on the part of the men to take that line. The most I could do was to let them down lightly: I could not of course guarantee them a livelihood for life.

My first move was to make an arrangement with the Forestry Department – or more accurately the Forestry Division of the Department of Lands. This involved a further intrusion on the privacy of Raheen which was already invaded by the establishment of a permanent hospital inside our bounds: how this came about will be related when we come to the Black & Tans.

Briefly my plan consisted of handing over on a long lease the greater part of the woods of Raheen to the Government. It was left to me to dispose of the growing timber and I agreed to transfer the land in question in three blocks, beginning in 1926. The total area so leased is something over 300 statute acres and the rent is a mere £65 a year, in itself a comment on inflation.

A decision which involved the cutting down of a great part of the woods of Raheen could not be made by me without long consideration and real sorrow. The charm of Raheen, apart from its surroundings of lake and mountain, lay in the woods – commercially of little value but aesthetically almost unique – part of them being ancient forest and part little more than clumps of birch and holly with open bracken-covered spaces between them. Regiments of conifers uniform in colour standing as it were to attention in long straight lines have no beauty comparable to the glades and furze bushes they have superseded. However, I saved some part of the old Raheen of my youth. From the first I insisted on retaining the wood through which the main avenue runs, for this happens to be a rare relic of the ancient primaeval forest of Ireland; to destroy this would be a crime to which I would not consent, a view I am happy to say shared by my son William who is the owner of Raheen since 1958. One oak tree we have which the late A. C. Forbes, the well-known authority on forestry, declared must have been there a thousand years ago – in the days when Brian Boru was established at Kincora, only eight miles away as the crow flies. These old oaks used to fascinate AE who made many pictures of them – one in particular near the 'Hollow Sound' he painted over and over again and it is no doubt to be seen adorning the walls of several American homes. In the heart of summer the forest is almost oppressive, but in the spring when the leaves are still light green and particularly in the depth of winter it is wonderful. The ferns which grow on the moss-covered bark of the huge twisted limbs of the oaks give a touch of green in winter and this, in the pale winter sunlight, seems to make a perfect harmony with the plum-covered twigs of the birches.

Before the date of handing over the third block I was so much concerned at the prospect of having to scarify the place still further – for the spoliation caused by the felling of the first two blocks seemed saddening enough – that I proposed to include a certain number of acres of poor quality farmland in the last section and to retain instead the wood which lies on the south side of the old house. Fortunately this was agreed to, so that

Raheen has not been nearly as much spoilt as it would have been had this too been turned into a commercial plantation of sitka spruce or larch.

CHAPTER IV

Introduction to Politics

In January 1913 I had, or thought I had, appendicitis. In fact I had a slight attack, but I was nervous of that malady because my brother Pat had recently had a bad time with it. It was left too long without an operation and as a result he was very seriously ill. When I first felt the pain which alarmed me I was for some reason or other on a visit to London. I very seldom left Clare in those days and do not remember what brought me there. I remember very well what I did. I went to the place where I was staying and looked up a directory which listed the names of Dublin surgeons. I did not know one from the other, Dublin at the time being as strange to me as London; Limerick was the only city I knew well. So I just picked out the name with the most letters after it (what simplicity), which happened to be that of William Taylor, and sent him a telegram to say that I would call to see him the next day. By the time I disembarked at Kingstown, as we then called Dun Laoghaire, I felt perfectly fit again but Taylor had no hesitation in saying that the appendix should be removed. After a brief visit home to Raheen I returned and coming to Dublin by a late train I made my way to Portobello Hospital to get a scolding from the night sister for arriving at such an unusual hour.

I made a quick recovery, in time to accompany my convalescent brother in a voyage which took us to Japan. This is a book on Ireland and an account of that journey through a very different Japan from that of today, interesting though it was, would be out of place here. Let me just briefly say that I crossed the country much of it on foot, so had a more intimate view of it than that of a tourist. The two lasting impressions left on my mind of a pleasant and friendly people are their insistence on personal cleanliness and their acceptance of nudity as natural in appropriate circumstances such as in mixed bathing; and, of their towns, the notable absence of sewage systems.

When I returned from that long absence I was reported in the Clare papers as being welcomed back to Raheen by the clergy and people of the place as 'fellow Catholic and fellow Nationalist', 'worthy descendant of the old Dalcassian clans' and so on. (I rather jib now at the word 'worthy'). My reply to their address was not of a kind to please any Unionist friends I had, though I had some disparaging things to say of Irish politicians. I expressed a view which was substantially that of Arthur Griffith, though I did not know it at the time, and I declared my belief that the Irish language was the greatest national asset we had.

Before that my first appearance in the public eye – a very limited public not extending beyond east Clare – was as a subscriber to William O'Brien's party fund in 1910 (William O'Brien the Co. Cork M.P. not the Labour man of the same name, of whom I later became a close friend). This small gesture was due less to any political affiliation on my part than to the fact that it was my friend Denis MacMahon of Scariff who was making the collection. Trivial though it was this move of mine seems to have been noted at the County Club.

County clubs were an integral part of Edwardian life with its rigid class distinctions, and a brief account of my connexion with one will help to depict one aspect of Irish life at the time.

During the three summers that I lived at Lahinch before going to Raheen, though I felt more at home with my namesakes the MacLysaghts at Kilfenora I was also a frequent visitor at Ennistymon House, the seat of the Macnamaras (now the Falls Hotel). Henry Macnamara was prominent as a Unionist landlord – Clare was remarkable for the high percentage of Gaelic-Irish names among the leading Protestant landlords. Through the Macnamaras I was at first tacitly accepted as belonging to the 'county'. It was Henry Macnamara who proposed me at the age of 21 for membership of the Clare County Club. The fact that my father was a mild Redmondite (so far as he was anything at that time) did not amount to a disqualification more especially as the family in Co. Cork ranked as 'minor gentry'. Mr Macnamara was doubtful of me when a year later he saw my name in a list of William O'Brien's supporters and in due course my nationalist views alienated from me all the class which then composed the membership of the club. A few years later my unpardonable offence was committed the day I took two men in Volunteer uniform into the club for tea. Anything that savoured of strong nationalism was taboo there. Even the County Court judge Mathew Bodkin (Tom Bodkin's father), who was appointed by the Liberal government to take the place of the notorious old Judge Adams, was liable to such indignities at the hands of the younger members as having his Redmondite boots filled with gravel when he left them outside his bedroom door to be cleaned.

The committee had no actual grounds for expelling me, but they did their best to make me resign, as for example when they formally expunged the name of Col. Maurice Moore from the visitors' register on some trivial technical ground which was in fact inoperative. His crime, apart from being a Catholic and a 'renegade', was that he was in Ennis for the purpose of opening the Feis there and had been offered the hospitality of the club for the night by me.

Edward Martyn, the founder of Sinn Féin, continued to frequent the Kildare Street Club, then the headquarters of the Ascendancy, after his obnoxiousness to its members was so strong that they expelled him and he had to take legal action to uphold his right to remain a member. It was indeed a *cause célèbre* about the year 1906 but I do not remember it myself. I have no such vein of assertiveness in my composition: thus I could make no use of the club socially after that and when as time went on I needed money for other purposes I jettisoned my *amour propre* and resigned. I could no longer afford to pay six guineas a year for the privilege of occasionally making use of a certain humble apartment or, shall I say, consulting a railway guide. I might have said using the telephone but that would be an anachronism because, if indeed there was one in the County Club in those days, the idea of telephoning simply never entered the head of anyone outside the offices of a large town. When a really urgent matter arose we sent a telegram.

Now my reason for mentioning that appendicitis episode at all is the fact that the absolute chance of my choosing Taylor to consult had far-reaching· consequences for me, since it was the means of introducing me into literary circles in Dublin. Not that Taylor himself was a member of the intelligentsia: probably the only two of them he knew even by sight were Oliver Gogarty, whom he was wont to describe contemptuously as 'that white-faced papish', and Bethel Solomons, the famous gynaecologist, then better known as a rugby international forward, who was also in the literary set or at least one of its entourage. I met the latter when I was in Portobello Hospital, we became friends, and I thus got to know in due course all the Dublin literary celebrities of the day.

The names of the men and women who constituted the literary society of Dublin in the years immediately preceding the first World War make an imposing list for a small country. George Moore, whose three volumes of *Hail and Farewell* were published between 1911 and 1914, has in his own entertaining but rather supercilious way, given a picture of the people with whom I now became acquainted. I met George Moore only after he had left Dublin, but I got to know very well two of the central figures of his trilogy, his brother Maurice and George Russell (AE). Two more completely different types than these could not be imagined. Maurice Moore, retired colonel of the Connaught Rangers, not unlike his elder brother in general appearance but without his look of old-maidhood, the veneer of the British military caste never really covering the Catholic and nationalist Irishman underneath; AE, some ten years younger than the even then white-haired Colonel Moore, still seemed an elderly man to me though in 1913 he was only 46. He never had an overbearing or authoritative manner, he possessed an air of wisdom and knowledge which coupled with his beard and bohemian appearance greatly impressed a young man from the country more than twenty years his junior. He was extraordinarily kind to young authors, and his encouragement of me, when he found that I was a budding rhymer whose work he was able to praise, meant a great deal to me. The centenary of his birth was the occasion of a number of articles and letters in the press. Mine appeared in the *Irish Press,* but there is little in it which I have not said somewhere in this book.

In those days he was still entirely unspoilt by the constant adulation which he received from his admirers at home and from the never-ending stream of English, Continental and American highbrow visitors to whom a call to AE's house at 17 Rathgar Avenue on a Sunday night was more essential than a visit to St Patrick's Cathedral or an inspection of the Book of Kells. AE became in fact a Dublin institution; and in time this, coupled with approaching old age, did have some effect on him. He became more impatient of interruption and, surest sign of advancing years as I should know, more given to repeating himself. Towards the end of his life I could make a good guess as to how he would greet me when I entered his room – unannounced as the custom was – some Sunday night. He might even introduce me to people whom I had been meeting from time to time under his roof and then, no matter what had been the subject of conversation before my arrival, he might interrupt it to describe a somewhat legendary incident which took place at Raheen one time when he was staying with us and painting the woods and lake. He told how, the heavens threatening rain and the half saved hay being upon the ground, I created such a vortex of energy in my endeavour to gather it in that not only was he himself drawn into it, who for all his editorship of a rural paper had never before taken part in rural work, but even Ed. Curtis, as he called the professor, and an elderly lady also staying in the house were impelled to assist.

Almost every day of the week some one like Sarah Purser or James Stephens kept open house for all who had the *entrée*. In spite of the great progress of the Gaelic League the atmosphere of these gatherings was mostly that associated with the Abbey Theatre and the Anglo-Irish literary revival, with in some cases, as at AE's and Con Curran's, a background of economics or politics; the Irish language, except perhaps as a factor in the latter, had little place in them.

In only one house at which I used to attend these evening salons whenever I was in Dublin was the background Gaelic. That was Stephen MacKenna's. MacKenna was not to me just one of the more or less distinguished people whom I met fairly frequently in the days between 1913 and 1918, like James Stephens, Padraic Colum, Alice Stopford Green, Maud Gonne, Constance Markievicz, Oliver Gogarty or Father Paddy Browne. My acquaintance with Stephen MacKenna had a definite influence on me and left a permanent effect. I say acquaintance rather than friendship advisedly although I knew both him and his wife well, because, while I did not realize it at the time, MacKenna stood more in the place of a father confessor to me than of an ordinary friend. His Catholicity indeed was far from orthodox, but he had nevertheless the characteristics which one associates with a priest of the finest type; or at any rate he had until constant sickness undermined his enthusiasm and left him in his later years broken and dispirited. No one else that I ever met could infuse me with the fervour, almost religious in its intensity, which he inspired in me for the Irish language: when he gave me Irish books like Henry's Grammar, he might have been a missionary presenting *The Imitation of Christ* to a convert; when he rated me for printing some pages of *droch-ghaedhilg* before I had sufficient mastery of the language to use it as a literary medium he was a confessor, I, at least at the moment of admonition, a humble penitent; and when he, as he sometimes did, waxed eloquent on the beauties of the Irish language and our duties towards it he filled me with the same ardour that a preacher of eloquence and patent sincerity can sometimes arouse in a Holy Week congregation.

Douglas Hyde on the other hand, though his apostleship of the Gaelic movement converted, one might almost say, the whole nation, had not the same inspiring effect on me personally as

MacKenna, who was never a public man at all. To some extent this may be due to the fact that when I first met Hyde I was already a keen disciple of the faith he preached. He therefore took my adhesion to the cause for granted and had no need for eloquence and persuasion. My recollection is of an extremely genial and hospitable old gentleman living in Adelaide Road near the Eye and Ear Hospital. How absurd it now sounds to speak of a man of 54, which he then was, as an old man; yet so he remains in my imagination, though nearly a quarter of a century was to elapse before, still vigorous in mind and body, he was unanimously and enthusiastically selected to be the first President of Ireland under the new 1937 Constitution.

Before the first World War politics in Ireland were still in the doldrums: the somewhat vague prospect of Home Rule did not stir the blood of young men as it was stirred a few years later when something worth fighting for was in prospect. The Rising woke me up. There is no lack of entries in my diary during the months of April and May 1916. George Russell (AE) was spending that Easter with us at Raheen. The late W. K. Magee (John Eglinton) in his book *Memoir of AE* (p. 115) made use of my account, made in my diary at the time, of our attempted journey to Dublin on Easter Tuesday. In those days we had no radio and on the Monday we knew nothing about the Rising. Those entries scribbled down at the moment without time for reflection express my first reaction, which can thus be summed up in one sentence: 'My heart is with them though my head's against.'

In the weeks that followed the long drawn out toll of executions and subsequent events had a profound effect on me. From that time on I felt I would have to be much more than the sympathetic Gaelic League spectator I had been hitherto. Indeed the effect of Easter Week on me, as upon the majority of other Irishmen who were not even Gaelic Leaguers, was just what Pearse and Connolly hoped and expected it would be: it is ample justification of what seemed to be a hopeless undertaking at the time. How thankful I was that I had not responded a year or two earlier to the exhortations to take part in the 'fight for the freedom of small nations' or to that passing fit of indignation I felt at the allegations published in the Bryce report of German atrocities against women and children in Belgium. Robert Barton, and other good Irishmen who had not his traditional allegiance to the British Empire, joined the army on such an impulse. Nor were we allowed to forget that it was the British army. Any attempt to make the Irish divisions distinctively Irish was resolutely frustrated by Lord Kitchener with, as Lloyd-George said afterwards, a stupidity which almost amounted to malignancy.

Those German atrocities were largely the inventions of clever propaganda, but we had yet to learn how unscrupulous a nation at war can be, however much it prides itself on its gentlemanly behaviour in normal times – to learn it if only by our own experience from 1916 onwards.

After Easter 1916, I resolved to take a part in politics which the nationalist sentiments I had from boyhood and my fairly prominent position in Co. Clare demanded of me. So far I had only appeared in the public eye as an advocate of everything the Gaelic League stood for, from speaking the language to buying Irish made goods – an advocate, I may add, who really did practise what he preached. The political aspect of Irish freedom now began actively to engage my attention.

The first practical step I took was to write a circular letter to a number of leading non-party men in Ireland stating my views on the existing situation and on the possibility of a solution of what was called 'The Irish Question'. My proposals really amounted to Dominion Status, which it must be remembered was regarded by John Redmond, John Dillon and the rest of the Irish Party as unattainable and was, of course, a far greater measure of freedom than the emasculated Home Rule Bill was designed to give us.

My letter, as might be expected, did not have quite the effect I desired, but it did indirectly bring about the formation of an unofficial body which called itself the Irish Conference Committee. As I was both young and inexperienced I realized that I was not the right person to convene a meeting and after several interviews in Limerick with Dermod O'Brien, the President of the Royal Hibernian Academy, I persuaded him both that my idea was a good one and that he was the man to issue the invitations. The proceedings of that body cannot be of any interest to anyone nowadays; it did, however, cause a certain number of intelligent Irishmen to study various constitutional questions thoroughly. The most active among them were Lord Monteagle, the father of Mary Spring-Rice of gun-running fame, and James Douglas, with whom I then formed a close friendship which lasted up to the date of his death in 1954.

Out of the Irish Conference Committee, when it had apparently proved abortive, arose what Lord Monteagle called somewhat horribly a study circle. This engaged in various activities and finally formed the nucleus of the body responsible for drawing

up the memorandum which Col. Moore and James Douglas (and
also AE for a day) took to London and showed to General Smuts
and many prominent people in England. This document, mainly
written by Moore, which really put the Irish or nationalist case
most excellently, had the signature of men as far asunder in views
as two baronets (Coote and Everard) on the one hand and James
MacNeill, Diarmuid Coffey, Moore and myself on the other.
Coffey and I and Joseph Johnston were deputed by the others to
put the memorandum in the form of a pamphlet with a view to
publication. We spent a week or so at it and succeeded in de-
imperializing it to such an extent that it did not command the
approval of detached minds as being the thing that was required.
AE was asked to rewrite it. One night early in May 1917 we met
(AE, Moore, Douglas, Johnston, Coffey and I – Monteagle was
not with us) to discuss his draft. AE had taken quite a different
line from that in the original memorandum, which had been first
drawn up as a kind of brief to which we could all speak, if we had
gone to London to meet the Dominion premiers as was originally
intended. He wrote in a perfectly detached way, outlining the
ideas of each of the three parties in Ireland, remonstrating with
each for its shortcomings and making an appeal to each. So far
his work was entirely original. His proposals for settlement were
substantially those of our first memorandum, the portion about
navy and army being taken word for word from Col. Moore's.
Now AE had produced a fine piece of writing which was his own.
The first part of it as well as the structure of the whole were the
result of his thinking. The conclusions and arguments were, however, almost entirely those of a previous document which was as
much Moore's as his. AE had shown his draft, among others, to
John Edward Healy, the editor of the *Irish Times*. Healy said that
he personally would like to publish it if he could persuade Arnott,
a prominent Unionist who was the proprietor of the paper. AE
signed it (without his signature Healy would not publish it) and
added a note to the effect that the ideas in it were the result of
discussions with us, mentioning our names. He did not wait for
the meeting at 8 p.m. to decide this. We all agreed that the document was excellent. Moore, however, practically said that AE
was acting somewhat dishonourably by publishing it over his own
name since he had founded it on a memorandum largely Moore's.
The peace and goodwill which the pamphlet urged on intolerant
Irishmen was lacking between them and AE became thoroughly
angry, which was quite uncharacteristic of him. He went to the
telephone, heedless of our requests for a few minutes considera-

tion and told Healy the thing was off. We all agreed that publication in the *Irish Times* first was desirable, especially as it was then a Unionist paper. Col. Moore gradually gave in as to the form of acknowledgement which would satisfy his claim to co-authorship. But AE was so upset that he would not listen to reason. Though when he cooled down he wrote a note of acknowledgement which Moore agreed to, he would not ring up Healy again or let us take a note to him. He spoke vaguely of seeing him on Monday. Moore was tactless, AE was cross; we four others being comparative youngsters were as powerless as no doubt Lord Monteagle would have been had he been with us.

It was a storm in a teacup as my next diary entry shows.

1 June, 1917

The unpleasantness recorded in my last entry was only a storm in a teacup, buidheachas le Dia.* The following day Col. Moore travelled down from Dublin with us for the christening of Fergus (no, Feargus, as it will be in Irish); Moore stood as his godfather. He told me he had written a conciliatory letter to AE which I afterwards heard from AE had completed his appeasement. I gather he too felt somewhat in the wrong. Matters are now in a most interesting position. The memorandum as written by AE appeared in the *Irish Times*. Some thirty people have issued a statement saying that they agree with it in the main: these include names as far asunder as Archbishop Walsh, Gavan Duffy, Mrs Green, Douglas Hyde, Edward Martyn, Horace Plunkett and some Unionists or should I say ex-Unionists. The names of the five of us who were connected with AE in this affair were specially mentioned by AE, though not in the *I Times* which suppressed them.

AE's memo was later published by Maunsels as a 32-page pamphlet entitled *Thoughts for a Convention.*

I cannot close this chapter without giving some account of Maunsels. As I have an appropriate diary entry, written many years later, I will quote that now.

30 March, 1959

I have to give a talk soon to the Bibliographical Society about Maunsels so to get my ideas clear in my head I'll make a reminiscent entry tonight. Once I have that done I'll not need a written script. An incident which occurred during a recent parish registers trip seems a good starting point.

*Thanks to God.

58

Last week returning from one of those journeys I went astray and found myself in a village which turned out to be Delvin. Not knowing where I was I went into a shop and asked the young man behind the counter the name of the place. 'This,' said he, 'is The Valley of the Squinting Windows.' 'Well,' I replied to his surprise, 'it wouldn't be called that only for me.'

The explanation of these apparently obscure remarks is this. Away back in 1917 I was not only chairman of Maunsels, the publishers, but also their general utility man which included reader. One of the manuscripts I had to read was entitled 'The Valley of the Squinting Windows' by a then entirely unknown author who used the pen-name Brinsley MacNamara. I saw at once that we had found a new writer of real promise, though I realized that his was the sort of book which might well cause a storm (as it did). Anyway we published it and so launched Brinsley MacNamara, alias John Weldon, on his literary career.

I suppose the publishing house of Maunsel & Co. Ltd. is now almost forgotten except by librarians and bibliophiles, yet for the first two decades of this century Maunsels was, one might almost say, synonymous with the Irish Literary Renaissance. Maunsels published one or more books by every worth-while Irish writer in English and indeed in Irish too. I happen to have kept a Maunsel catalogue of 1919: there are 96 authors in it and of these more than half are still well known. I may mention a dozen or so of them, recalled almost at random – Bernard Shaw, George Moore, George Russell (AE), Seumas O'Sullivan, James Connolly, Pádraic Colum, Lennox Robinson, James Stephens and even Eamonn de Valera. I jotted those down from memory; on looking at the catalogue I find others equally memorable – J. M. Synge, Stephen Gwynn and Pádraig Ó Conaire to mention only three. Our one book by W. B. Yeats was published some years before I joined the firm.

I joined the firm as a director in January 1916 – a very junior director with no qualifications beyond the authorship of one small book of country rhymes: actually my qualification was that my father put some £300 capital into the firm in my name. The trouble with Maunsels was that making a profit always seemed to be a secondary consideration, the primary object being to publish Irish books of literary merit in Ireland and moreover to produce them well. George Roberts – managing director and technical expert – definitely could do that. He was an ex-Abbey actor with no business training, but he certainly knew how to choose and use type and how to lay out a title page.

So of course the firm was always pulling the divil by the tail.

Soon after I joined we had an unexpected windfall. Our premises were then a couple of dingy upstairs rooms at 96 Middle Abbey Street, our staff, with Roberts, one Miss Nailor (typist and book-keeper) and, believe it or not, Arthur Shields as – what will I call him – super office boy perhaps. I think it was later that Séamus Johnson came in as salesman. I was living at home in Co. Clare and only spent part of my time at Maunsels; my work there became more exacting afterwards. Well, the address Middle Abbey Street and the date 1916 give a clue to what occurred. At Easter No. 96 was one of the buildings destroyed as a result of British shell fire and, ironically enough, the firm which had in its own small way done its share in creating the spirit which brought about the Rising was duly compensated by the British government for loss of stocks, and to add to the irony the said stocks included not only a considerable quantity of old sheets nearing the remainder stage but also what might have been regarded as semi-treasonable works.

Mem. When talking, stress that the name is pronounced Mansel. In Munster where it is well known it is called Monsel rather than Mansel. Actually there was never any Maunsel in the firm. The name was taken for some reason from Joe Hone, the well known writer who died a few years ago: he was a first director and his second name was Maunsel.

With the office and all its contents in ashes it was necessary to decide what to do. I came in useful there. It happened this way. I must tell the audience that my family are farmers etc. in Co. Clare. Prices were bad in the country and we reckoned that if we had a shop in Dublin we could sell our produce in it to better advantage. So in 1915 we did open a shop, at 50 Lower Baggot Street. But we reckoned without the effect of the War – World War I – which was greatly to reduce the discrepancy between prices in Co. Clare and prices in Dublin. We were nothing if not resourceful. Denis MacMahon, who ran the shop, and I, who ran from place to place, both had a taste for books so what we did was to turn half our country produce shop into a book-shop which, after an experimental trial over Christmas, we continued as The Irish Bookshop. Customers were much intrigued at finding butter or potatoes on one counter and Abbey plays or Yeats poems on another. James Stephens, who lived nearby, used to call it 'the fairy shop'.

Immediately after Easter Week Maunsels took over the first

floor of 50 Lower Baggot Street and soon after they had the whole house except the flat when we gave up the farm shop and the bookshop was sold to a company consisting of several well-known people – Diarmuid Coffey was one of them and P. S. O'Hegarty was employed as manager. They operated for a good many years at 54 Dawson Street.

There were a number of reasons why Maunsels didn't make profits. We had little capital and, as I said before, we were more interested in literature than in sales; and probably the best reason of all, we were not the type of people who do make money. Who were we? Besides Roberts and myself there was Joe Hone a writer, certainly not a business man. Nor was Tom Bodkin, who was a director for a while but left us in what I felt was a fit of respectability. Incidentally I may mention that we published a book of his entitled *May it please your lordships* which never got the recognition it deserved; his translations from the French poets in it are near perfection. His place was taken by Neill Watson, definitely a business man but he came too late.

We often held informal board meetings in the summer on the strand at Dalkey where Roberts lived – in and out of the sea with George's kids (including the now well known Trades Union leader Ruaidhri) running around us, a comical sight no doubt. Joe was tall and lanky, I was thin and wiry, George short and more or less the shape of an egg topped by a tawny beard. He grew that at my instigation. I remember on one of the few occasions we had George Moore in the office he looked disapprovingly at the stubble on our George's chin and after our visitor had gone I suggested that he might as well let it grow altogether.

Some of our authors were often in the office, AE and James Stephens especially. Some came occasionally, when for example they wanted to be paid royalties which had fallen into arrears. One day Pádraig Ó Conaire called and offered us a book of short stories in Irish called *Seacht mBuaidh an Eirghe Amach*. The overdraft was stretched to its limit and he wanted cash down, so I bought the copyright from him there and then myself for something less than £50, never expecting to see a penny of it again, though in actual fact it was quite successful for an Irish language book and I reckon that in the end I just about got my money back. Sean O'Casey was little known then. He had to persuade us to take his *History of the Citizen Army*. Why he called himself P. O. Cathasaigh, not Sean, I cannot remember. Séamus Johnson has a better memory than I have and it is he rather than I might have been asked to give this proposed talk to the Bibl. Soc. I don't think Bernard Shaw ever called; if he did I was not there at the time. He sent us one memorable telegram.

In that he instructed us to destroy the whole edition of his 'War Issues for Irishmen', which was ready for publication by us. The preface is dated 10 November, 1918; the telegram came on November 11, the day of the armistice. The result is that there are I think only five copies of this work of Shaw's in existence. The five copies we did not destroy were released in 1949. Denis had kept one which he disposed of at a nominal price to the British Museum; one is in the American Library of Congress, and one in the National Library here; I have one still; and I seem to remember that P. S. O'Hegarty got hold of one (I am not quite sure of that) wherever it is now.

Well, in view of the kind of firm Maunsels was and the kind of work we did our financial position was usually more or less critical and sometimes liquidation seemed to loom ahead. During one of these crises I had a brainwave which I discussed with Joe and Denis, though I didn't say a word to George at that stage. My idea was that while we had all the authors, and so the prestige, and also had a good technician in Roberts, we had no money and little business ability; at the same time there was another firm in Dublin which had capital and a flourishing business in mainly educational publishing, but few authors of note. Surely we had there the makings of a successful amalgamation. Joe and I went to see Mr Lyon, the managing director of the Talbot Press (a subsidiary of the Educational Company) who fully agreed with our proposal but stipulated that while he would be glad to take on George Roberts in a permanent position as a printing expert he would not favour having him as a director. Back we went to George, as I thought with our plan a *fait accompli;* George asked for a week to think it over. At the end of the week he came in with £20,000 – well, not exactly, but he had a guarantee that, if he floated a public company to be called Maunsel and Roberts Ltd., this sum would be underwritten by – better not name them in this talk because, believe it or not, £19,350 had to be found by the underwriters, whose head man naturally got into trouble over it. Of the ridiculous £650 subscribed by the public £250 came from Neill Watson's old nurse who on the strength of his name thus invested her life savings. What a fool I was to allow my name to be associated with it. If Neill Watson and I had not it would probably have fallen through and our alternative scheme been implemented. Anyway after our swift resignation the new company launched out into stationery and other unMaunsel-like activities and before very long ended in bankruptcy. Neill, I need hardly say, refunded the £250 I mentioned. So in an atmosphere of exercise books and slate pencils ended an undertaking which was once a bright spot in the resurgent Ireland of the first quarter of the century.

That was not the end of George Roberts, however: he left Dublin and managed to start on his own in London. His experiences with Maunsels must have taught him much, since he eventually made good there. Anyway whatever about him as a business man he was a likeable character and I have the happiest remembrance of him as such.

CHAPTER V

Clare elects de Valera

One day in mid-June 1917 I was saving hay with the rest of the men in the field called Melody's, one of those beside the Killaloe road which we had so laboriously reclaimed. In spite of the exciting times in which we were already living (though they were quiet compared with what was to follow two or three years later) my mind was entirely occupied with the homely problem of whether to begin tramming the hay that evening or to make it up into cocks and let it save for another day. You can imagine a fine summer's day, our view bounded to north and south by the slopes of Slieve Aughty and Slieve Bernagh with Lough Derg stretching away out of sight to the east, and eleven men busy with forks – a big meitheal to see in a meadow in that part of the world. I chanced to look up and I beheld a sight never before seen in my day in a Clare meadow: a layman approaching clad in black frock coat and tall hat – a small little man but one who when he came near seemed to have a look of determination. He introduced himself as Laurence Ginnell and the man with him was Eoin MacNeill. I had never seen either of them before. They came to canvass our votes in the coming East Clare election. I and the men with me promised our full support, which we duly gave.

The oppressive measures of Sir John Maxwell, which continued after his recall in November 1916, had finally roused the country from its former lethargy. Nevertheless the Irish Parliamentary Party quite failed to appreciate the revolution which had taken place beneath the surface and, in the absence of a general election since 1910, still claimed to represent the Irish people.

East Clare was not the first of those by-elections of 1917 which foreshadowed their almost total eclipse the following year. After the one in Co. Cork, which Sinn Féin, still unorganized as a political party, did not contest, two others, North Roscommon and South Longford, soon followed, and in both of these the Redmondite candidate was defeated by the Sinn Féiner. In South

*In this chapter I have made extensive use of two articles I contributed to the *Irish Times* in 1967.

Longford, which was thought to be a Parliamentary Party strong-hold, the successful Sinn Féin candidate, Joseph MacGuinness, was actually a man still in jail for his part in the revolutionary movement. Nevertheless in neither of these was public attention, at home or abroad, centred on the campaign and its result to anything like the extent it was in the case of East Clare.

There were several reasons for this. The results in the two previous by-elections had undoubtedly stimulated interest. People were becoming aware of the possibility of what did actually happen the following year, and East Clare seemed to be a test case. Then there was the personality of the two candidates: on the one side Patrick Lynch a well-known K.C., who was himself a Clareman with family and other connexions throughout the constituency which made the chances look odds-on in his favour; on the other Edward or Éamon de Valera, then a little-known man whose claim to consideration was his notable part in the 1916 Rising and his reprieve from the death sentence by reason, it was thought, of the fact that he was an American citizen. Indeed he was labelled as a foreigner by some of his opponents in the· by-election, though this had little effect in view of his Co. Limerick background and his recent activities. There was also the fact that the name first seriously proposed as Sinn Féin candidate was Eoin MacNeill, whose action at Easter was responsible for practically confining the rising to Dublin.

Though the term Sinn Féin was widely used in connexion with this and the earlier by-elections, Sinn Féin was not yet formally established as a political party. Consequently the proceedings which led to the selection of an opponent to Patrick Lynch were unusual. Several preliminary meetings of known republicans were held at which various names were suggested including two little known Claremen (who got no seconders) and Peader Clancy who also got little support. Then at the end of May a meeting of the groups interested was held at the Old Ground Hotel, Ennis, to arrange for a convention. Eoin MacNeill was the only serious rival to de Valera. MacNeill had the backing of those of the Catholic clergy who were not partisans of Lynch, but the representatives of the I.R.B. and the Volunteers who had worked untiringly for de Valera would not have MacNeill. The result was that at a convention on June 14th, 'Edward de Valera, the hero of Ringsend' was finally selected; and from that on he had the unanimous support of all who opposed the Parliamentary Party. He was not released from jail till three days later and did not immediately accept nomination. It is interesting to recall that when he did so he clearly stated that notwithstanding MacNeill's attempt to stop the Easter Rising he would welcome the assistance of Eoin MacNeill in the campaign.

The East Clare election was front-page news, or it may be more accurate to say that the result was: Dev the outsider received 5,010 votes, the favourite 2,035.

The Freeman's Journal, the organ of the Parliamentary Party, did not attempt to belittle the effect of the result on the 'national cause', beyond expressing the view that Clare had repudiated with contempt the principles of O'Connell, whose historic election in 1828 gave Clare the proud name of the Banner County. The editor stressed the fact that it was the first election in which the issue was put straight to the electors. He also admitted that it was fought out fairly. *The Irish News* (Belfast), Joe Devlin's organ, faced the situation equally frankly. *The Independent* which only a year earlier had been quite rabid in its denunciation of the 1916 men, used the occasion to pour scorn on the Redmondites.

The Irish Times, which was then a Unionist paper – how greatly it has changed since those days – said: 'He who runs may read the immediate lesson of the East Clare election. It signifies the rise of a new party which must be henceforth an important, if not a controlling, factor in Nationalist politics. The Sinn Féin victories in North Roscommon and South Longford were remarkable; but nobody could have deduced from them the crushing character of Mr de Valera's victory in East Clare. His own followers were surprised and the official Nationalists were dumbfounded when the poll was declared. . . . The Sinn Féin policy, as explained by Mr de Valera with the utmost frankness, demands an independent Irish Republic, into which Unionist Ulster and all other minorities are to be dragged by force. It contemplates another rebellion – if that should seem necessary – at some moment when England's hands will be full of her own troubles. This policy has captured East Clare, triumphed over the memory of a devoted Irish soldier (William Redmond), defeated the authority of the Catholic Church, and swept the Nationalist Party out of a seat which it had held without opposition for twenty-two years.'

Shortly after the East Clare election the setting up of the Irish Convention (which will be the subject of my next chapter) was being used to try to convince the world, and particularly the United States, that Ireland was at last being allowed to decide her own destiny. The English dailies were evidently concerned because of the support the East Clare result gave to the Irish-American papers which were doing their best to expose this fallacy. One of the former, the London *Daily Express* took a different line. Disregarding the fact that de Valera repeatedly stated unequivocally that the aim of the side he represented was an Irish Republic their special correspondents wrote: 'When the Sinn Féin movement sets itself to the very necessary business of presenting its very enthusiastic followers with a programme and starts out to carry through such a programme, Mr de Valera will lose his place. He is not a politician. This may speak well of his moral character but it will eventually depose him as a leader of a political movement and he is chary of late of taking recourse to the rifle.' Mr de Valera not a politician! Has any political prophet ever been more wide of the mark?

Reverting to reactions in Ireland I quote part of a letter written to the *Irish Times* by Colonel O'Callaghan-Westropp because, coming as it did from a local resident who was actually a former Unionist candidate in our constituency and was of a landlord family associated with the notorious Bodyke evictions, his tribute to Mr de Valera himself and to the way the campaign was conducted on our part must carry weight.

'The gospel of Sinn Féin,' he wrote, 'as preached in East Clare, is essentially national and non-party, and it was wholly free from incitements to class or religious hatred, from abuse of opponents, and from personalities of the bitter and objectionable kind which formerly characterized similar contests, and this clean fighting was so widely appreciated that it must have been worth many hundreds, perhaps thousands, of votes to de Valera.

'I did not vote. As a King's officer I could not support a republican while, as a loyal man, I could not help to add one to a party whose chief organizer described severing the last link that binds us with Great Britain as a "great and desirable end". We may leave poor Mr Redmond out of consideration. That able and excellent man has for more than seven years been deposed from the leadership, as distinct from Parliamentary chairmanship, of the official Nationalist Party. In Mr Redmond's place sits the gentleman who never wearies of threatening Unionist minorities with the fate which will be reserved to them under Home Rule.

'To the Unionist this is naturally less attractive than the wide forbearance of de Valera, who seems to have adopted Parnell's formula, "We cannot spare a single Irishman", and who avoided antagonizing any of his countrymen. Again, to the Unionist, there is not much to choose between Sinn Féin which opposes recruiting for the British Army and the constitutional Nationalist party, whose *de facto* leader announces: "I never stood on a recruiting platform and I never shall." I have not heard of any Unionist who voted for de Valera. Some voted for his opponent as the more moderate man, but many abstained. . . . The fathers voted for de Valera because they believed that he, by risking his life and liberty in Easter Week, had saved their sons from wounds and death at the hands of Germany and her allies. A further source of Sinn Féin strength was the belief that an Irish Republic would escape entirely from the load of war debt. We had been told that the Sinn Feiners were all madmen and rowdies, and I have had several letters from distant places condoling with me on the terrible time we were going through in Clare. As a matter of fact, the tone of conduct of the election would have done honour to South Co. Dublin, and in Clare we had good reason to be proud of ourselves.'

Having paid tribute to Mr Lynch in his desire for order, Colonel O'Callaghan-Westropp proceeds:

'When decent people saw the restraint and good temper of those rowdies they had been warned against a quite natural revulsion of feeling set in. I was also much struck by the barrenness of the Nationalist appeal. Electors were continually besought to remember what the Party had done for them in the past; its action in the present and the future did not appear to bear reference. Commandant de Valera is surely a man to be reckoned with, and, if Sinn Féin can produce many candidates such as he, we are on the eve of great events. He stands for the purest nationality, unsullied by class hatred, uncorrupted by appeals to greed, and while every word he utters is a cause of offence to the West Briton, may not we Irish hope that so great a fire may light us on the road to nobler things, rather than consume the land we all love in a senseless conflagration?'

This by-election was the first parliamentary contest in which I personally took more than a passing interest. There are now few left of those of us East Clare people who as young men in our twenties turned out with enthusiasm to back the stranger from Dublin (or, as he preferred it himself, from Co. Limerick). Perhaps I may recall a few incidents which, though of no importance, may help to recreate the atmosphere of the time.

One evening Mr de Valera, with supporters from Dublin including Darrell Figgis, was due to arrive at Bodyke to address a public meeting. It happened that we had Joe Hone and his friend Warre B. Wells, staying with us at Raheen in their capacity of political commentators. Now Joe was tall, thin and bespectacled and Wells, like Figgis, had a red beard. Mr de Valera's appearance was then only vaguely known, so it is not to be wondered at that when we arrived by car just before the meeting was due to begin we were greeted with enthusiastic cheers: the people thought I was after bringing Dev and Figgis. I was just mounting the platform to try to explain the position, when fortunately the real V.I.P.s turned up.

On the day of the poll I and the thirty men employed by my father went to Tuamgraney in a body to vote. I have often told my friends that we marched out with Denis MacMahon and myself carrying between us a large banner bearing the words: 'What Clare says today Ireland says tomorrow: Vote for de Valera.' Denis assured me the other day that we did no such thing, but we did erect a large placard bearing these words at the entrance gate. I think I am right in stating that our motor-car was the only one from our area in constant use on de Valera's side.

Another incident that I recollect clearly was Stephen O'Mara arriving from Limerick at our house, where he had come for a meal before joining in the fray: when I went ouside to meet him the first thing he did was to show me a couple of bullet-holes in the bonnet of his car. 'I got that reception at Broadford on my way out,' he said, 'maybe it was only meant as a warning.'

The contest was not without its humorous side as when, following a scornful reference by a Lynch supporter to his opponents as a few little children in Tulla, a large contingent of hefty men from Tulla marched in to an Ennis meeting, with a banner announcing themselves as 'Tulla's little children'.

The shooting at Stephen O'Mara's car was not a typical incident of the election. On our side one or two cases of intimidation were brought into court, but, as the letters and articles I have quoted testify, the fight was a clean one. It has been stated that a notable feature of this election was the division of opinion and allegiance among the clergy. I refer of course to the Catholic clergy, as Clare is the county with the smallest proportion of Protestants in Ireland.

The statement that the older men were solid for Lynch is not in accordance with the facts. Undoubtedly a number of well-known parish-priests were vehement in their support of him. For example Father Hayes, P.P. of Feakle, a parish close to us, in a strongly worded and much reported speech deplored the fact that many of the younger priests were so 'misguided' as openly to express their support for the 'revolutionary' candidate. On the other hand having regard to the patriotic line taken at an earlier stage by the two bishops in our part of the country, Dr Fogarty and Dr O'Dwyer, the attitude of the younger clergy was not to be wondered at.

In actual fact a number of the parish priests were enthusiastic supporters of Mr de Valera, none more so than Father Scanlan of Scariff. Indeed his enthusiasm introduced an element of comedy into at least one large election meeting.

This was held at Scariff on a Sunday early in the campaign and its success did much to encourage undecided voters. It was a memorable occasion. Everything was arranged for it to take place in the Square at 2 p.m. At about 10.30 a car arrived in Scariff. Fortunately Denis MacMahon was there at the time, as he was one of the few people who knew de Valera personally or even by sight. He was appalled, on recognizing him as one of the occupants, to learn that they intended to hold a meeting at the church gate as the people came out from Mass. However, when Denis rather vigorously protested, Mr de Valera realized the position and said he would do anything the Scariff people wanted. So he was directed back to Tuamgraney, where he remained at Malone's pub till the appropriate time. He was then met by a crowd half way along the Drewsboro road which connects Tuamgraney and Scariff.

Someone had produced a handcart for the purpose of carrying Mr de Valera in state up to the Square and rather reluctantly he took his seat on the chair provided for the purpose. After a minute or two Father Scanlan decided that it would be appropriate for him to join the candidate on the cart. Unfortunately one of the four handles by which it was carried was weak, the yoke collapsed under the extra weight and the two of them were deposited on the road. They picked themselves up and walked the rest of the way sedately. Father Scanlan's tendency to be theatrical made a hit that day. After some introductory remarks as chairman of the meeting he turned to the stranger sitting beside him and said in a loud voice: 'Valaira, give me your hand. Valaira,' he went on, still omitting the 'de', 'You have given me your hand and I,' he added striking his chest, 'in return give you my heart and the hearts of my people.' It sounds melodramatic now but it evoked a mighty and genuine cheer in which, if I remember rightly, a contingent of Lynch's followers who were at the meeting joined.

Both sides worked very hard during the three weeks before polling day on July 10th, and meetings were held all over the constituency. It extended from the Shannon to a point some miles west of Ennis and northwards to the coastline of Galway

Bay; so in fact it embraced part of what is normally regarded as West Clare. Mr de Valera unequivocally stated that he stood for an all-Ireland republic. Understandably the fact that he had been condemned for his notable part in the Easter Rising and that Mr Lynch had been Crown Prosecutor for Co. Kerry was not to be forgotten: its electioneering value is well illustrated in a cartoon by Grace Plunkett (widow of the executed Joseph Plunkett) which was used as an election poster.

However, this personal approach was far from the main plank in the platform, which was definite acceptance of the aims stated in the 1916 Proclamation. The Nationalists, as the Parliamentary Party men called themselves, were more orthodox in the posters they issued: the only thing at all unusual in this respect was a reminder, accompanying their exhortations to vote for Lynch, that the ballot was secret.

In the event, the result surprised even the most optimistic of us. As I have already said, its importance was generally recognized. The release in London in 1967 of State Papers of this period for public inspection brings to light one which shows how seriously it was regarded in Government circles. This is a memorandum of July 14th, from Lord Wimborne, the Lord Lieutenant, to the Cabinet. It reads as follows:

'The Sinn Féin victory in East Clare is a fact of cardinal significance, and has precipitated events. Following as it does on a course of extreme leniency and conciliation which culminated in the general amnesty of political prisoners and tacit tolerance of seditious and secessionist propaganda, it marks the definite failure of the policy to rehabilitate constitutional nationalism or disarm Sinn Féin defiance to English rule. After making all deductions for local influence and the general revolt against the Redmondite party machine, the fact remains that in a remarkably well conducted political contest sustained by excellent candidates on both sides, the electors on a singularly·frank issue of self-government within the Empire versus an independent Irish Republic, have overwhelmingly pronounced for the latter.' (Ref. Cab. 24/20/ 1416).

The same collection of documents contains a letter, also of 14th July, from Patrick Lynch to Edward Duke, the Chief Secretary, in the course of which he said: 'I have come to the conclusion that the country is passing through a phase of excitement which will not last. The only thing to fan the flame and put the country in a blaze would be repressive measures of any description.' Having warned of the danger of attempting to enforce

71

conscription in Ireland, he adds: 'I have no fear of the future of Ireland if the Government are not misled by people who do not understand the real situation.'

It is of interest to recall that the same Patrick Lynch, de Valera's opponent, eventually became Attorney-General in Mr de Valera's Fianna Fáil government of the 1930s.

From 1917, until he retired from active politics to become President of Ireland in 1959, Éamon de Valera continuously represented Clare in Dáil Éireann, being returned at the head of the poll on every occasion since he decided to re-enter the Dáil in 1927. In the 1966 Presidential election the large majority he had in Clare just turned the scales in his favour. Clare has been faithful to Mr de Valera. He on his part always showed a special interest not only in the present-day affairs of the county but also in the history and culture of Thomond.*

*The anglicized form of Tuathmhumhan (north Munster), the old name of Co. Clare and the adjacent parts of Cos. Limerick and Tipperary.

CHAPTER VI

The Irish Convention

I now come to my first actual participation in the political arena. Early in 1917, the European war situation seemed serious for Britain, and the prime minister, Lloyd George, was therefore particularly anxious to do everything he could to influence American opinion favourably, at a time when the United States was still hesitating about joining the Allies. Knowing that the Irish element in the United States was of considerable political importance he decided to do something to propitiate them and with this (I think it will now be admitted) almost solely in mind he promised 'to let the Irish people decide their own future' and in due course announced the establishment of a Convention to implement this.

The British Government's gesture in unconditionally releasing the prisoners interned in connexion with the events of Easter 1916 was undoubtedly intended to create a favourable atmosphere for the assembling of the Convention, but in fact it had very little effect in that direction.

Lloyd George was clever: he so constituted the Convention that it appeared to an outsider unacquainted with conditions in Ireland to be fairly representative of Irish opinion generally. It was to consist of a hundred members. The four political parties, the Irish Parliamentary Party, the Ulster Unionists, the Southern Unionists and Sinn Féin, were allotted five seats each, Labour (in practice northern Labour only, as Dublin-based unions refused to take part) had seven, there were four Catholic and two Protestant bishops or archbishops, and the head of the Presbyterian church, while the Irish peers and the chambers of commerce each had three representatives apart from nominated members. Fifteen were nominated as individuals, of whom the best known were Lord Dunraven, Lord Granard, Lord McDonnell, Dr Mahaffy of Trinity College, William Martin Murphy, Sir Horace Plunkett, George Russell (AE) and Sir

*In writing this chapter I have made considerable use of an article I wrote in the *Capuchin Annual* 1968, vol. 35, pp. 345-50.

Bertram Windle of University College, Cork. The remaining forty-five seats were occupied by mayors and chairmen of local government bodies.

Sinn Féin, understandably, refused the invitation to participate. The results of the by-elections in North Roscommon, South Longford, Clare and Kilkenny made it reasonably certain that Sinn Féin would sweep the country at the next general election (as in fact it did the following year) and to have only five seats out of one hundred would leave them quite powerless in the Convention, while at the same time their participation would let it appear that all sections of the community were fairly represented. In this connexion it must be remembered that the Convention largely consisted of local government representatives who had all been elected before 1914, and so were, apart from some northern Unionists, Redmondites to a man. Its composition, coupled with the fact that the Unionists had a virtual pledge from Lloyd George that north-east Ulster would not be coerced into an Irish parliament, doomed the Convention to failure from the outset. Consequently the Convention has received very little attention from historians.

There are however, some points of interest which may be worth recalling. I was, of course, personally of no importance at all; I was a young man, still in my twenties, in an assembly of elderly men and I was little known outside County Clare. How then, it may well be asked, did I come to be a member of the Convention. I was nominated as an individual who, while having no definite connexion with Sinn Féin as a political party, was known to be sympathetic with its aims. The leaders of Sinn Féin whom I consulted before accepting nomination, were glad of this means of having an unofficial liaison with the Convention. In fact I was in constant touch with them throughout the six months I was a member of it. Our usual meeting place was James MacNeill's house. The men I most often met there were Eoin MacNeill and Bulmer Hobson, and also James Douglas (who had no party affiliation). I was disappointed that Mr de Valera did not come to take part in our consultations. He evidently regarded the Convention as useless. In August I got instructions (I still have the note from Séan T. O'Kelly which conveys them) to get hold of de Valera and bring him to meet AE at his office in Merrion Square. I arrived at Connacht Street early and he was still in bed. Mrs de Valera opened the door and let me in. We talked while he was getting up and I took an immediate liking to her. I never saw her to speak to again in

74

the sixty years which have elapsed since then. On our journey across the city on the top of a tram we carried on our conversation in Irish, Dev avoiding any reference to Convention matters. I remember that tram ride clearly but, strangely enough, I can recollect very little of the discussion in AE's room. A brief note in my diary says that Dev was cautious in dealing with a stranger (AE) and careful not to express any definite views.

Apart from the fact that George Russell (AE) was an outstanding personality and I was not, the reason for our nomination was presumably somewhat similar though it was understood that he was far less committed politically than I was; he had, in fact, no contact with Sinn Féin except in so far as I kept him in touch with their views. His admirable pamphlet, *Thoughts for a Convention*, let everyone see that he understood them.

The first meeting of the Convention was on 25 July, 1917. I have no need to look up my diary to recall what was to me the most memorable incident of that day. That was the concluding words of the speech of Mr H. E. Duke, then Chief Secretary for Ireland, who presided until we had elected a chairman. Having delivered a series of Broadbentian clichés he said by way of peroration: 'Gentlemen, *nil desperandum reipublicae*'. After a pause he translated – for the benefit of those of us who did not know Latin – thus: 'never despair of the republic'. The effect of this innocent gaffe on the majority of his audience can be imagined.

After a few months it became apparent to me that there was no possibility of the Convention's having any useful result from our point of view. At an early stage of the proceedings I made a speech, most of which I venture to quote here as it will show how comparatively moderate a standpoint was regarded by my elders as extreme, despite the lessons of 1916. Sir Horace Plunkett in his private diary (quoted by Alan Denson in his *Letters from AE* p. 233) described it as 'a badly constructed ten minutes shocker about Sinn Féin and its wondrous and horrible doings'. In his confidential report to King George V he quoted most of the speech and said that the Convention was glad to hear me declare my attitude so frankly, though he added 'to some of his hearers the declaration sounded too much like a threat and too little like a warning, as he obviously intended it to be'.

Having referred rather diffidently to my age – a mere youth compared to all the others – I said: 'It is clear to me that my function here will be to remind you of Sinn Féin. Mr Russell, in the pamphlet which has been mentioned several times during this debate, after an equally sympathetic exposition of the Unionist point of view, describes the inner meaning of Sinn Féin with great insight. The political faith he expounds there, reinforced by economic arguments which are outside the scope of what I have to say today, represents my view. Now those, I emphasize, are the views of the constituencies.

'This is no passing phase to be contemptuously brushed aside, as one speaker did. Nor is it a contemptible fact to be recognized but deprecated, which has been the attitude of a number of previous speakers here. With the ideals and principles of Sinn Féin I am heart and soul at one; and I am bound to regard this as a hostile assembly. My presence here in this Convention after that avowal is evidence enough that I recognize the ideals of others and hope for a settlement from this Convention. I earnestly hope for a settlement because I know that, if no settlement is arrived at, the consequences will be appalling.

'If the Convention fails, it will require revolution and bloodshed to arrive at the inevitable result, Irish freedom. I say the result is inevitable; you have only to consider the tendencies of today. . . .

'I spoke of bloodshed and upheaval; perhaps this will take the form of sporadic outbreaks all over the country rather than an organized insurrection.

'The people as a whole do not want revolution and the country is longing for a settlement. But such a spirit is abroad today – as I know from my intimate connexion with many parts of the country – that if it be not appeased, it will break loose again . . . as the Ulster delegates well know – if they do not care to admit it even to themselves – it will involve Ulster as much as the other provinces. . . .

'I do not fear the ultimate results of this revolution, but as an individual – I am a farmer and a business man – I contemplate such an immediate prospect with apprehension.

'It can be avoided. How? By no other means than by the action of the Unionists in this assembly. You have it in your power. . . .

'I have said the country is longing for a settlement. It is. It is true that Sinn Féin is demanding a republic – complete separation. Some men there are who would undoubtedly die for this. But the great bulk of Sinn Féin in the country wants only complete freedom for Ireland to work out her own destiny in her own way, without constant interference, benevolent or malign, by another nation. Sinn Féin is claiming absolute independence because the world – America and Russia especially – is asking: what is the claim of Ireland among the nations? But Sinn Féin is not, now at least, intransigent. It may soon be too late. Sinn Féin, the most powerful portion of the country in numbers and if I may say so without offence, in youth, has not yet taken up an attitude which you could regard as impossible. They have stated their full claim but I say with the greatest confidence that they would accept a settlement arrived at by this Convention if the solution were a bold and far-reaching one. . . .'

(I then went on to refer to some of the tentative proposals for limited home rule which had been put forward by Mr Murphy and Lord MacDonnell: and to Lord Londonderry's and Mr Anderson's objections on the grounds that they were not sufficiently subordinate.)

'Even full dominion status is itself a compromise, a half-way house between the two extremes of Irish thought . . . I believe that the extreme which I partially represent will make a compromise – on details, not on first principles – but rest assured it will not go beyond a certain point.

'Three possible results of this Convention would push the waverers in the country into the Sinn Féin ranks and drive the whole great body of Sinn Féin (many of you I fear do not, or will not, recognize its strength) into the arms of implacable extremists. You can arrive at no settlement; you can offer a bad settlement; or you may delay so long on the way to a good settlement that the result will be the same. Or, on the other hand, you can produce a swift and wise settlement and then we will have, perhaps alone among the nations at this time, peace.

'Mr Anderson says it would be risky and dangerous to interfere with the status quo. I warn Mr Anderson and his friends that it will be dangerous not to interfere with it, drastically.'

I was followed at the rostrum by Doctor Bernard, Protestant Archbishop of Dublin who rebuked – I might almost say castigated – me for my presumption. I don't think he actually called me an impertinent whipper-snapper; I forget the exact words with which he summed me up and dismissed me. The Catholic bishops on the other hand merely thought my speech injudicious.

When Sir Horace Plunkett wrote in his private diary I am sure he never imagined any of it would ever appear in print. He obviously made his entries on the spur of the moment and they are often rather intemperate. On 31 December 1917 for example we read (Denson *op. cit.* 233) that Russell and Lysaght who visited him in his office 'were in a very bad temper and talked as if they were determined to wreck the Convention'. AE was far from adopting such an attitude, as can be seen from his admirable letters to Sir Horace of 1 February and 3 February (Denson *op. cit.* 136, 137). I quote the last few lines of the second of these. 'The English arm them (the Ulster Unionists) with promises and send them in to humbug us and tell the world they are allowing Ireland to settle its own destiny. The Sinn Féiners were right in their intuition from the first. If I had followed my intuition from the first I would have remained away also. A man must be either an Irishman or an Englishman in this matter. I am Irish.'

Plunkett, who was an intimate friend of AE's, had certainly no hostility to me either. In this case I am sure he was actuated only by his anxiety to avoid anything which would endanger the successful outcome of the Convention, for he had high hopes of it even at a stage when it was obvious to most of us that they were certain not to be realized. He was in fact very friendly to me. I spent several weekends at Kilteragh, his house at Foxrock; he was most hospitable and was greatly helped in this by his cousin Lady Fingal.

His selection as chairman, thought at first to be a compromise of doubtful wisdom, was a happy one. His manner and lisping way of speaking were against him, but his devotion to the job and unexpected firmness on the one occasion when an attempt was made to cold-shoulder him made up for that.

Though I was active on Committee work and made the Convention a whole time job, I spoke very little at the full meetings, apart from the speech I have quoted. I did make one other considerable contribution. This was a 36 page printed memorandum, the prefatory note to which explains why it took that form instead of a speech. As the note is quite brief I quote it: 'Much of the series of debates just concluded consisted in discussion of Ireland's financial position. In this memorandum my aim has been to collect together and co-ordinate into one whole the arguments which have been used by various speakers and to develop further such of them as have not received the detailed attention they deserved. I have added some arguments and conclusions which have not been voiced in the Convention . . . I feel that perhaps an apology is needed for putting my views before the members of the Convention in this way instead of by means of a speech, I can only say that to deliver the contents of this memorandum as a speech would take two hours and that I am no speaker. The most brilliant orator could hardly fail to tire his audience with so long and detailed a statement.'

My diary entries are concerned mainly with the attitudes of various parties in the frustrating debates and negotiations which took place particularly in the committees and sub-committees. These naturally include here and there comments on the personnel of the Convention. I had nothing personal to record about such well-known men as Lord (formerly Sir Anthony) Mac-Donnell, Lord Dunraven and Bishop Crozier or even our own bishops MacRory and O'Donnell, though the last named merits frequent mention as the advocate of financial independence. John Redmond I regarded as weak, Andrew Jameson as sensible. Actually the three whom, apart from my personal friends Sir Horace Plunkett and A.E., I now remember most clearly are the tough old William Martin Murphy, who gave me advice ('never explain') which I did not follow, and two who exasperated me. One was Mahaffy of Trinity College. His outlook is too well-known to need description here – I will dismiss him by quoting his allusion to Diarmuid Coffey, who was one of the secretaries of the Convention, as 'that rascally associate of the woman Markievicz'. My other *bête noir* was H. T. Barrie, the leader of the Ulster Unionists. It was not his persistent blocking of progress by tacitly relying on Lloyd George's promises (after all that was normal politics), it was his air of looking on at a lot of chatterboxes wasting time and the unctuous platitudes he uttered when he did speak that got me. Even A.E., who was the kindest and most charitable of men, confided to me that he found Barrie's company 'degrading'.

I had personal friends too in the secretariat. One was Plunkett's secretary, Cruise O'Brien, father of Conor Cruise O'Brien. Particularly memorable was his facility in mimicking the voices of some of the prominent members of the Convention such as Mahaffy, Southborough and Barrie. I remember one evening I spent at his house when he entertained us by retiring behind a screen and carrying on a conversation between Plunkett and R. A. Anderson so true to life that it was hard to believe these two men were not there. My two other friends figure in two diary entries which I will quote here as they provide some variation from long forgotten and abortive politics.

August 7, 1917
    Though I have only got to know Erskine Childers, author

79

of *The Riddle of the Sands* and *The Framework of Home Rule*
in the past few weeks I already feel that I have made a new
friend. He and his American wife – I haven't made up my
mind about her yet – are staying at the Coffeys' in Harcourt
Terrace. He has come over from England as one of the
Convention Secretariat (the most effective of them I pro-
phesy: he has brains as well as the requisite knowledge). I
really like him personally, though his very English ways do
irritate me (unreasonably as usual) at times. I would expect
him to address his wife as 'Mother' but in fact I don't think
he does that. E.C. may be half Irish by virtue of his mother
(he is a cousin of Bob Barton's) but he is nonetheless a
typical Englishman. I chuckle a little to myself when I go
round to Harcourt Terrace in the evenings, as I do nearly
every night, and see not only the two Childerses manifesting
their unity sitting holding hands on the sofa but also in the
room that hard-faced and unkempt old aristocrat Mrs Coffey:
how on earth did that super-Lestrange come to marry the not
so well born Catholic George Coffey? I fancy at any rate that
she weaned him from his faith and she certainly brought up
Diarmuid a Protestant, though allowing him to be baptized a
Catholic. That formidable old lady is a remarkable enough
figure; and Diarmuid, who with Denis McM[ahon] I count
my best friend, is even more unusual in appearance, six foot
three inches in height, less than ten stone in weight and black
bearded though not yet thirty years of age.

This strange appearance enhanced by his habit when in the
country of wearing knickerbockers and stockings, the latter
hanging in festoons around his calfless spindleshanks, led to
an amusing incident recently. He had a free week from the
Convention so, having spent a day or two at Raheen, we paid
a visit to Edward Martyn at Tullira. The weather was good
and we decided to have a long walk first, to Kinvarra in fact.
The simple R.I.C. men of that place evidently suspected that
the weird looking being with me must be some kind of sinister
foreign spy and promptly took him to their barracks, whence I
had much difficulty in extracting him. No doubt my own
appearance is not such as to instil confidence in a guardian of
law and order, particularly my black hat which my father says
makes one look like a cross between a Christian Brother and
a Spanish onion seller.

We had started our walk from Gort (having got a motor
lift that far) and when at last after our seventeen mile walk,

tired and footsore, we reached Tullira late for dinner the scene we came upon is one I will always remember. The big drawing room in the summer twilight was lighted only by the candles on the grand piano. At it sat Vincent O'Brien playing the fugues of Bach – he plays them all and the preludes, night after night each year, I believe. In the gloom attentively listening were Martyn himself and, perhaps with less intense appreciation, one O'Hanlon a playwright. We dropped unobtrusively into the nearest chairs and for my part I forgot my weariness and remained entranced for the hour or so O'Brien continued his rendering of Bach.

During our long walk we found that Irish was everywhere understood and gladly spoken by the people to us, which was most heartening.

This entry continues with two further pages dealing with Convention matters – mainly members interviewed and consultations with representatives of Sinn Féin.

Monday, October 8, 1917

Since my last entry much has happened. I've had four days working hard at Raheen where accumulated arrears relating to both farm and nurseries meant working fourteen hours a day partly due to Harry Orchard's misfortune (he went more or less off his head, was taken to Belfast and locked up there, and is now free again and in England – some time I must describe Denis's trying experiences getting him up to Dublin). I am now in the only place where I ever seem to have time these days to write more than a short entry in this diary, viz. a railway train.

Thomas Ashe has been killed by forcible feeding, which has created an almost unprecedented state of excitement and indignation in the country. His funeral was, I believe, greater than Parnell's. In direct contravention of the D.O.R.A.* regulations volunteers in uniform attended it in military formation. Even when they fired a volley over the grave they were unmolested by the authorities who as usual act, or refrain from action, too late to get any credit. I have avoided all social functions indulged in by the Convention. I did accept an invitation to dinner at Dr MacRory's house in Belfast where I was an unimportant unit in a large party; and another to a small private dinner party with Mr Duke. I was anxious for a chance to give the latter my views as to how the Government

*Defence of the Realm Act.

should behave if they wanted peace (this was before the Ashe calamity). He devoted the whole evening after dinner to me tête à tête: I did my best, but I got little good of him, although his attention to what I said was flattering from a man in his position to a young unknown like me: he is just a Broadbent without Broadbent's liberalism. As I am on the subject of dinner parties I would like to recall another one: it was at Stephen Gwynn's house in Ailesbury Road. I was introduced to some grand lady and after we had parted I overheard her remark: 'Is that young man really a Sinn Féiner, he seems quite a normal person to me'.

Otherwise I have gone nowhere. Even if I liked entertainments such as those given by the Lord Lieutenant, the Lord Mayor and so on I would not go because of the King's health and singing 'God Save the King', which I regard now as much as ever as a provocative party tune. At the Lord Mayor's banquet in Belfast they did the accursed thing twice and poor Joe Devlin (whom I don't like much but have to sympathize with at times) mournfully told me he had to follow suit at his dinner and even warned me not to come on that account.

The Convention last week paid an official visit to Cork. I went for one day only. The journey down from Dublin was remarkable. Goulding, who is chairman of the G.S.W.R., provided a special train. My father, who travelled with us, said it was the best train he'd ever been in; and he has certainly used them in all parts of the world. We left Kingsbridge at 2 and arrived at Glanmire Cork at 5, having stopped for ten minutes at Thurles 'to pick up water and an Archbishop', as Plunkett remarked in his pawky way. I did not return by the special but I hear it made even better time going to Dublin, averaging 63½ m.p.h. excluding the stop.

I suppose it would be hardly fair to blame the pioneers of eighty years ago for what now looks like lack of vision. To them the main desideratum was a line of railway with as few gradients as possible. The result on the main line of railway in Ireland is deplorable. Visitors whose first view of the Irish countryside is obtained from the windows of the Dublin-Cork mail get a very bad first impression – compare it with the picture presented to those who came into Waterford, as we did in my childhood before the Rosslare route was devised to save a little time and thereby destroy leisure and comfort. Except near Dublin and Cork the main line runs through poor illkempt fields, the cold damp land being prolific in little but rushes. It avoids the towns, too: even in the unfortunate route it follows, with Thurles and Mallow the only places of any importance it passes through, it could at least have added Portarlington and Tipperary had not these places been left a mile or two on one side. I fancy this will be a point of importance some day for the introduction of motor cars must adversely affect the railways; and the influx of foreign visitors which may be expected after the war if we settle down – what the French call *tourisme* – will not be helped by the fact that our principal railway is at pains to bring them through the least attractive stretch of country in the four provinces. Had it joined up the principal towns between Dublin and Cork and gone via Carlow, Kilkenny and Clonmel, just as short a route if less level, it would have given travellers something to look at during the whole journey and at the same time fulfilled the prime purpose of a railway which is to serve the country's centres of population, not merely to be an organization for collecting emigrants from the poorer country districts.

I went to Cork because it was freely rumoured that there would be a strong anti-Convention demonstration on the part of the local Sinn Féiners. The Lord Mayor of Cork spoke to me of this with great anxiety as far back as the Belfast visit. Indeed, though I personally thought anything beyond some disturbances by rowdies unlikely, I did make a point of seeing Eoin MacNeill on the subject. There was an enormous Sinn Féin meeting and demonstration the Sunday before we went down and as fortunately it was not proscribed a good deal of steam was let off there. As a result of my conversation with McN several of the speakers on the Sunday definitely warned the people not to interfere and to leave the Convention severely alone. I felt, however, especially before those speeches were made, that as the only even quasi-Sinn Féin representative on the Convention I should put in an appearance. Nothing happened, of course, except a certain amount of not unjustified counter demonstration following on the mob cheers with which Redmond was greeted the first day. From what I hear from others who were there I gather that this was much exaggerated by the newspapers, though Joe Devlin, always particularly unpopular in Cork, did get rather a hostile reception at Queenstown.

To go into details of the proceedings which occupied some eight months would be tedious and to summarize them in a paragraph or two is not easy. However, with the help of the diaries I kept at the time, it is possible to do so in a general way.

After much time spent in discussion, first in full session and then by a 'Grand Committee' of twenty (of whom I was one) and various sub-committees, an alignment emerged. Apart from AE and myself who constantly urged full dominion status (with safeguards for the Protestant minority) there were four schools of thought: that led by Dr O'Donnell, Bishop of Raphoe, and William Martin Murphy, who advocated a majority report in favour of a modified form of dominion status; John Redmond's followers, who would accept the Home Rule Act of 1914; the non-possumus Ulster Unionists; and the southern Unionists, whose chief spokesman was Lord Midleton. The last was all the time in close touch with the Government in London, as was clear from his repeated warnings that it would be useless to ask for too much because the British Government would not agree to anything like dominion status. (He might have added: in spite of their lip-service to the principle of self-determination). I may mention that on the subject of possible partition, so far as we considered it at all, no one, except probably the Ulster Unionists, envisaged anything more than the exclusion, even temporarily, of more than four counties; Fermanagh and Tyrone were regarded in the same light as Donegal, Monaghan and Cavan.

Early in January 1918 when the Convention was still procrastinating (largely due to Plunkett's desperate attempts to prevent collapse) my Sinn Féin advisers agreed that the time had come for me to resign. I had explained to Lloyd George in my letter accepting nomination that in view of the constitution of the Convention I might find it necessary to do so. Our idea was to take this opportunity of publicly explaining the true position by a letter to the papers. Before taking this final step I wrote to Lloyd George asking him for a definition of the 'substantial agreement' he required from the Convention if its recommendations were to be implemented. His reply was non-committal and unsatisfactory.

The effect of the letter from me which appeared in the *Independent* and the *Freeman's Journal* on 31 January, a fortnight after I wrote it, was impaired not only by that delay but also by the fact that it was extensively cut by the censor. We were anxious that AE would act in conjunction with me but, perhaps because he did not wish to be too closely identified with Sinn Féin, he did not do so – in fact, he resigned independently shortly afterwards. His trenchant letter of explanation to

Lloyd George appears in the book of his correspondence which I have mentioned several times above.

Our resignations, though the real cause of them was suppressed, may have helped to bring things to a head in the Convention.

The final reports which were presented soon after are printed in a White Paper (*Cmd.* 9019) which consists of a general report on the proceedings by Sir Horace Plunkett with reports or notes by various sections of the Convention showing no more than a certain amount of agreement among the Redmondites and the Southern Unionists on a truncated home rule proposal. One of these notes was signed by Dr Mahaffy and the Protestant Archbishop of Dublin wherein they expressed the opinion that coercion of Ulster was unthinkable and the partition of Ireland disastrous and recommended in general terms a federal scheme on the Swiss model.

These were ignored by the Government in London; and the stirring events which followed in the next few years amply justified the predictions in my 'impertinent' speech.

In October 1919, some time after the report of the Convention had been published I wrote two letters to the editor of the London *Times* which I quote below. The last sentence of the second of these makes a fitting conclusion to this chapter.

Throughout the long sittings of the Irish Convention there was an air of unreality about it which many of its members, I think, failed fully to perceive. This was derived from the Convention's complete lack of popular sanction and constituted the chief point of difference between that assembly and similar conferences in other states. I suppose it was because I strove to emphasize this (and its corollary the great need of a speedy conclusion of our work) that your correspondent describes me as 'the self-appointed herald of the Irish proletariat'. It is not, however, in that capacity, but as an ordinary unit of the Irish electorate that I now wish to make one observation on his first article.

It is hardly fair in an account which for detached impartiality (as between various sections of the Convention) might have been written by Lord Southborough himself, to dismiss the fact of Sinn Féin's abstention as a mere piece of ill-natured intransigence. The leaders of Sinn Féin made it clear at the time that they were prepared to take part in an Irish convention in which they would have representation proportionate to their strength in the country and provided that no possible solution of the question to be considered should be excluded from discussion by the terms of reference. It is hard to see what harm could have been done by allowing the Convention to thrash out the pros and cons of an independent status for Ireland; but, apart from that, the essential point was that Sinn Féin was offered only five seats in an assembly intended to comprise over 100 members although, as your correspondent states, they represent practically three-fourths of the country.

31 October, 1919

I had no thought in writing to you other than to correct what I considered to be a mis-statement in your correspondent's first article on the Irish Convention, but Lord Southborough's letter in your issue of 30th inst. calls for a further one from me; in fact to be silent would be discourteous. I am afraid, however, that his idea of an unofficial conference is not practicable, certainly as far as I am concerned. There are few indeed in Ireland today who believe in the possibility of any good coming out of the old method of negotiation; some did in 1917 – the change of mood can only be ascribed to Government policy. I am not in a position – having no connexion with any party – to promote such a conference as Lord Southborough suggests, but in any case, even if I were, I would be debarred by the fact, so typical of Irish affairs, that the friends with whom I would like to consult are mostly in gaol.

CHAPTER VII

The Conscription Crisis

Anyone reading the foregoing chapters covering the period 1915 to 1918 will no doubt be struck by the fact that there is no direct reference in them to the World War, the first in which all the great powers (except China if at the time China can be so classified) were engaged.

My attitude to the war was, I think, typical of Irish people, of Irish people that is who had no close relative or friend 'at the front', as the saying was. To me it was something remote and no concern of mine except in so far as it indirectly affected Ireland. It was not till the war was near its end that it affected us directly, when East Clare was placed under martial law, the first so-called 'military area' in Ireland.

It seem advisable, therefore, to deal briefly with the subject by quoting three entries which I made in my diary at the time.

June 3, 1918
Politicians, anxious to placate English opinion, lay stress on the fact that 170,000 Irishmen have joined the army since August 1914; that there are many Irish in English regiments and that the U.S.A. troops and Navy are very largely made up of Irish-Americans. These are facts, of course, but the psychology of Irish recruiting is by no means simple. There is no doubt that at the beginning, probably owing to propaganda about German Hunnishness in Belgium there was a wave of enthusiasm for the cause of the Allies. Many joined the army because of Redmond's action in pledging Ireland – though without obtaining Ireland's consent by consultation with anyone here. Bob Barton, for instance, now a member of the Sinn Féin executive, joined because he really believed at the time that enlistment would further Ireland's cause. Everyone knows of what Lloyd-George himself described as the 'malignities' of the War Office in dealing with Ireland in this matter. These were, of course, one of the causes of the cessation of recruiting. The reasons which produced recruiting itself are more

complex. As I said, John Redmond's prestige influenced some men, a spirit of adventure drew many, while unemployment, for there has been no war work – Gretna Greens and the rest – in Ireland, is probably responsible for more of the 170,000 than anything. Coyne's may not be a typical case, but it is something of a caricature and like all caricatures, it has a basis of truth.

Many Irish soldiers are undoubtedly more or less Sinn Féiners, though perhaps few were so at the time of their enlistment. Coyne was not the only soldier, released at the time of the East Clare election in the belief that they would vote for the Government candidate, who actually supported De Valera. On one occasion when I was travelling to Dublin on my roundabout route at the time when martial law began in Clare, I was in a carriage with a number of soldiers. They were from West Clare (all had some Irish). All these were far from antagonistic to Sinn Féin, even the boy who was, of all regiments, in the Sherwood Foresters, though not in the battalion which was so cut up during Easter Week. The Irish soldiers (not officers) that I have met would certainly be Sinn Féiners if they were not in the army, though none of them love 'the Hun'; nor does the average Sinn Féiner either. The people at home on their part are perfectly friendly to those of them who are in the army, notwithstanding the allegations of treachery hinted at by the extremist newspapers (which, I must say, wisely do not make much of that point). Boys of military age, even prominent members of Sinn Féin clubs, do not boycott natives of their parish home on leave but foregather with them and listen with interest to their stories of modern warfare. There is a very strong distinction between the relationship between the country people and the returned soldiers on the one hand and the alien soldiers who are the instruments of martial law here on the other. These are left severely alone, except by a few of the lowest class girls (and very few of these even will have much to say to them). That, at least, is the case in Clare, though I was told last night at AE's by an English lady who is studying co-operation in Ireland, that there is considerable fraternization in Co. Donegal where coast defence is the British Army's function, not the enforcement of martial law as it is with us.

This lady in spite of the atmosphere of detached criticism which she must have felt in Ireland still believes completely in the British war aims as expressed in Lloyd George's speeches and she is still unaffected by such events as the publication of the secret treaties. The British public will swallow anything, e.g. the Government defence in the Maurice affair and the 'German plot'. The letters I get now and then from typical and normally decent Englishmen like C. W. Allen shew how little real desire there is for truth in England at present. That, of course, is a tribute to the success of their propaganda machine; and it no doubt strengthens them as a nation in their determination not to be beaten. The result is still a toss up and for my part I still feel neutral. If the Germans do win, how will it affect us? We can feel sure they will do nothing for love of us but in their own interests, perhaps – this, however, is leading me into the sphere of pure speculation. In any case, I've no time for more of that tonight.

But before I go to bed I must record in this 'diary' how, rather more than twelve months ago, John Coyne came to join the army.

He was born in Connemara and as soon as he realized our interest in the Irish language (but not before) told us that he never spoke English till he was twelve years of age. He was a first class worker but his value was largely discounted by the fact that drink made him utterly unreliable since he seldom turned in to work on a Monday, and might go off any day without warning. We reckoned this was bad for the *esprit de corps* of the staff (yes, such did exist then). He was sacked more than once but taken back on some excuse. Finally all reasons, real or faked, for reinstating him were exhausted and we only gave him intermittent piece work.

It is here Harry Orchard* comes into the picture again. When he stayed with us on leave he was full of the idea that Irishmen should join the British army. This view I combated; but when it took the form of trying to get John Coyne to do so I found it hard to interfere, knowing as I did that his impoverished family would receive a large separation allowance and I would be rid of a perplexing problem which would have been easily soluble but for the plight of his good wife and many children. Harry proceeded in a most pertinaceous way to try and argue, coax and browbeat John into enlisting. The war seemed then quite likely to be coming to an end, and even John was beginning to realize the difference between being a spalpeen and a man with family responsibilities – for John, though he

---

*Harry's unusual subsequent adventures and those of his son Colm are told in another book of mine entitled *Leathanaigh Om' Dhiallann* which is due for publication soon.

abused his wife when he was drunk, was quite obviously fond of her and his family, while she strangely enough seemed to love him.

Whatever his motive he decided that enlistment was worthy of consideration. He consulted me and I told him I could not advise anyone to join the British army but that in his case I could not advise him not to. He felt that this ensured at least my tacit acceptance of some interest in his family in his absence. (I was, I may mention, godfather to one of his sons who was christened in Irish.) To increase this sense of security, however, he cleverly succeeded in throwing on me considerably more responsibility for his action in enlisting than I meant to accept. One day, when Harry had John sufficiently primed with whiskey, he wired to the recruiting sergeant at Killaloe to come out and he himself donned his officer's uniform in order fully to attest his recruit for fear of any last minute hitch. The ceremony was to take place at the old house and I thought no more about it beyond some doubt as to whether John Coyne would turn up at the appointed time. I did not get out of it so easily however, for an hour or so after the time arranged two weary khaki-clad figures and Coyne, ragged and well under the influence, arrived at my own house, Coyne protesting loudly and incoherently that he would not do a damn thing unless I was there. So reluctantly I had to turn one of the rooms for the occasion into a recruiting Office.

Then began a strange scene, half comic half sad. 'I'll not do a bloody thing for them buggers unless Mr Lysaght tells me,' roared John. 'He's my boss, I know no other one.' I said mildly that he was his own master but that he had gone so far he could hardly turn back. After some preliminaries, I having to fill in the papers and even show him where to mark his X, for he could not write, the proceeding went on thus. The oath had to be taken; it could only be administered if I read it out sentence by sentence, John repeating them after me. Between us we succeeded in taking a very thorough oath of disloyalty, leaving out words as we went through it. Harry was fussy the sergeant amused.

The former somewhat pompously congratulated John on now being a soldier. All he said in reply as he drank off his final glass of whiskey was: 'Gimme a gun till I shoot the first bloody Englishman I meet.' His end was tragical: a year ago he was due to return to duty on a given day but of course outstayed his leave with the result that he left Ireland by the mailship

Leinster, which was torpedoed that very night.

Go ndéineadh Dia trócaire ortha go léir [May God have mercy on the souls of all of them].

Saturday, 28 September, 1918

Only a couple of months ago, Curzon's announcement that Home Rule and conscription for Ireland had been abandoned together made us feel that the hundreds of thousands of Irishmen of military age, including myself, who solemnly pledged ourselves to resist to the utmost the imposition of conscription by any authority other than an Irish Parliament would not be called upon to implement that pledge. However – and this was really of more practical import – French said he must have 50,000 more voluntary recruits by October 1st, or failing that conscription must be enforced. Although it will mean upheaval and bloodshed, I am glad that the optimism of Colonel (no inverted commas for him now!) Lynch on this point was misplaced. How utterly unscrupulous is the Government we shall have to fight I need not emphasize. This diary is full of examples of the outrageous régime under which we live – especially here in Co. Clare, in what is called 'No. 1 Military Area'.

Now that the danger is imminent, I ask myself two questions: how should I resist and why should I resist?

The answer to the latter is that it's a matter of principle. Personally I will no doubt be in an exempted category for I am a farmer, a married man and blind of one eye; but that does not matter: it is a national issue and we must all stand together. My attitude in this war as I have frequently said here, is neutral and I steadfastly refuse to be coerced into fighting for Ireland's hereditary enemy – even if I wanted to fight for the Allies the only way I could do so would be as a unit in the British Army. The Mansion House Conference has put our position forcibly and comprehensively even if its pronouncement was a trifle wordy. It must have weight outside Ireland (though I believe it has been suppressed by practically all English newspapers) because any body on which de Valera, Dillon and Healy worked together with the direct co-operation of Labour and the approval of the Hierarchy is undeniably representative of the whole nation (except, of course, the Unionists). As to the *How,* exempted or not it is clear that I will be up against it very early in the campaign, whatever form it takes. To begin with, I am firmly resolved what I will not do: I will not put on a

British uniform; I will not drill; and I will not fill up any papers connected with the conscription or myself or any of our men. If, as I expect, resistance includes the withholding of food supplies as well perhaps as a general strike, I will, until I am arrested, carry out the instructions of the Mansion House Conference which – with the principal Sinn Féin leaders under lock and key – will mean in effect William O'Brien, Tom Johnson and one or two of the more active and courageous bishops.

Among the papers the late William O'Brien gave me when we were compiling his book *Forth the Banners Go* I found recently the following note on the subject of the Mansion House Conference. It needs amplification and he is no longer with us to provide it. Nevertheless, I think it is of sufficient interest to include here.

'When de Valera and Griffith were arrested the question arose as to who were to replace them. These had been appointed by Sinn Féin but de Valera of course represented also the Volunteers: their substitutes Tom Kelly and John MacNeill did not. Tom Kelly resigned after one meeting. Then Michael Collins, Duggan and Dick Mulcahy came to a meeting and, not being welcomed by the Irish Party and delegates, were greeted in stony silence. Healy then suggested that he might interview them privately.'

28 January, 1919

It is somewhat contrary to the generally accepted view of Ireland, and especially of Clare, that Dick Forsyth, a British officer on leave, should be so tremendously popular here and indeed that he should be staying with us at all. He is a Scottish highlander, but the real explanation is that we have no antagonism to individuals whatever – as a speaker said at the meeting in Dublin to demand the release of the prisoners, we actually welcome individual foreign soldiers; what we resist is an army of occupation, and that is what Ireland is still experiencing though the Great War is over. Meanwhile Dáil Éireann has assembled and, thank God, has carried out the business of its first sitting entirely in Irish, a big change indeed from the conditions of a few years ago. I am entirely with the Republican party; I am doubtful about the immediate future, Peace Conference and so on, but am sanguine of our ultimate success. Just one thing occurs to me to mention before I put this diary away: an example of how our claim for self-determination of small nations – championed by Britain in the case of the Czechs – is misrepresented by politicians and newspapers there. In quoting statistics for last year's general election they give the total votes cast for and against Sinn Féin only in contested elections, completely ignoring the 25 constituencies where Sinn Féin candidates were returned unopposed, thus presenting an entirely misleading picture.

CHAPTER VIII

The Black & Tans: personal experiences

In the year 1918 there was a considerable difference of objective among the leaders of the groups that had superseded the old Parliamentary Party. By degrees, however, largely owing to the influence of Éamon de Valera, the various discordant elements were brought into at least temporary harmony and the most united and determined effort ever made by the Irish people in their struggle to get free of British control was begun.

In East Clare we had a foretaste of the war conditions which became general a year later after the affair at Soloheadbeg had unofficially begun the gue.illa warfare. Our area was put under martial law at the beginning of 1918 and I noted briefly in my diary incidents which, while less brutal than those which became normal later, seemed at the time the grossest interference with the liberty of the subject. We were not, to take one mild example, permitted to deliver our butter to Killaloe railway station, unless whoever brought it was prepared to declare that he was not a Sinn Féiner. I had a very stormy interview with the District Inspector there when I tried to deliver the butter myself after our men had been stopped. When the same question was put to me I asserted that I was an out and out Sinn Féiner. In the circumstances I would have said this even had it not been true. As a result I was forbidden for a while to leave Raheen. I went to Dublin, however, while that prohibition was in force, first six miles across the lake in a boat to Dromineer and thence by road to Nenagh to get a train; I came back by train to Ennis via Athenry and home from there (23 miles) by road. I thus became more or less a marked man and when the situation became more serious the next year I had very little peace, although the rôle I was instructed to play throughout – in the eyes of the enemy – was that of an innocuous employer of labour, at the most mildly sympathetic with the popular cause. Our local enemy, of course, saw through this and acted accordingly, but it passed muster for some time with the authorities at British headquarters.

Like every other Catholic in our parish – in which there was then only one Protestant family – I took the anti-conscription pledge in April 1918, but that in itself did nothing to focus attention on me. However, I was eventually included in the Auxiliaries' 'black list' of persons to be 'done in', and I was lucky to learn of this in time through the friendly warning of one Dalton, an ex-policeman, who discovered it when calling to the Black & Tan barracks at Tulla in connexion with his R.I.C. pension. That however was not till after November, 1920. I first put my foot into it in a very foolish manner about a year before that. I was a member of the Dáil Industrial Resources Commission and on one occasion I was travelling with Darrell Figgis, Patrick Walsh and someone else in Clare on the business of that branch of the Republic's activities. I was still, however, officially classed as a 'law-abiding citizen'. We were held up by Black & Tans and Figgis was taken aside and interrogated. With the Tans was a man in plain clothes whom I was fool enough to believe was a prisoner of theirs. We were surrounded by armed men and he happened, intentionally as I realised afterwards, to get beside me several yards away from the nearest Tan. We fell into conversation. Never guessing who he was and deceived by a remark of his, I said with outspoken thoughtlessness that I had no use for semi-military policemen in Ireland and did not care how many of them were shot. I cannot imagine why he did not arrest me on the spot, for who was he but District Inspector Glynn of the R.I.C. I suppose he could hardly believe his ears, for he went straight on to Fr. Scanlan, the parish priest of Scariff, and asked him was I quite sane. At that stage the British were concentrating on the I.R.A. and did not interfere with the Dáil Commission or the Arbitration Courts, so I heard no more of the matter. I suppose Father Scanlan told him I was harmless. Our commission was not declared illegal until January 1920, when we held a meeting in Cork in secret after being forcibly prevented from doing so at the place publicly appointed. Though it was proscribed, needless to say we continued our work on the commission with the exception of one or two non Sinn Féin members who resigned when it came under the ban of the British authorities. An official report on the work of that commission was published later.

I have quite a number of entries in my diaries for the momentous years 1918–1921 but for the most part they are rather hastily scribbled because after 1918 I could not keep anything in the nature of a diary or note book with me. In the course of 26 raids many of my most interesting papers were taken away and I never saw them again.

I will have much to say about the misdeeds of the Auxiliaries and Black & Tans. I would like to record here that my strictures do not apply nearly so strongly to the Army. On one occasion, before the position became so acute that my diaries had to be cached, a raid was carried out on our house by an army contingent. I was not there at the time but Denis MacMahon was. The commanding officer found a diary of mine (fortunately not the current one) and evidently intended to take it away. Denis protested against the seizure of a purely private document. The colonel, or whatever he was, said it looked interesting and he would like to read it. He promised he would bring it back and much to Denis's surprise, a few days later an army lorry drove up to the hall door and the colonel waited till Denis had been brought in to accept formal return of the said diary. No one could picture an Auxiliary doing that.

I know from what I wrote at the time that I was becoming increasingly worried as to whether I was doing a full man's part in the rôle which was assigned to me. Father William Hackett, S.J., who was a great friend of mine, insisted that I was much more useful to the Irish Republic carrying on with the work I was doing than behind barbed wire or with a rifle in my hand. I found his advice a relief for he was a man whose opinion and advice I felt was really very valuable. So keen a Republican was he that he was later banished by the Provincial of the Jesuit Society to Australia on account of his outspoken opposition to the Treaty. It might be something to look back at to have been a prisoner at Frongoch or Ballykinlar but on the other hand I was undoubtedly much more useful free than interned.

We were accustomed at Raheen to raids, ill usage and terrorism but up to this no one connected with the place had actually been killed. The shooting on Killaloe bridge early in November 1920 of Denis MacMahon's brother Michael (Brod) with three other Scariff volunteers (Alphie Rogers, Martin Kildea and Michael Egan) while prisoners in the hands of the Auxiliaries therefore came as something of a shock to us, even though we thought we were hardened to all ordinary feelings of horror. I forget whether they were alleged to have been trying to escape. It does not matter, for that was the excuse used to account for every murder of a prisoner, except when (even more cynically) he was reported to have been shot by extremists on his own side, as they said about Lord Mayor MacCurtáin of Cork.

H. W. Nevinson in a book called *Changes and Chances* tells how he visited Raheen that November and found us all very much upset by this barbarous end to four of our comrades. I was not intimate with Michael MacMahon in the same way that I was with his brother Denis, who was then and is now my closest friend, but I knew and liked him well. He did not work for us at Raheen; his job was to manage, with his father, one of the two principal stores in Scariff. It was there we dealt for all our requirements until we started a co-operative store at Raheen and he was one of my best allies and helpers in my efforts to revive the Irish language as the spoken tongue of East Clare. I have an Irish prayer book of his which until the old mass books were superseded I used and still value highly.

Within a few days I was to experience a still sharper and more personal sense of loss. I was lucky having at Raheen two young men who were not only members of our staff but also really personal friends of my own. I have already mentioned Denis MacMahon. Denis became a partner in the Raheen business for a time. I arranged this more as a gesture of friendship than for any great financial benefit he was likely to gain by it. The other was Conor Clune, or MacClune as he preferred to be called. The fact that he was an employee did not of course prevent us from being friends and so we were. What particularly attracted me to Conor was our mutual enthusiasm for Irish. Though he was not actually a native speaker he had been sent as a boy to Ring and with him I was able to use Irish only. Apart from his having a pleasant personality he fitted in exactly with my plans for surrounding my little son Fergus (who was born in April 1917) with Irish speakers. Here I may mention incidentally that in this I was quite successful for he could not speak English till he was six years old and though he and I have spent a great deal of time together, especially up till the time he was twenty, we have never yet had a conversation in anything but Irish unless there was a third person present whose ignorance of Irish made it necessary to use English.

By November 1920, conditions were such that I felt that the Raheen motor car would surely be commandeered or smashed up by Crown forces if I kept it on the road any longer, so I decided to dismantle and hide it. The best place to do that, I thought, was in Dublin and in due course it found its way into a back lane near Baggot Street where one Nugent ran an obscure garage. Later on I put it on the road again and lent it to Michael Brennan, the leader of the Volunteers in Co. Clare, on whose ability, both as a military commander and as an administrator of civil affairs, I based the character of Daithy O'Broin in my novel

97

Toil Dé. The man called T.D. in that novel had also a foundation in real life, being suggested to me by that fine Clareman J. D. Moloney. I will have more to say about Michael Brennan in the next chapter.

The bringing of that old motor car to Dublin led to an event which has since got a great deal of publicity. It is a long story but of sufficient interest to be told in some detail.

It so happened that the Raheen Co-op accounts were due for annual audit at the time. It was arranged that Pat Hayes should come with me to Dublin with the books, but a last minute change had to be made because he was wanted at home in connexion with the coroner's inquest on Michael MacMahon and the other lads – the verdict, by the way, was wilful murder by Crown forces – and so Conor Clune took his place. It was thus mere chance that Conor came to Dublin at all.

We arrived in Dublin without incident on the Saturday evening, November 20th, and after spending the evening together we parted. He had lodgings in Haddington Road and did not sleep in my flat in Fitzwilliam Street as Denis MacMahon used to. We agreed to go to Mass together at Haddington Road church the next morning and afterwards to go to the big football match at Croke Park. Conor did not turn up. I went to his lodgings but was told he had not slept there. This was most disturbing. If it had been Denis or Pat Hayes who had not slept in his own bed I would have thought little of it. Denis MacMahon was hand in glove with the Volunteers and Pat Hayes who was adjutant of the East Clare Battalion did, with my knowledge, all the work connected therewith in our office at Raheen. Pat Hayes proved himself a man of character and in spite of repeated interrogations on the occasions of the many raids on Raheen – such questionings were no kid glove affairs – no one ever got a word out of him. Conor on the other hand was not 'in the know' at all. His usefulness lay in his devotion to the Irish language and it was this which proved his undoing. What actually happened was that he went to see a man called John O'Connell at Vaughan's hotel after leaving me on the Saturday evening. His business was a matter connected with the Gaelic League, but it so happened that Michael Collins and other leading members of the Volunteers, who frequently used Vaughan's Hotel as a rendezvous, were there at the time. The house was surrounded and they escaped by their usual channel but Conor, not being one of them, found himself alone when the Auxiliaries burst in and he was arrested. Dorothy McArdle in her book *The Irish Republic* says that Clune was

98

arrested on Sunday night with McKee and Clancy. Actually he was arrested on Saturday night, as I have said, and it was mere chance which put him with them in the guard room in the Castle, where prisoners were lodged after being brought in. Thus fate placed him in their company on the night of 1920's Bloody Sunday and caused him to be murdered along with them. It has also earned for him a posthumous fame, for as Volunteer Conor Clune his name is coupled in the anniversary celebrations with those doughty fighters Peadar Clancy and Dick McKee. Technically he can be so termed since he was a member of the National Volunteers before they disintegrated, and in any case I hold that he died for Ireland as surely as any of those who fell in battle.

Conor was particular about the form of his name, which has the prefix Mac not O. There is no question about this in regard to the Clare surname Clune, which is incorporated in the place name Ballymaclune in the heart of the traditional and present homeland of that sept. MacClúin has long been accepted as the correct modern form in Irish: Father Seoirse MacClúin so spells it on the title page of his well known book *Réilthíní Óir*. In April 1968, after the 1916 commemorative Mass in the Castle Chapel, members of the families of Clancy, McKee and Clune had been invited to go to the guard-room (which was too small to accommodate more than a few people) to attend the ceremonial opening of that room as a memorial to the three men murdered by the Auxiliaries after Bloody Sunday. The Clunes said to me that on this occasion I was virtually as much a Clune as they were and they brought me in with them. I was surprised and annoyed to see his name given as Ó Clúin under Conor's portrait. My impulse was to stand up on the spot and protest against what was, unwittingly, an insult to Conor's memory, but Eilís Clune restrained me. Ó Cluain does exist as a name but it is that of a Co. Wexford family entirely distinct from Clune of Co. Clare.

This has now been corrected by the Board of Works. Its representatives in 1968 cannot be blamed for the error as they were simply following the form used on the plaque on the wall outside, which was erected in 1939 evidently without any step being taken to ascertain what the name should be in Irish. It is in such an out of the way place that I imagine few people have ever taken much notice of it. I do not remember even looking at it myself before this question arose.

I was also surprised and disappointed to see that the bullet marks in the wall had been obliterated: that wall is now freshly plastered. Those marks were part of the history of the guard-room. When later I was in the hands of the Auxiliaries there they gloatingly pointed them out as indicating where Conor and the other two had been shot: evidently as a refinement of mental torture some shots deliberately missed their target.

That Sunday I was quite in the dark as to his movements. I went to Croke Park and stood outside the entrance in the hope that I might meet him there. I turned away having no heart to watch the football without him, only a few minutes before the shooting began when, as everyone knows, the crowd was fired on without the slightest provocation and twelve were killed and sixty odd wounded. I had a lucky escape there but in those days a miss was as good as a mile and my only concern was to find Conor. On the next day, Monday, I went to Mr Denroche, our family solicitor and friend, for advice. While I was in his office we heard a stop-press being shouted by the newsboys in the street outside. At that time stop press editions were not mere catch-pennies and a clerk was sent out for a copy. From it we learned that Peadar Clancy, Dick Mackee and a man called T. C. Clune had been shot dead in the Castle. Could this be Conor Clune, though his initial was not T? We feared so. Mr Denroche rang up every hospital in Dublin and did all that one man could do. He received point blank denials of any knowledge of the matter even from the place where Conor's body was actually then lying. Mr Denroche was both persistent and, what was more important, influential and eventually he learned that the bodies of those three men were at King George V Hospital. He went with me to the hospital but at that stage I was not allowed to view the bodies. We had to get a friendly military doctor to do this for us. Naturally it was impossible to identify a dead man from a mere description, but at length I was able to be reasonably sure that we had located poor Conor by certain of his effects which were shown to me. Application had then to be made to get possession of the body for burial. Up to that I had with me in Mr Denroche, a dependable and elderly man to whom the military showed some respect. From that on I had to act alone. When the order to remove the body was obtained, I went with a hearse to King George V Hospital. It was late November and it was already dark before I arrived. Endless and unnecessary delay followed. At long last I was told I could remove the remains but that I must go to the mortuary. I did so. Several bodies were lying there, all covered with sheets. I was brought to one and it was uncovered. 'Is that your man?' I was asked. The corpse bore a superficial resemblance to Conor and as I had no idea I was being put through a test I hesitated a moment. Could a man be so changed in death? 'No,' I answered then. The next dead man had a small moustache so I had no hesitation in saying that he was not the right one. Thirdly we came to Conor himself and I claimed him. The other two. I realized afterwards, were McKee and Clancy.

As I shall show immediately the pretence that those three had been shot while trying to escape was patently absurd. But I am bound to say that the statement which was afterwards made by Dorothy McArdle in *The Irish Republic* to the effect that their faces were so battered about as to be almost unrecognizable and horrible to look at is quite untrue. Frank O'Connor repeats it in his book on Michael Collins, *The Big Fellow*. I remember those pale dead faces as if I had looked at them yesterday. They were not disfigured. Our case is strong enough: such hearsay inaccuracies, fortunately few, tend to weaken rather than strengthen it.

By the time I at last got possession of Conor's body and had the coffin on the hearse it was already almost curfew hour. We went to Westland Row church and deposited the coffin there: I then had to make my way back to Fitzwilliam Street in the dark and silent streets. I was unlikely to be shot at sight for being out after curfew, because there were always occasional people to be seen who had received permits to be out for some special reason. I, of course, had no permit. However I met no one and with the feeling that I had accomplished the first step in my job I went to bed.

It was only the first step however. The next morning I had an ordeal before me. I got Dr William Pearson, who had been a military doctor and a colonel in the British army during the War, to accompany me to Westland Row or at least to a stable in a house on the other side of what is now Pearse Street. There we unscrewed the coffin which I had removed from Westland Row church and took out the body of what had been one of my best friends. I stood by while Dr Pearson carefully examined the wounds and noted down exactly where each bullet had entered the body. There were thirteen bullet holes in his chest. Pearson's report made it perfectly clear that the official statement that Conor was shot while trying to escape was a fabrication.*

As I was in Dublin and they were not, the Clune family had to leave all this work to me. I remember with thanks that I had the assistance of Frank O'Dea the brother of my friend Father John, who like the Clunes hailed from Quin, Co. Clare. He made all the

*See N.L. Ms. 5368 for details. See also the Auxiliary's remark to me (p. 108 *infra*) for confirmation of this.

arrangements for the funeral so far as the Dublin end of it was concerned. We said farewell to the mortal remains of Conor MacClune when the motor hearse O'Dea had hired disappeared at the end of Westland Row that morning.

Then I realized that I had been through a fierce strain for several days. There was more to come, however.

The very day of Conor's funeral at Quin the biggest raid ever made upon Raheen was carried out. Prior to the events I am now relating I was unknown to the British authorities in Dublin. As far as Clare was concerned I was more or less 'on the run'. The co-ordinating of the various units of the British Forces in Ireland at that time was slight. Thus I could be marked down by the Auxiliaries of Killaloe for death and at the same time be quite unknown to the Auxiliaries in Dublin, that is to those units of Auxiliaries who carried out those sentences of death which were not officially ordained though always officially condoned. My family had moved to France in the previous September.

Every man in Raheen had, in spite of the prohibition of such gatherings, gone to Quin on the day of Conor's funeral. The Auxiliaries and Tans who came to Raheen in several lorries thus met no one but some women and children. They proceeded to empty my private house of its moveable contents, even going to the length of hacking a picture out of its frame. The Auxiliaries had only one good quality – courage; otherwise, although they were all supposed to be ex-officers of the British Army, they were on a level with the vandals who in peaceful times amuse themselves by breaking up seats and destroying trees in a public park. They returned again on the next day. So clean a sweep did they make of our house that having filled every available suitcase and portmanteau they then got hold of pillow cases off the beds and stuffed these with clothes.

After their departure the place was more or less a wreck, much of the destruction being quite wanton. They left a trail after them as they went. Thus the legs of a pair of pyjamas of mine were found on the avenue and further on a photograph which had been thrown out and the frame retained. I was telling Father Sherwin about this raid: so much a commonplace of everyday life were such recitals that he listened with no more than common politeness to my tale, until I mentioned that the discarded photograph was one of himself. Then he seemed more interested. In actual fact, most of these clothes belonged to my father. He was in Australia having left his surplus clothes at my house, since Hazelwood was at the time being renovated; they were all looted by the Auxiliaries as well as any ladies' clothes the house contained. The latter gave rise to the anecdote which I used in my novel *Toil Dé* but may perhaps be permitted to tell again.

Two women, camp-followers let us call them of the Auxiliaries, fell into a heated argument on the bridge at Killaloe. A slanging match ensued in which one combatant delivered the *coup de grace* with these words: 'Well,' says she, 'I may not be married, but at any rate I am not wearing Mrs MacLysaght's furs.'

My mother was not the woman to lie down under what she considered an injustice. Her behaviour during the three years 1919, 1920 and 1921 was such as to make me very proud of her. Apart from the war she deserves the greatest credit for the way in which, though she only started to learn Irish at the age of fifty-four, she valiantly managed to keep up with my young children in that language. However we are dealing now with the Irish struggle for independence and, though the cultivation of the Irish language was certainly an aspect of this, my mother did her part well in more dangerous fields*

After the big November raids she was filled with indignation and went to Dublin to protest. So determined was she in the face of persistent refusals to listen to her in more than the most perfunctory way, that at last, after several hours literally sitting in the cold upon the doorstep of General Tudor's office in the Castle, she eventually saw him personally and gave him a piece of her mind. The excuse he offered for the looting was that the linings of the clothes had to be searched for hidden documents and his men had not time to do it on the spot. This statement of his afterwards proved of great value to us because when, after the Treaty, we brought our case before the Shaw-Thomas Commission with a claim to compensation for destruction by British military forces, we won it on the technical point that the damage was an 'act of war' as stated by Gen. Tudor. My mother's

---

*Denis MacMahon has often helped me in connexion with my memories of those exciting times. When he had read this chapter he expressed annoyance, saying that I had wronged my mother by not mentioning one of the most courageous of her actions, namely the time she went to Killaloe to beard the notoriously dangerous auxiliary Col. Andrews in his den after one of the worst raids: when he denied her accusations she pointed to one of his men who was in the room and said 'That man there was in it and he was about the worst of a bad lot' or words to that effect. If she had not been an elderly lady of sixty she would hardly have got home without being beaten up. I might add that the substance of this account was given to me not by herself but by Siobháin MacMahon (Denis's wife) who drove her to Killaloe in the pony trap and was with her during the interview.

testimony on this was a point of prime importance, because compensation was not payable in cases of mere looting, and resulted in our receiving over £1,000 compensation for the damage done by the Auxiliaries at the time of Conor Clune's funeral. This included £180 for our motor boat; they took it out on the lake and sank it in deep water there. That, of course, was a perfectly justifiable act on their part for the same boat had often been effectively used in helping the Volunteers. The system adopted was such that no opposition was made to that part of our claim.

At the time my mother was bearding Tudor in his den there was no question of compensation – such ideas belonged to a time when hostilities had ceased. Her object was to do what she could to curb the outrageous exploits of the Auxiliaries, and to fix responsibility on irresponsible men who were always able to plead that they could not exercise complete control over subordinates liable to see red under the continual strain of ambushes etc. etc.

On the Irish side indeed the war was waged with two weapons; in a word we may say, bullets were supplemented with 'Bulletins'. The frightfulness of the Auxiliaries and the more cowardly bad work of the Black & Tans, nerve-racking though it was to us who had to live under it, was in fact steadily telling in our favour as the facts began to leak out. And this they did in spite of the severest censorship. Gradually not only America, where we expected sympathy, but even the more liberal minded people in England began to realize that what were the perfectly legitimate aspirations of the Irish people were, within a year or two of the war which was ostensibly fought for the freedom and self-determination of small nations, being ruthlessly suppressed by naked and barbarous force. The Ministry of Propaganda run by Erskine Childers was in fact a very vital element on the Irish side.

The official republican publication, the *Irish Bulletin*, was probably the principal means by which the truth was made known to the outside world. I received my copy of this regularly from its first issue in November 1919. With remarkable carelessness, my mother one day when conditions were at their worst – February 1921 – took two numbers of the 'Bulletin' with her to read in the train which she boarded at Killaloe station. The train was stopped on the way to Limerick; the passengers were searched and she was court-martialled for this minor offence. Her sentence was one month with an alternative of a fine of £20. Now it so happened that this court-martial at Limerick took place on the very day my father returned from Australia. I regret to say that he paid the fine for her, saying that he could never let his wife go off to jail the very day he returned after five months' absence. It may be said in extenuation that he had been out of the country during all the period of the most intensive Black & Tan and Auxiliary campaign and could not be expected to feel just as we did who had been through it all. I was not present at the court-martial or I would certainly have done my best to dissuade him. My mother, determined character though she was, never had a mind of her own where he was concerned.

She gave evidence before the American Commission of Enquiry and the purport of this is printed in their extensive Report. That Report was in itself another powerful antidote to British misrepresentation. What largely contributed to driving a peacefully-inclined man like myself into rebellion was the British attitude towards us: the assumption that the whole lot of us were a pack of murdering cornerboys.

Even after the murder of Conor Clune I was still instructed to play the part of a respectable employer with perhaps some sympathy with Sinn Féin. I had no time to suffer much reaction from the strain of the previous week, for a few days later Mrs Desmond FitzGerald sought me out and told me that I was expected to turn Conor's death to account. Desmond FitzGerald was the Minister for Propaganda at the time. I was not satisfied with her vague message but on getting definite intructions from FitzGerald and Arthur Griffith I crossed over to London with the object of exposing in every way I could the cold-blooded murder of a non-combatant in the person of my friend and employee Conor Clune. In my capacity as an employer I had written a few days earlier a factually accurate letter to the London *Times* which they printed under the heading 'The case of Mr Clune'. I quote it: –

You published in *The Times* of Wednesday, 24th inst., under the heading of 'Murder Gang Members' statements about my friend Mr Clune who was shot while in custody of Crown forces on Monday last. The statement which you published as an official report, and which therefore I am sure was issued as such, is untrue in all the important particulars relating to Mr Clune.

For seven years Mr Clune has been employed by my firm as head clerk in our office at Raheen, Co. Clare. Of late he has also been my intimate friend so that I can speak about him with entire confidence. He was not a member of the I.R.A. and never had been: the official report states that he was a lieutenant in the Clare brigade, I.R.A. The official report refers to a notebook found on him and supposed to incriminate him. The supposedly dangerous names in it – common ones like Tracey and Collins – must be those entered in the ordinary course of his work, of men in our employment or of persons with whom we have business relations. All our office staff have similar note-books which are part of our system of management. The notes about obtaining passports were those connected with procuring passports for my wife and family to go to France recently and some other members of my family to go to South Africa.

Mr Clune came to Dublin with me in my motorcar on Friday. He was arrested on Saturday night. He came on business connected with his accountancy work. He spent Saturday up to 3 p.m. with me; he asked me to go to a theatre with him which unfortunately I was unable to do, and had arranged to spend all Sunday with me. So much for his movements of which we are officially informed he was unable to give a satisfactory account. It is important to know, in case it should be alleged that the business which brought him to Dublin was a cloak for other activities, that it was only at the last moment, owing to purely personal reasons, that I substituted Mr Clune for another member of the staff who was to have come with me. It is unfortunate that the responsible Press have no means of checking official reports issued from Dublin Castle and that no enquiry such as you have demanded is held at which the truth of any official statement can be tested.

In the foregoing letter I deliberately did not give the reason why my family had to go to France nor did I mention how it came about that Conor chanced to be arrested (as I have recounted on p. 98 above).

In London I began by calling to make an appointment with Sir John Simon. He was then in Opposition and a few months later was very active in attacking the Government on its policy of 'frightfulness' in Ireland. I have no record of what form of introduction I had nor can I remember how I succeeded in interviewing several important public men. Surprisingly I had breakfast with Sir John Simon at his house and later on lunched with him at some kind of office in a legal atmosphere. He was very sympathetic but regarded the case from the point of view of how much anti-Lloyd-George capital could be made out of it. He was remarkably hospitable and friendly to a young stranger and at

The Black & Tans: personal experiences

the same time impressed me with his quick grasp of essentials, a quality common to all really successful barristers. Later I had no difficulty in seeing Sir Oswald Mosely, who seemed at the time to be a 'coming man'. I remember being struck by the incongruity of, on the one hand, his luxurious dwelling and super-aristocratic wife and on the other of his membership of the Labour Party. More difficult to come at was Mr Asquith. I called at his house and was told by the butler that he was not available; but, having point blank refused to leave till I saw him, I was left to wait for at least 1½ hours. The butler was clearly uneasy because he kept reappearing in the hall where I was: it was a droll position for in the circumstances I could hardly ask him to show me the loo. Mr Asquith's attitude was fully in keeping with the phrase which will always be associated with his name, 'Wait and see'. I left after a few minutes convinced that he would completely forget about me and the death of Conor Clune as soon as the door closed behind me. After other interviews with various newspaper men and private individuals I returned to Dublin and reported.

These moves on my part were apparently known to the authorities. They knew where I was accustomed to work by day but fortunately were unaware of where I slept. They thought I occupied the flat over Maunsel's publishing offices and the night after I returned the Auxiliaries raided this and told Mrs Robertson, who lived there, that they wanted me. Next morning when I went to the office she came down to tell me this. Before I had time to decide what to do, while I was attending to some very urgent business matters which had accumulated in my absence, a tender drew up at the door outside and in a few minutes I was arrested and driven swiftly away down Baggot Street. As usual a small crowd had collected, among whom were my fellow-workers from Maunsel's office. I waved good-bye to them and remember only two things before I found myself in the guard room at the Castle: one was the intense cold of driving very fast in a vehicle without a wind-screen and the other was waving to an acquaintance in Grafton Street – a person who was not remarkable for sympathy with the Republic!

I have described that guard room and its occupants in *Toil Dé*. Some lurid details descriptive of Auxiliary behaviour which I included in the manuscript were omitted when it was published. As regards myself, I did, like Diarmuid in the book, eventually give in and address my captor as 'Sir' but continued to wear my Fáinne.* The incident of the rifle left lying on the unoccupied bed

*The emblem indicative of ability and inclination to speak Irish.

was fact. Another matter not mentioned in *Toil Dé* but referred to earlier in this chapter was that the Auxiliary in charge gloatingly pointed to the bullet holes in the wall which he stated had been made at the time 'that friend of yours, Clune, was finished off'. They would obviously have liked to give me the same treatment if they could have got away with it with the same certainty they had felt during the high tension of the 'Bloody Sunday' week-end. They had a special hatred for anyone who attempted to expose their misdoings and I had just been so engaged in London, as they evidently knew. My recollection was that it was Mr Denroche who somehow got me released. Here I have another example of the value of having Denis MacMahon to check my sometimes faulty memory. As Denis reminds me Mr Denroche did not hear of my arrest that day. The fact was that in Maunsel's office we had a man named Johnson who was there when I was taken away: he went immediately to see a man he knew, a Mr Bolton who had some standing with the authorities. Denis assures me that it was his influence, not Mr Denroche's, that secured my release after barely 24 hours in custody.

I was glad to get out of their clutches. At any rate, though it meant risking a journey through the dark streets during curfew hours I wisely refused an escort. Such 'escorts' had a way of removing 'Shinners' conveniently and in the weeks following they were not likely to be asked any questions which could not be evaded about a fracas in the streets; and they were sure of tacit approval from Hamar Greenwood, the Chief Secretary, who was as unprincipled, or should I say credulous, as his predecessor, Ian MacPherson.

I was not molested on my way to my flat in Upper Fitzwilliam Street and so ended the most eventful month of my life.

I can recall many other incidents in which I was involved. If I relate two of these it will be enough to complete the picture of life in Ireland as I saw it during the years 1916 to 1921.

I went to France once in 1920 for a brief visit to my family. For that purpose I needed a passport: mine was out of date and the local police refused to recommend its renewal, so Denis said he would go to the Castle and see if he could do anything about it. He went there and asked to see Sir James MacMahon. Before him in the waiting room were two other men, one of whom was the Lord Mayor of Dublin. When both of these were told that Sir James was not there, and had eventually been got rid of, the official in charge asked Denis had he an appointment. 'I haven't,' said he, 'I came to see Sir James.' Denis's casual approach and his name being MacMahon must have made the man think that he was a relative of the V.I.P. for he forthwith took him to the private office and left him standing inside the door. The Under-Secretary continued his work without looking up, thinking presumably that the official was there. When he did look up he saw a stranger. On hearing his name, instead of firing Denis out, he became friendly, and the upshot was that the passport was sent to me without delay.

On my way back from the South of France I called to see Seán T. O'Kelly in Paris, where he was acting as Irish representative. He gave me a dispatch to deliver in Dublin. I returned via Cork and decided to spend a night at Raheen before going on to Dublin. At that time the direct railway line from Cork to Limerick was still in operation. When my train stopped at Croom I saw that there was a big squad of Auxiliaries and Tans on the platform and it soon became apparent that their job was to search the passengers. Now I had Sean T's letter tucked away inside my shoe, inside my sock in fact. Before they reached me I noticed that the searching seemed pretty thorough, though I saw only one man actually made to take off his boots: still I felt I could not take any chances. It so happened that I had two very personal letters, written in Irish (of no political significance but much treasured by me) in a pocket inside my waistcoat, which might have been designed as a hiding-place. When my turn came to be searched I managed to make what I hoped would look like an involuntary gesture towards that pocket; and my ruse succeeded. When they found the letters they evidently assumed that being written in Irish they must be treasonable and, as I had hoped, they neglected to search me much further. They detained me and when the train had gone on they kept me in the R.I.C. barracks while they took what steps they could to find out what the letters contained. I have no idea how they did so, if they did. I know that having got my name and address from the label on my baggage they let me go after a few hours without my precious letters but with Seán T's intact.

The other incident I have in mind is of more general interest. As I have mentioned earlier in this account Pat Hayes was the adjutant of the East Clare Brigade and his paper work in that capacity was done in our office. One day word came to him that the commanding officer of the Auxiliaries at Killaloe was intending to have the Workhouse at Scariff occupied by a contingent of his men as a barracks. It was decided to forestall this move by burning down the Workhouse. This decision was complicated by the fact that the District Hospital was an integral part of the Workhouse block of buildings, so that the disposal of the patients in it was definitely an urgent problem. We had only twelve hours to carry out the necessary operation. The large old house at Raheen, since we had gone to live in the new one, had been converted into three dwellings and the office. The occupants of the three flats (to use a modern word) had to be got out at a moment's notice and their families brought to relatives' houses in the neighbourhood, and the majority of the hospital patients with their beds etc. brought over from Scariff and installed in the vacated rooms – as secretly as possible lest by some chance the Auxiliaries at Killaloe might get wind of it. Well, it went without a hitch and when the British forces arrived in the morning, to find the road to Tuamgraney and Scariff blocked, we were all at home innocently preparing to go out for the normal day's work on the land. When they came to our house I simulated astonishment at the sight of the black paper ashes which were floating around us like snowflakes in the breeze, more than a mile as the crow flies from the scene of the conflagration. With all the Raheen staff and some neighbours who were roped in I was forced to spend much of the day under armed guard clearing the blocked road. We had reason to be pleased with ourselves as no garrison was established at Scariff then or later.

Quite recently I received in my capacity of chairman of the Manuscripts Commission a letter enquiring where the Rural District Council and other local records kept at the Scariff Workhouse are to be found. On learning the facts our correspondent rang me up personally and blamed me for their loss. In 1920 I was not concerned with archives and if I had been I doubt if I would have given them more than a passing thought on that exciting night. I confess that when I saw the black 'snowflakes' falling the next morning it never occurred to me that we had destroyed anything of historical value. Writing now, more than fifty years later, I should add that even though they only dated back to 1898 such records are worthy of preservation or at any rate of examination before being destroyed.

CHAPTER IX

The East Clare Brigade

In the last chapter I recounted some of my own comparatively unimportant experiences in the War of Independence. In this I will give some account of our East Clare Brigade. I was not an active volunteer in it but I co-operated with it; I was a 'backroom boy', as the last incident in the previous chapter will illustrate. Its adjutant (Pat Hayes) used my office for all his confidential paper work and I played the part assigned to me throughout those three crucial years. So I was pleased, if rather surprised, to have been included in the reunion of the East Clare Old I.R.A. which took place at Knapogue Castle in April 1968. I am proud of the I.R.A. of my day. This book is not the place for comment on the I.R.A. of today.

Most people under sixty find it hard to realize the spirit, at once enthusiastic and indomitable, which then permeated almost our entire population, and many of those who shared that exhilarating experience cannot now recapture it. Nevertheless I believe that spirit is still latent and could be rekindled if suitable circumstances should arise.

I will try to tell how we all felt in those unforgettable years. I say 'all' and that word is perhaps the keynote, for after 1916 there was a unity of purpose actuating us which is unique in Irish history. In that period there were no informers and no potential Quislings. In those parts of the country where English influence was strong there were of course not a few whose sympathies were with the enemy, but I doubt if there were a dozen such in East Clare, and these if they existed, remained quiescent and kept their thoughts to themselves for fear of the consequences of their attitude. I can only speak from first-hand knowledge for Co. Clare. There we had complete confidence in our leaders, whose coolness and courage was an inspiration to us. Nor was the courage confined to our leaders and the flying columns which acted under their direct orders, for had not courage and complete trustworthiness been found among the people generally the actual fighting men would soon have been

111

captured and the whole campaign brought to a speedy and ignominious end. As we know, the combination of a small well-directed and fearless body of the Volunteers* acting with the co-operation of the whole civilian population was almost incredibly successful, though how long the fight could have been continued had not the Truce come when it did in July, 1921 is a matter of doubt. If any further proof of the whole-hearted support of the people were wanted it would be furnished by the remarkable response on the part of the small farmers – never too eager to subscribe to sentimental causes – when Michael Collins launched the First Dáil Loan. Very few of us expected ever to see our money again, though in fact it was all repaid a few years later.

In Clare, and particularly around Tuamgraney and Scariff, we had a foretaste of what was to come, sooner than most of the country, because as early as February 1918 this district was put under martial law. A curfew was enforced and the whole community was harassed by the petty tyrants in command, particularly those who actually lived in the town. When I say the town I am referring to Scariff and Tuamgraney together, for, though in different parishes and quite distinct in the minds of the local people, the two places are contiguous and appear to be one: the older hotel, the Guards' barracks, the Vocational School, the creamery, one of the largest in Ireland, and the large chipboard factory (Scariff's main industrial concern), as well as the street of houses they stand in, all of which are counted as Scariff, are actually in Tuamgraney parish.

I could fill pages with examples of the exasperating effects of this régime. Later on, however, when the Black and Tans and Auxiliaries came on the scene, as a frankly hostile and terrorizing force, the martial law of 1918 seemed mild in retrospect, for the most part a matter of inconvenience and indignity compared with this new and continuous danger to life and property which was to follow.

The lot of the civilian population was very different from that of the I.R.A. but it is no disparagement of the I.R.A. to say that it was the solid backing they got from the people which made their success possible. The participation of the non-combatants – if that is not a contradiction in terms – is a feature of guerilla warfare; and I think that a sketch of the conditions under which

*The designation 'I.R.A.' was at first seldom used for the men we called 'The Volunteers' but by degrees after they became the official army of the Dáil it was generally adopted.

the ordinary man then lived will make a fitting background for the main picture.

As is well known, after the General Election of 1918 and the subsequent setting up of the First Dáil Éireann the long-awaited Independence of Ireland was formally and solemnly declared by that body, the first Irish Parliament in which Catholics sat since 1689. The British Government, predictably, ignored the Declaration and regarded Dáil Éireann as an illegal and treasonable assembly. They tried to continue functioning as the only government of Ireland. The people of Ireland, excluding the Unionists of Belfast and north-eastern counties, gave their allegiance to the Dáil. In places like Dublin, where the armed forces of the Crown were sufficiently strong, the British continued to make a semblance of carrying on constitutional government and the Irish authority had to work 'underground'; in others more remote, the 'King's writ' simply did not run and the machinery of government was openly operated by the Dáil Ministries. Co. Clare was one of these. We paid no taxes to the British revenue, we took our law cases to the courts set up by the Dáil; in short we avoided the complications arising from the existence of two rival authorities. Nevertheless, though this was so, we were somewhat in the position of an 'occupied' country. The County Council, for example, which had declared its allegiance to Dáil Éireann, could not (on account of the close attentions of the British military quartered in Ennis and other places in the county) hold regular meetings, but was obliged to conduct its business *sub rosa* at great personal risk to its members. I had the greatest admiration for those men and particularly for their chairman, who was none other than the redoubtable Michael Brennan. The way he managed to attend, and attend most efficiently, to civic affairs while the main burden of the military campaign was on his shoulders, was amazing. In this connexion the help he got from the fearless and indefatigable J. D. Molony, the vice-chairman of the Council, and also from Michael Carey, the secretary, must always be remembered.

It is hardly necessary to say that it was impossible for us at Raheen to carry on our normal avocations in a normal way. We had, for example, to abandon the working of a large tillage field lying alongside the main road lest our men be killed or wounded by the Auxiliaries who used to make forays at breakneck speed out from Killaloe, firing indiscriminately from their lorries as they went; the weekly wages (which at the time greatly exceeded our receipts, so complete was the dislocation of normal business) had to be paid irregularly and by surreptitious methods lest the pay packets be appropriated by uniformed marauders; work on the farm itself was spasmodic as several of the staff often operated by night as members of the I.R.A. – only the flying columns were full-time soldiers. I was not actually beaten up by Crown forces, as were many, including several of our own men; nor was my house burned down at a moment's notice as were those of some of my neighbours; but I know how it feels to be woken at early dawn by peremptory banging on the door and to sit for hours in chilly night attire while a search is being made, knowing full well that if by chance a certain secret hiding place is discovered I am 'for it'.

I had many adventures but my personal experiences, exciting though I found them myself, were small beer compared with those of hundreds of other better men than I; and I mention them to illustrate how far from peaceful was the life of the ordinary man. In actual fact I hardly saw Clare, except for a few clandestine visits, from the end of November, 1920 till the following May, because, as I have said, I was arrested as the result of my actions following the murder of Conor Clune, and after my release I was warned through an R.I.C. pensioner whose sympathies were with us, that I had a prominent place on the local Auxiliaries' black list. During the last couple of months before the Truce, however, they were so much occupied with their always abortive attempts to capture Michael Brennan and his flying column that they paid less attention to non-combatants as such, though more savage than ever towards them when they suspected them of lending active assistance.

Leaving aside Dublin and large urban districts where the conditions were so different that comparison with rural places is valueless, East Clare has much to its credit, probably indeed more than any other area in Ireland. I am thinking not only of the actual fighting but also of the lead given to the rest of the country. It is my aim to tell what was done in that respect as well as to give some account of the military activities of the Volunteers.

Clare was rather slow in starting. It is true that in 1913 and 1914 a considerable number of companies were formed. All over the country they sprang into being, following the establishment of the Ulster Volunteers by Sir Edward Carson, without any interference on the part of the British authorities. The gun-running, Bachelor's Walk and other interesting events of that time, are a matter of history, and they do not concern Co. Clare directly. Suffice it to say that these companies were ephemeral, though the drilling done by them, very thoroughly in certain cases, was of value because it gave some preliminary training to those individual volunteers who subsequently joined the ranks of the genuine fighting men and did something more useful than mere drilling. The body known as the National Volunteers, to which these early companies belonged, can be disregarded because as such they contributed nothing to the fight for independence; in fact they had ceased to exist long before 1918, when the 'shooting war' began in earnest.

Let us then forget the National (or Redmondite) Volunteers and glance at the beginnings and development of the East Clare Brigade.

I suggested some years ago to General Michael Brennan that he should write the account I am now attempting. With undue modesty he disclaimed the necessary literary skill to do it. He did the next best thing, however; he lent me his very extensive notes and talked to me at length about them. I have also had conversations with several other prominent members of the East Clare Brigade to supplement the information obtained from Gen. Brennan. This arrangement has one advantage, were he to have contributed this himself he would undoubtedly have hidden his own light under a bushel. There is no need for me to minimize his exploits and those of us who were in East Clare between 1917 and 1921 know that the story of the East Clare Brigade cannot be written without following the career of Michael Brennan. I am not concerned here with anything which occurred after 1921.

The Brennans' home is at Meelick, which though in Clare is very close to the city of Limerick; and Michael's earliest contacts with the national movement were in Limerick itself where as a mere boy, too young to be admitted without special permission, he was sworn in as a member of the I.R.B. in 1911. His beginnings were thus in a revolutionary atmosphere with nothing of the milk and water quality which characterized contemporary politics.

The first Volunteer company to be formed in Clare was that of Meelick, followed soon after by Oatfield, a place nearby: both were organized by the Brennans – Michael, his elder brother Paddy and Austin, the other boy of the family. Some other companies were established but not much progress was made before 1916. Nevertheless the nucleus of a fighting force had been created; and these volunteers mobilized in several places for action in Easter Week, over a hundred men, for example, concentrating at Bunratty. Eoin MacNeill's countermanding of the Rising prevented a nation-wide outbreak; it left the Volunteer units in the country uncertain what to do. Individuals here and there tried to take some action but all concerted plans were inevitably disorganized and in most places, including Co. Clare, isolated attempts to participate just fizzled out. Those who were known to the police as prominent Volunteers became marked men, and soon after Easter Week they were arrested and did not seé Clare again until they were released some ten months later; some of them spent most of the two following years in jails and prison camps.

The men of East Clare managed to strike more than one effective blow in the struggle for independence. The importance of their actions has received very little recognition and it should be stated clearly and with emphasis.

They were the first in this phase of the national struggle to adopt as a deliberate policy the course of non-recognition of the British courts. They argued that in the past Irish 'rebels', by availing themselves of legal aid at their trials, had made a double mistake; for to plead at all was tantamount to admitting the right of the court to try them; and to employ counsel for that purpose meant dissipating financial resources which could be very much better spent in advancing the cause in other ways. This idea was then so novel that its wisdom was not realized at first, but in due course it was universally adopted and East Clare should have the credit of initiating it in Ireland.

Another idea which emanated from the same source was the organized use of the hunger-strike weapon. In this case there was again a two-fold objective; first to maintain a continuous struggle even when in prison, and secondly to keep up the morale of the men by making them feel that they were 'doing their bit' all the time. The moral effect of being on the offensive rather than on the defensive was important. Organized hunger strikes were resorted to at the least provocation and the only time the men felt that no progress was being made was when the prison authorities granted every demand put forward. In that case, fortunately for those who were carrying on this gunless warfare, the prisoners were shortly afterwards removed to another jail where one or two minor privileges won in their previous place of captivity were withdrawn and it was possible thus to find a reason for once more employing this method of embarrassing and worrying their captors. These heroic tactics, culminating as they did in the death of Thomas Ashe and Terence MacSwiney, not only had the effect of attracting world-wide attention and causing the authorities grave disquiet, but also did a great deal to mould public opinion in Ireland and to create that spirit of determination which was such a great factor in our ultimate success.

The East Clare election result was declared on July 12th, 1917 and organized drilling was carried out in many parts of Clare on the following Sunday. Peadar O'Loughlin of Liscannor and the three Brennan brothers were arrested and charged with illegal drilling and tried by court-martial in Cork. They refused to recognize the court and were sentenced to two years hard labour. After ten days of hunger strike they were transferred to Mountjoy Prison where they were joined by more than thirty others, mostly from Clare. When they went on hunger strike there they were forcibly fed, but, as we know, the government gave in when Tom Ashe died.

Later on, too, when our men were back again on active service and the Black and Tan terror was at its height, Clare blazed the trail and more than once gave a lead to the country. When, for example, the rather pusillanimous 'peace resolution' of the Galway Co. Council came up for consideration by the Clare Co. Council (in secret session, of course), the latter resolved that the proper way to treat the document was to burn it and forthwith did so.

Yet again in the purely practical sphere East Clare gave a lead in at least one respect. When the Auxiliaries came on the scene it was soon realized that they differed from the ordinary Black and Tans inasmuch as they were clever as well as being tough. Their technique necessitated the working out of an elaborate system of protection. A watching system was devised covering the country right up to their bases. In addition to the systematic obstruction of roads, which was a feature of the war in all parts of the country, the East Clare leaders hit upon a novel plan. Local volunteers were posted day and night at various points ready to give the signal the moment a raiding party left their base. Thus when the column was located in the Scariff area, a bonfire ready for ignition was lighted on the side of the Slieve Bernagh mountains above Ogonnelloe to show that the raiders had left Killaloe. This bonfire was clearly visible on the other side of Lough Derg anywhere between Scariff and Whitegate. The local scouts in this area at once aroused the column who assembled at an agreed mobilization point. In the same way other areas in East Clare where the column operated were covered. This system worked admirably; and G.H.Q. issued a copy of the East Clare Protection Order as a model to all other brigades.

Meanwhile martial law had been proclaimed in Co. Clare; once again our county was in the van – and on January 21, 1919, the first shots of what has come to be known as the Black & Tan war were fired at Soloheadbeg, Co. Tipperary, closely followed at Knocklong by the rescue of Seán Hogan from the train in which he was being conveyed as a prisoner.

East Clare was made a separate brigade early in 1919, with Michael Brennan as brigadier. Paddy Brennan had resigned his command owing to his dissatisfaction with G.H.Q. His reasons need not be recorded here; in any case it was felt with some justification that G.H.Q. was neglecting the Clare Brigade, especially in the matter of supplying arms and ammunition. Our men argued that Co. Cork was getting more than their fair share. No one denied that supplies were very scarce or that Cork would make good use of them, but nevertheless it was a fact that hardly any rifles at all came west of the Shannon, and a war, even a guerilla war, cannot be conducted with revolvers and home-made bombs alone. A special grievance lay in the fact that of the thirty rifles which my father had procured for the Raheen National Volunteers, and which had been by tacit consent transferred to G.H.Q. (I.V.) in 1916, not one was returned to Co. Clare when serious fighting began two years later. It is a matter for regret that they ever went to Dublin at all, but had this not been done at the time they would have been lost altogether.

Throughout the whole campaign this shortage of arms and ammunition was one of the chief difficulties with which the East Clare Volunteers had to contend. If the units of the 'flying column' were eventually all armed with rifles it was only because they succeeded in capturing them from the enemy; at no time up to the Truce were more than a very few of the part-time men so equipped, and as a result nothing in the nature of a battle proper could be attempted. Circumstances necessitated purely guerilla tactics. This meant using the mobile column for frequent attacks on so-called police barracks (actually military posts) with the dual object of capturing arms and ammunition and of making the enemy concentrate his forces in as few places as possible. The mobile units ambushes kept the greatly superior numbers of the British forces in a constant state of uncertainty and anxiety. The local volunteers took some part in these attacks and ambushes; but their main function was to impart local knowledge, to act as scouts and to carry out the important task of blocking roads by felling trees, knocking walls down, and so on, so as to slow the movements of military lorries and give the mobile column time to retire into the mountains after the operation had been carried out.

In considering this campaign it must always be borne in mind that its primary object was to make the government of Ireland by Great Britain an impossibility and so to win the independence to which our country had a moral right and which according to accepted democratic principles, should have been obtained without recourse to arms at all.

The campaign, then, consisted of a series of these attacks and ambushes, some successful, in a military sense, some not, but all successful in furthering the object outlined in the previous paragraph. Not many of our men were killed in actual engagements. Some were murdered in cold blood, the most notorious case being that of Volunteers Michael MacMahon (Denis's brother), Alphonsus Rodgers, Martin Kildea and Michael Egan, who had been captured while asleep in Egan's house near Whitegate and a few nights later were shot on Killaloe bridge while in the custody of the Auxiliaries there. The usual excuse was made that they were shot while attempting to escape, but the circumstances of their 'liquidation' were such as to make this plea even more implausible than was customary in such cases.

How utterly false these 'official reports' were I can assert from first-hand knowledge. On an earlier page I have given incontrovertible proof that Conor Clune, who was shot 'attempting to escape' from Dublin Castle, was in fact stood against a wall and summarily executed while an untried prisoner.

If the number killed in action in East Clare was small, a good many were wounded. Michael Brennan himself was severely injured in an engagement at O'Brien's Bridge, and for a long time he was very much hampered by a broken right arm.

This chapter does not purport to give a connected account of the military actions which took place in East Clare between 1918 and 1921: my aim is just to give a general idea of how the campaign was carried out.

Readers unacquainted with Co. Clare, and especially those who do not know Ireland at all, will find it hard to visualize the scene I want to put before them: a countryside of small farms each with its own dwellinghouse – seldom two close together;

small fields and innumerable fences, either stone walls or ditches (as we call the clay banks topped with furze or thorn quicks); very little flat ground, for all that country slopes down to the shores of Lough Derg or up to the mountains, northwards to Slieve Aughty and Co. Galway, south and south-west to Slieve Bernagh, on the other side of which lies the City of Limerick – only on the west is there any kind of plain, away to Ennis and beyond towards the bare hills fronting the Atlantic. In this terrain the reader must picture a small band of resolute men constantly on the move for the best part of three years after it was decided that no armed Volunteer should permit himself to be arrested, rarely sleeping for more than two nights in the same bed, often in sheds or haybarns, usually sleeping fully dressed to be ready for the sudden emergencies which had to be met – one of their number caused a good deal of amusement by always bringing his pyjamas with him! Often, too, the clothes in which they slept were saturated with rain. 1921 was an exceptionally fine summer but they had three winters of hardship, involving not only mud, broken sleep and hair-breadth escapes but also great tests of endurance. None but the trained and hardy men of the mobile column could have stood the strain; imagine, for example, sixteen hours constantly on the move, surrounded on all sides by hostile troops, without food, and no less than 36 miles covered in the time. This exploit, which took place during and after the engagement at Mountshannon early in 1921, is reminiscent of the famous march of O'Donnell's men in 1601 on their way to the epoch-making and disastrous Battle of Kinsale. In that campaign as has so often happened in history, the English were repeatedly defeated, but they won the last and decisive battle. History, however, did not repeat itself in 1921.

The personnel of the column was not confined to the farming community who might be expected to be best able to stand hardship and severe physical exertion. Three of the four men who died on Killaloe bridge worked in shops at Scariff, and one of the most active members who shared that most testing Mountshannon experience was the late James Hogan, Professor of History at University College, Cork.

As I have already said, high praise must also be given to the civilian population. For an act of cool courage it would be hard to beat that of a young boy, O'Grady by name. He was out one morning engaged in gathering mushrooms or some such boyish occupation; knowing that a party of Volunteers were sleeping in a certain farmhouse nearby and seeing the Tans arrive in their lorries to surround the suspected house, he calmly set off to warn the sleeping men. Though challenged and ordered to stop he broke into a run. Bullets whistled past his head and even through his cap. He had to cross a ditch under fire. Still he kept on and reached his objective, only slightly wounded, in time: the sound of the shots had already roused the men he was determined to save. As usual they were billeted in a house on a farm abutting on wild mountainous country and so were able to slip away before the encircling cordon was formed.

On another occasion they were saved by the presence of mind of two girls. This time the position seemed nearly hopeless. The locality was surrounded by a large body of Auxiliaries and Black & Tans. Their temporary headquarters was established at the avenue gate of the very house in which Michael Brennan, James Hogan and other leading men of the column were lodged. These men were completely exhausted after an exceptionally arduous march across country from Caher to Meelick where they reached the house in question (Punch's) at 1 a.m. It was while they were still asleep later that morning that the enemy arrived. Seeing this the two Miss Punches went to their gate and having got into conversation with the officers and established an apparently friendly relationship with them they invited them into the house for tea and drinks. As the day advanced, with the worn out men still asleep upstairs, more British officers dropped in. The leaders awoke to the sounds of music and loud laughter from downstairs. By late afternoon the party in the Punch's drawingroom was jolly, almost rowdy. Still the girls kept up their part, playing the piano and dispensing drinks. Hungry though they were the men above could not stir. Eventually when every other house in the cordoned area had been thoroughly searched the British forces withdrew. Thanks to the quick thinking of the Punch girls, the only house not searched was the one in which the badly wanted leaders actually were.

The attacking of barracks was a comparatively straightforward job which could be carried out according to plan and at a chosen time. Sometimes the bombs which were used to breach the roof of the building and set it on fire failed to do their work and the defenders were able to hold out; at other times an otherwise successful attack was accounted a failure because no arms and ammunition had been captured, and the taking of a mere building and the infliction of casualties had little value beyond its moral effect. That, of course, was considerable; but as a military operation ambushes were undoubtedly more effective. They were also a greater test of courage and discipline, for not only had they to be carried out by day but they also involved long hours of nerve-racking waiting.

As I have said this chapter is intended to give a general impression not a chronological account of the campaign. There were a number of military actions – such as those at Glenwood, with reprisals on the neighbouring farmhouses which quickly followed, and at Kilrush when the East Clare Brigade made history outside their own territory: had I taken part in them myself I might give a detailed description of them to help me present the reader with a more vivid picture. They were achievements of note; but while in no way minimizing the military value of such engagements I think that future students of the period will be inclined to emphasize two rather different aspects of the matter. Take, for example, the Kilrush affair. The men involved marched 200 miles in eight days, with a major scrap in the middle of the week. I say marched; by which I mean to convey that they covered the ground in military formation, using the roads – and that by day; whereas a year earlier it would have been necessary for them to proceed furtively at dead of night. The case in point is thus an illustration of the physical fitness of the mobile columns and the efficiency of their intelligence service on the one hand and on the other of the whole-hearted co-operation of the entire civilian population.

The East Clare Brigade was noteworthy for more than its daring, its tenacity and its endurance. It was an example to the country in the matter of morale and discipline. Firm leadership which never gave arbitrary or unreasonable commands resulted in East Clare having a very fine record. For instance, to take a comparatively trivial example; tired men, naturally enough, when living under a constant nervous strain, were inclined when they got the chance of a short respite to have a few more drinks than was advisable and so would relax the constant watchfulness required in the kind of warfare they were waging. Very wisely their leaders thought that as total prohibition would only mean clandestine disobedience each man should be strictly limited to two pints: this order worked out very well in practice. And in the wider aspect it can be claimed that their record was not blemished by a single really regrettable incident. No prisoner was harmed – General Lucas was in their custody for several weeks. No informer was summarily liquidated – one R.I.C. pensioner whom they had good reason to believe was a spy was spared, though the rank and file were anxious that he should get his deserts. (Incidentally it may be mentioned that his guilt was proved after the Truce). In due course he was arrested on another charge and was forced to spend two years in confinement as some slight retribution for his crime. A number of people whose traditional sympathies were not with the 'rebels' – both Unionist landlords and strong supporters of Redmond – expressed their admiration of the conduct of the Volunteers in East Clare, notably Lord Dunboyne (whose house was used for an important secret meeting of the County Council) and Col. Farrell (whose house was occupied for a time in his absence). In this connexion it is only fair to recall the honourable behaviour of several convinced Unionists, notably the county surveyor at Ennis and the doctor in Limerick who had Michael Brennan under his care after he had been wounded.

It seems to be somewhat invidious thus to refer by name to some persons in this negative way – I do so, of course, because a vague statement unsupported by evidence carries little weight – while at the same time passing over without individual mention so many of the leading men of the mobile columns.

General Brennan told me that while over two hundred men served with the East Clare Flying Column at one time or another, owing to the shortage of arms and billeting difficulties the number actually with the Column at any one time seldom exceeded twenty-five. These were picked from about sixty experienced men, all of whom rated as 'regulars'. In addition to the brigade column each of the six battalions had a local active service unit armed with shotguns, revolvers and a rifle or two. These battalion units could hit hard when opportunity offered – for example the attack on the Black & Tan garrison in Feakle when two R.I.C. men were killed and several wounded, and the attack on troops guarding an aeroplane at Cratloe when a British sergeant was killed and some of his men wounded.

With the help of several active participants I did in fact prepare what I hoped was a complete list of all those who served in the East Clare Brigade, but it was almost inevitable that at this length of time some names which should have been included will have been left out. It is now deposited in the Manuscripts Department of the National Library.

By way of conclusion to this appreciation of Michael Brennan and his men I cannot do better than to state two facts without comment. They were called upon to go outside their own area in order to put new life into the disorganized Volunteer force in an adjacent county; and during the whole 2½ years of active campaigning they scarcely ever missed Mass on Sundays and Holy days, though by attending they usually took their lives in their hands. What greater tribute to their military prowess and to their personal high character could be paid to that fine body of men of whom we are so justly proud?

Above left: myself aged four-and-a-half, dressed for a fancy dress party. *Above right:* my father, mother and I, at Hazelwood in 1934. *Below left:* with my wife Mamie, and our sons William, Pat and Brian, taken in 1947. *Below right:* a drawing of me by my grand-daughter Damaris.

Above: Raheen House in 1908 before it was renovated. *Below:* the view of Lough Derg from the lawn of the house, with Iniscaltra (Holy Island) in the distance.

Above lef
Castle, L
in my lat
c. 1927.

Above: at Clonboy in 1909. Myself on the steps, with Ernest Brown, old Mrs. Brown and Constance Brown in the car with Paddy Mulready of the Raheen staff. *Below:* one aspect of the early activities at Raheen was nursery work: lining out forest tree seedlings before the introduction of modern machinery.

Above: a view of part of the primeval forest at Raheen, 1978. *Below:* the Garden of Remembrance at Tuamgraney, which commemorates the local people who died in the 1918–1920 Black and Tan campaign.

Al
Be
M
on

Above: the transfer of the Office of Arms to the Irish Government. *L. to r. front:* myself; Thomas Derrig, Minister for Education; T. U. Sadleir, the Acting Ulster king of Arms at the time of the transfer; Éamon de Valera, Taoiseach. *Behind:* Dr. R. J. Hayes, Director of the National Library. *Below:* part of the photograph taken at the reunion of surviving members of the East Clare Brigade of the Volunteers of 1920 at Knappogue Castle in 1968. It included some associated county councillors of that date and one or two 'backroom boys', such as myself. Space would not permit the use of the entire picture. I am standing six from the left, and the commanding officer, General Michael Brennan is seated three from the right.

Above: the presentation of the Devoy papers to the National Library in 1954. *L. to r.:* Desmond Ryan, Frank Robbins, William O'Brien, Dr. R. J. Hayes, myself. *Below:* with President de Valera at the conferring of my Hon.LL.D. by the National University of Ireland in 1972. (I earned my Litt.D. in 1941.)

CHAPTER X

Truce and Treaty

The fact that after a protracted and dialectic correspondence between Mr de Valera and Mr Lloyd George a formula had at length been found which could serve as a basis for peace negotiations seemed to the man in the street to augur that the negotiations themselves would end in an agreement. Indeed those who were not in the know were quite confident that there would be no renewal of war. Had I not been away during most of that anxious time I would no doubt have realized how critical the situation was. After the arrangement of the truce I went to France to join my family there, but first I saw Michael Brennan and told him to recall me if hostilities were likely to be resumed, when I could be counted on for any service he thought best to demand of me. After that I had no contact with leading Republicans till the Treaty was actually signed. When I returned from France in October all my energies were needed to deal with the innumerable matters of a thoroughly disorganized business which awaited my attention after two months' absence.

I was at Raheen when the news that the Treaty had been signed came through. I confess that I did not scrutinize its terms with close attention: I shared with everyone I met a sense of relief at the coming of peace and delight at the prospect of at last having the native government which had been my dream since boyhood. So far as I analysed my attitude at all it can be summed up in the words "What is good enough for Michael Collins is good enough for me." In his words, though we had not yet heard them, we felt 'This is freedom to achieve freedom'.

On November 29, Mr de Valera started on a tour of Clare and south Galway, which was to last six days. It was arranged that he and his numerous retinue together with Michael Brennan and the staff of the 1st Western Division H.Q. should dine at Raheen on December 2 before going on to stay the night as the guest of the Bishop of Clonfert at Loughrea. So the official printed itinerary states, but only some of them came: events in London were becoming too critical and de Valera hastened back to Dublin.

He was in Clare again on the day the news of the Treaty was published. His laconic proclamation came as a rude shock to us – by us I mean to the little group comprising Denis MacMahon, Pádraig Ó Cadhla, Pat Hayes and myself, who at first happily and then with increasing foreboding discussed the situation in that remote corner of the west of Ireland.

I hurried off to Dublin, careless once more of ordinary business affairs and only anxious to get the latest and most authentic information.

I soon realized that the situation was even worse than we had feared, and for the first time in my life I knew what it was to be overwhelmed by pessimism: a split seemed inevitable, after all our years of united effort. I was so anxious not to cast away substance for shadow that it took me some time to grasp the viewpoint of those who preferred to continue what was bound, now that there was a division in our ranks, to be a hopeless contest with Britain rather than accept the half independence offered by the Treaty as it stood. Conversations with my friends Gavan Duffy and Robert Barton helped me to understand, though not to agree with, the anti-Treaty attitude. Another great friend of mine, Father Willie Hackett, was so unmeasured in his denunciation of Collins and Griffith that his extreme view produced in me a strong reaction in their favour.

The two salient facts seemed to be that our delegation in London could probably have safely called Lloyd George's bluff in threatening a resumption of 'immediate and terrible war' by insisting on a few days respite to consult with Dublin; and secondly that, if we had to face it, the prospect of a successful outcome of the fighting was bleak; for, apart from shortage of arms, the same wholehearted co-operation from the people in general could hardly be expected after five months relaxation from the horrors we had experienced, especially in view of the fact that something which had the support of a majority in the Dáil had actually been achieved.

William O'Brien, Connolly's friend and co-worker, was in close touch with both sides during the crisis which was precipitated by the signing of the Treaty. Some years later I got to know him very well and I frequently urged him to write his memoirs. It was not, however, till he was eighty that he agreed to do so, and then only if I would collaborate with him by recording what he had to say on a tape-recorder and editing the result in book form. This was published in 1969 under the title *Forth the Banners Go* (his choice not mine). In it he has little to say about the Treaty split;

but many years before the book was published he did tell me
what he thought of the situation and of the people concerned. I
am therefore putting here the diary entry in which I noted what
he said, and his comments on that entry after I had given it to
him to read.

Friday, 25 April, 1952

If there is one man in Ireland who should write his memoirs
that man is William O'Brien. I will try to record here fairly
accurately the conversation I had with him to-day. It started at
lunch with a discussion of P. S. O'Hegarty's provocative book
The Victory of Sinn Féin which brought us of course to an
assessment of de Valera's part in the events which led up to
the Civil War. William O'Brien has made some notes but I
doubt if he'll ever put them in extended and continuous form.
He has been behind the scenes so much since before 1916 that
his knowledge is very extensive and his freedom from bias in
the sphere of politics indisputable. He is certainly not hostile
to Dev and Dev is very friendly to him. No doubt Mrs de
Valera's remark to his sister Miss O'Brien on being introduced
to her at a recent gathering in honour of Ethna Carbery's 50th
anniversary (her death) viz 'Oh, William O'Brien, why my
husband always consults him when he's in a difficulty' was
hyperbolical, but it had a basis – witness Dev's remarks in the
Dáil on Wednesday on the subject of William O'Brien and the
Central Bank.

William O'Brien is quite definitely of the opinion that de
Valera was wrong in his actions in the 1921–22 period. Having
read Dev's letters to Lloyd George three times at long intervals
over the years he feels more than ever that implicit in them
was the possibility of accepting something less than a completely independent republic. This view he thinks is supported
by such expressions as 'We are not doctrinaire republicans' and
his request to Griffith to 'get me out of the strait-jacket of the
Republic'. Apropos of that O'Brien himself heard Griffith at
the Mansion House Conference in April 1922 say across the
table to Dev: 'Did you not ask me to get you out of the strait-
jacket' etc. which Dev did not categorically deny then, or when
later (? in the Dáil) he was again taxed with it. Further, the
appointment of Arthur Griffith as chairman of the delegation –
a man known not to be a republican, seems to William O'Brien
to be a clear indication that some compromise was envisaged.
In fact he thinks that in November–December 1921 de Valera

changed his outlook somewhat, Childers being an immoderate influence on him. Austin Stack, too, could sway him. Paddy O'Keeffe (he of 'rattling dead bones' fame), who according to William O'Brien has an excellent memory, told O'Brien of an incident which he said was the origin of Stack's hostility to Collins. Be that as it may, the incident no doubt took place. Michael Collins 'a wonder man' (according to William O'Brien with whom I agree) was the real able man on the Irish side, clearsighted, methodical, hardworking. When other Ministers let things slide, as happened and will always happen when men who are primarily brave soldiers have to be administrators also, people all went to Collins to get them done. This day Collins showed Stack three or four letters unanswered by his department (Home Affairs) which could have been passed on to him at Finance. Austin Stack took deep offence at the disparaging way Michael Collins said so in the presence of several other people and over his nightly pint of stout with others of the same type Stack expressed his fury.

My own thoughts, as O'Brien talked, went to a job I've been doing quite recently in the Library, viz, sorting and numbering a collection of letters from Michael Collins to Austin Stack (1919) which came to us from Mrs Stack. They are couched in friendly almost affectionate terms.*

William O'Brien considered, again rightly I think, that Collins was the man of the movement and that Dorothy MacArdle's conclusion that the Army was the creation of Cathal Brugha is quite wrong: Collins made it and it was to him that its most active members looked. O'Brien named Dick Mulcahy, G. O'Sullivan, D. O'Hegarty, McGrath and others in this connexion.

I raised the point often made by those who opposed the Treaty: why did not the delegates risk Lloyd George's threat of 'immediate and terrible war' and report back to Dublin on

*Nearly twenty years after this diary entry was made the excellent book *Michael Collins: the Lost Leader* by Margery Forester was published and in it his relationship with Austin Stack and their gradual estrangement is dealt with very ably. At times Miss Forester seems almost too anxious to show her impartiality, as for example where she suggests the possibility that McKee, Clancy and Clune might have been shot while attempting to escape. My first-hand evidence, had she consulted me, would have made the position quite clear. You have only to look at the guard-room with its one door leading to the Castle yard, covered day and night by the armed auxiliaries on duty, to realize the impossibility of any such attempt; and, apart from that, there were the actual words spoken to me by one of them, which I quoted in Chapter VIII, p. 108.

that Monday night rather than sign then and there, since their instructions were to sign nothing without referring it to Dublin? The answer to that, William O'Brien says, is that they were in Dublin on the previous Saturday when the situation was discussed at great length, and the delegates thought they had got from the British the further concessions decided on as a *sine qua non* at the Saturday meeting.

I cannot remember all our conversation. We hardly discussed the Civil War at all. I'd like to see just how wise old William O'Brien feels about the executions. He thinks the English tricked us, that Birkenhead told Griffith and Collins (? all the delegates) that if Craig & Co. did not fall into line they, the English, would make it so difficult for them that they could not carry on. This was understood to mean at least Tyrone and Fermanagh would be transferred to the Free State for he (Birkenhead or one of them) said that under the Treaty it would be impossible for the County Council of Fermanagh (or was it Tyrone) to be suppressed (which of course it was).

The two major follies we agreed were: first, agreeing to go into the Boundary Commission when Craig had refused (minor follies being accepting Feetham as chairman and appointing MacNeill as our representative); and secondly, the 1925 agreement which made the border permanent with a show of right on Britain's side. That, says William O'Brien, is the attitude of the British Labour Party – 'Ye agreed unequivocally and finally to a permanent border, I.F.S., N.I. and G.B. together in conference and to set the seal on the bargain, the amount of the I.F.S. undetermined share of the National Debt was agreed to and paid.' Of course, Collins and Griffith were not in on that: they had been killed by the non-cooperators – Griffith, says William O'Brien, as surely as Collins.

Cosgrave should have had more sense, he feels, but we must make some allowance for the effects of the civil war on mental outlook, ability and initiative. He was reasonably able, not just a soldier pitchforked by accident into politics like Brugha or McKeon.

Well, I wish I could remember the rest but I have put down a good deal of it. He is off to the Channel Islands now so I will not be having my regular Friday meal with him till June 6th (D.V.). Since the Dolphin closed we only meet once a week instead of twice as heretofore.

Soft rain to-day. As much grass already in the Lawn Field as there was just one month later last year.

William O'Brien wrote me the following statement on 21st July 1952 (after he had read my diary entry of April 25th, which he says was a remarkably accurate account of what he'd said).

*

'I have been told by a member of the First Dáil that at the first meeting of the Dáil which he attended following his return from the U.S.A. de Valera said or hinted of the necessity of 'slowing down', as the British had by no means done their worst against us. In illustration of this he referred to 'Sherman's Ride' in the U.S.A. Civil War.

'De Valera said in the Dáil in 1921 that the Oath meant to him 'doing the best he could for Ireland', and that 'they were not doctrinaire republicans'.

'When de Valera announced at a Cabinet Meeting the names of the delegation to meet the British, three members of the Cabinet (Griffith, Cosgrave and Collins) were in favour of de Valera himself going, three (Stack, Brugha and Barton) were against, and de Valera decided by his own vote against. My authority for this is W. T. Cosgrave, who said the issue was discussed for two hours in the Cabinet, that he (Cosgrave) raised the matter again in the full Dáil when the names were submitted and kept the debate going for a long time. De Valera selected Griffith as chairman of the delegation, although Griffith fought against declaring the Republic as the objective in the Constitution in 1917, and de Valera himself wrote the compromise which was inserted in the Constitution of Sinn Féin in Oct. 1917, and which was agreed to before that at a private conference held in Cathal Brugha's house some time after the East Clare election.

'Following the signing of the Treaty and after the Dáil had. approved of it, a conference was convened in the Dublin Mansion House in April 1922 by Archbishop Byrne, Lord Mayor O'Neill and Stephen O'Mara, Senr. De Valera and Brugha and Griffith and Collins attended. As it was understood that agreement was unlikely, the Irish Labour Party and Trade Union Congress National Executive sent Messrs. Thomas Johnson, Cathal O'Shannon and myself, and during the discussion while they were present Griffith said across the table to de Valera 'Did you not ask met to get you out of the strait-jacket of the Republic?' De Valera did not deny this but said he would like to explain. The Archbishop intervened (as feeling was very strained) at this stage. All parties were standing at the time as the conference was breaking up. This statement was repeated in public by Griffith at either the Sinn Féin Convention or the Dáil and was never denied by de Valera.

'As regards the provision in the instructions to the delegation that they were not to sign without submitting the document to the Cabinet in Dublin it should be borne in mind that a draft of proposals was discussed for a whole day on Saturday, December 3rd and various amendments suggested and de Valera suggested a form of oath which he would be willing to agree to and the Secretary to the Cabinet (O'Hegarty) made a note of the terms which were fairly close to the oath in the Treaty. The delegation apparently believed they got these amendments in substance in the Treaty. The Treaty was approved by a majority of the Dáil Cabinet, by a majority of the Dáil, by a majority of the I.R.A. G.H.Q. and by a majority of the people in so far as the people were able to express their opinion in the 'Pact Election' of June 1922.'

I append an entry I made in my diary many years later which is worth recording, though its historical value is diminished by the fact that I got this only at second hand.

1 March, 1970

I regret that I did not make a note at the time of what William O'Brien told me about James Connolly's death. He said that some years later he met one of the men who comprised the firing squad detailed to execute Connolly and this man told him that Connolly was not shot sitting in his wheelchair but that with a great effort he raised himself up in a semistanding position saying something to the effect that it was more dignified to be shot standing – I forget the words he quoted. This is an interesting statement, but unfortunately I did not ask William the man's name, and now that it has struck me that it is essential to have it, if this piece of news is to be more than hearsay, William O'Brien is no longer alive to answer a question.

In spite of the atmosphere of strained uncertainty and impending tragedy which pervaded Dublin that December I found an occasional element of comedy in it too. One night, for example, I went to the Standard Hotel with Michael and Paddy Brennan. The place was full of T.D.s for the Dáil was to meet next day to decide the vital question of ratification. The room we were in was a babel. Everyone was talking, some earnestly, some excitedly, more no doubt as a safety valve for taut feelings than with any thought of being attentively listened to. The issue, however, was still in doubt and Deputies whose votes were uncertain were being anxiously canvassed by both sides. I was myself with a party of Claremen which included two T.Ds. Miss Mary MacSwiney spotted us and imagining that I was a T.D. myself, and that being with the Brennans I must be pro-Treaty, she pinned me into a corner and began to harangue me in words which I forget but which from her public pronouncements can easily be imagined. I do not even remember whether, in the rather brutal words used by Pádraig Ó Caoimh in the Dáil, she 'rattled her brother's dead bones' in my face. I do remember that she would not let me get a word in edgeways for some minutes and that, when at last I managed to convey that my attempted interruptions were only an endeavour to let her know that I was not a T.D. and that she was wasting time on a mere man in the street, she was quite vexed.

The result of the endless debate which followed is a matter of history. My own comments at the time made in my diary are of no great interest. I am rather surprised that I wrote so favourably of Cathal Brugha, for I never liked his stubborn type. Nevertheless though I disagreed with him I certainly feel that when later on he was killed in action in the Civil War he died for Ireland according to his own lights. I was very critical of a personal friend of my own too, Erskine Childers, whose extreme and heroic attitude I rather resented in one whom I regarded as an English convert to our cause. Nevertheless that did not prevent us from remaining friends. That deplorable Civil War was responsible for his execution in circumstances which even the tension of the time could not to my mind possibly justify. But I am anticipating: the Civil War was still to come.

The next important event in which I was to some extent concerned was the General Election of 1922. Though I was intensely interested in political questions behind the scenes I was not at all keen on becoming a politician. I felt, however, that holding the position I did at the time in Clare it was my duty to stand for the Dáil. I decided, therefore, to go forward and I did not hesitate to do so as an Independent for I have never been able to identify myself wholly with any party (as distinct from a united national movement); moreover, as my election address indicates, I was relying on my own personal reputation to get elected; and I hope I am not being boastful when I say that my name stood high at the time. Having made up my mind to this course I saw no reason to withdraw when the Election Pact which was made between de Valera and Collins was announced, as it appeared to include the proviso that Independent candidates might go forward irrespective of the Pact. So on nomination day I went off to Ennis and my papers were duly handed in to the sheriff. The latest hour for doing this was 12 noon. Shortly after 11.30 I saw Éamon de Valera enter the room in the Court House in which I and the other candidates and their agents were. He came over to me at once. I was not unknown to him. The last time he had seen me was the occasion of our visit to AE which I have already described in Chapter VI. When he came over to me in the sheriff's room the President, or rather the ex-President as he was in 1922, therefore greeted me in a friendly manner as one he already knew. He addressed me in English but as we were both wearing the Fáinne I replied in Irish and we continued to talk in that language for some minutes. Father O'Flynn had already pressed me to withdraw my candidature. They both argued that it was not in the interest of the country that independents should stand in that election and that it was my duty to retire from the contest. As I personally disliked the very thought of electioneering I was not averse from being persuaded by them and the upshot of these conversations was that at five minutes to twelve I walked over to the sheriff and withdrew my papers. Nevertheless while I was convinced by them that the Pact was necessary in the then critical situation I did not change my view that it was incumbent on men in my position who had always been nationalists to take their part in the political life of the country, even though like me they had no inclination for a political career. My supporters disagreed with my action. However, a few months later I became a member of the Senate, being one of those elected by the Dáil, thanks to the support of Michael Brennan and other Clare deputies. I am now the only survivor of that body.

Soon after the Pact Election the Civil War began. That is a matter of history and not one upon which I care to dwell. I was an eye witness of the one terrible event which the healing effect of time can never repair. The material damage has long been made good and the country soon recovered from the waste of many millions of money; the lovely ten arch bridge at Mallow, replaced by an ugly iron structure, may conceivably be rebuilt some time in the future; in due course the tragic loss of life, including such men as Michael Collins and Erskine Childers, will be no more than a sad memory, but nothing can ever restore the loss sustained by the destruction of the Public Record Office.

On June 30th I was in my office at 24 Mountjoy Square,

making the preliminary arrangements for our projected paper *An Sguab*. I happened to cross the room and stood for a moment looking out of the window. Suddenly I saw a huge black column of smoke rise high into the air a mile or so to the west and a second later heard a reverberating crash.

I did not know then that folly had blown to smithereens the accumulated historical material of seven centuries. When I realized that, I knew for the first time what it was like to feel vindictive against some of my fellow-countrymen, though on reflection I understood that the participants were quite unaware of the consequences of their action.

So far as I was personally concerned in this national loss the position was not so bad. For years before that Mr Tennyson Groves, the well known researcher, had been recording for my father every reference he came across to our name in the ancient records preserved in the Public Record Office at the Four Courts. Practically all the sources there from which he obtained this information have ceased to exist in the original. Mr Groves' copies of relevant Chancery and Exchequer Bills, Summomister Rolls, Exigents, Outlawries etc. are now lodged at the Public Record Office where they form part of the small collection of the records of the past which the officials at the P.R.O. have been able to get together, not as a replacement of what was destroyed but rather as a reminder of the irreparable loss sustained.

My time continued to be divided between Dublin, Raheen and Hazelwood. The Civil War affected the daily life of a non-combatant like myself far more in Co. Cork than in Co. Clare, or even in Dublin where, after the few days of intensive fighting in which Cathal Brugha was killed, the shootings and ambushes were less frequent and nerve-racking than those to which we had become accustomed under the Black & Tan régime. On the other hand, of course, we were not sustained by the spirit which imbued us before the Truce; during the Civil War every shot I heard fired depressed me still more, since it meant one more bullet aimed by one Irishman at another.

In east Clare we were spared the horrors of Civil War because almost to a man we followed Michael Brennan's support of Michael Collins, and the anti-Treaty forces were practically non-existent there. Though at the time in many places the lives of Free State T.D.s and Senators were at risk no such consideration entered my head: as an indication of that I may mention that we had lost the key to our front door and never troubled to replace it during all that period.

In Mallow we could not forget the Civil War. Co. Cork was almost the last place to come under the control of the Free State government; and even when there was no actual fighting going on the gaping wreck of the beautiful ten-arch bridge, which cut off railway communication between Cork and every place north of Mallow, was there as a perpetual reminder of the complete disorganization of the normal life of the country. I have no inclination to dwell on that unhappy time. As far as I was personally concerned, apart from a feeling of sadness which never quite amounted to despair, it did no more than cause me a considerable amount of inconvenience in travelling. Looking back on it now one cannot escape from the fact that the Civil War left a legacy of bitterness more harmful than the very extensive economic damage it did to the country. This has lingered on up to the present day. I was greatly pleased when a few years ago Tom Barry, a doughty opponent of Michael Collins in the Civil War, took part in the annual ceremony at Béal na mBlath where Collins was killed, thus dissociating himself from the continued hostile boycott of this tribute to his memory.

I cannot describe myself as really impartial as I regarded Michael Collins with something akin to hero-worship. Events have proved him right, but it must not be forgotten that at the time, more than fifty years ago, no one foresaw that the far flung and apparently indestructible British Empire would have disintegrated within our lifetime.

I was still much more interested in the preservation of the Irish language than in political formulae. The Treaty split and its sequel did without doubt result in our throwing away what may prove to have been the last chance of saving the Irish language as a vernacular in Ireland. Can we ever hope to see again the enthusiasm which manifested itself in 1921 for the Irish language? There was a general belief that with the departure of the British – and the widespread feeling after July 1921 was that they were at last going to hand over the destinies of the country to a native government – Irish would come into its own, and many people who had no love for it in itself, or indeed for the traditions it embodied, set themselves to learn Irish because they felt they would be handicapped without it. The split blew that spirit to atoms as surely as the explosion at the Four Courts made dust of the archives in the Public Record Office.

To quote a comparatively recent diary entry would be appropriate here. (It is a translation from an entry in Irish.)

135

Christmas 1970

The re-issue of *Cúrsaí Thomáis* nearly half a century after it was first published is an incentive to write an entry in this diary.

After fifty years of self-government, under Taoiseachs who profess to regard the revival of Irish as a top priority, one asks oneself is the position better than it was in 1921. The essential fact is that the fíor-ghaedhealtacht has become smaller. There has been progress in some respects, certainly. More young people have a smattering of Irish – the Department of Education has seen to that – but with most of them it fades from lack of use. Progress of a kind is to be seen in the newspapers: *The Irish Press* and *The Irish Times* commendably print regular columns in Irish by Brendán Ó hEithir and other well known people; but I wonder how far these are read; for myself their use of many lengthy words not to be found in Dinneen's dictionary makes the reading of them somewhat laborious. Similarly I find the new abbreviated spelling hampering (though that is my fault not theirs). I must admit that when I looked at my own novel reprinted in that spelling I found it quite troublesome to read, though it contains very few words not current in everyday Munster Irish. Nearly everybody tells me that they find the RTE newsreaders in Irish hard to follow. For the benefit of the majority of listeners should they not be instructed to read less rapidly?

CHAPTER XI

The first Senate

If you are a busy man and spend nine or ten hours a week travelling, as I had to between Dublin, Clare and Cork, those hours are practically wasted in a motor car, whereas in a train they can be used for writing and reading. While I was a member of the Senate I had also the advantage of travelling to and from Dublin on a free voucher; and in those early days the Senate met frequently without the long intervals which characterized it subsequently.

The Senate of the Irish Free State has come in for a certain amount of adverse criticism, some of it justified but much of it the result of mere ignorance and prejudice. I was a member of it for the first three years of its existence. During that time it did a lot of useful if unostentatious work, mostly in the direction of improving legislation which often came up from the Dáil in a somewhat half-baked condition. Actually during those three years the Senate passed 534 amendments to bills received from the Dáil: 503 of these were accepted by the Dáil in full and most of the remaining thirty-one led to consequential Dáil amendments.

The first Senate consisted of thirty members elected by the Dáil, of whom I was one, and thirty nominated by the President. The latter were principally composed of men of the ex-landlord class or business men, mostly Protestants: their selection was the redemption of Arthur Griffith's promise to give the old 'Southern Unionist' interest representation in an Irish Parliament.

As for me, I constituted myself a sort of watch-dog on behalf of the Irish language there, and at the first meeting I made a short speech in Irish. I think there were only four Senators beside myself capable of following a speech in Irish so I was really addressing myself to a few officials and reporters. I contributed very little to the commonweal by being a senator. My two definite attempts to accomplish something in the way of positive legislation were a failure. I made a speech urging the government to adopt the principle of Premium Bonds. I think it was a good suggestion, in fact it was officially introduced about thirty years later; but it was rejected by Mr Cosgrave on the ground that the State was

not yet firmly enough established to do anything at all unortho-
dox. My second attempt took the form of a regularly drafted Bill.
It proposed to substitute certain Church Holy Days, already kept
throughout Ireland, or at any rate rural Ireland, as holidays, in
place of English Bank Holidays. August 15th, for example, was to
supersede the first Monday in August. It was opposed by the
representatives of the banks, as any innovation bringing them
out of line with England would have been, and by Labour who
insisted that public holidays should always fall upon Mondays. So
my Bill was rejected at the second reading stage. The Catholic
support upon which I had counted was entirely lukewarm.

Even though Labour were partly the means of ignominiously
defeating my bill I saw their point of view. I always worked quite
independently but more often than not I voted with Labour.
Though conservative by nature, I had a leaning towards Socialism
of a mild and Fabian type – none of the Labour representatives
in the Senate were extremists – and my attitude towards the Free
State was exactly that of the Labour Party who, while expressing
belief in the desirability and the right of Ireland to complete
independence, saw no reason why they should hold aloof from a
properly elected Dáil and, once there, participation in the Senate
automatically followed. In fact my attitude in 1922 was practically
that of Mr de Valera in 1932.

The atmosphere of the Senate in those early years was often
painfully unIrish and only two members, Col Moore and Mrs
Wyse Power, spoke against the election of the Orangeman Lord
Glenavy, better known as James H. Campbell, when he was proposed as Chairman. Personally, I said nothing. There was no
formal vote taken.

I would enjoy giving some sketches of the Senate and its personnel but I fear that I would be working with lifeless material.
Even Campbell, in his day a Unionist as prominent as Carson or
Craig – they might have been called the three Cs – is already
forgotten. The thought of him, however, still makes me chuckle.
His methods in the chair were inimitable. He had the quick wits
of a successful barrister and his contempt for his fellow senators
was scarcely veiled. If he wanted to play golf at 5.30 p.m. I could
be sure the senate would rise at 5.00. As two of the staff were
friends of mine I often knew his plans beforehand, but though
I tried several times to get the better of him, he always scored off
me and when Maurice Moore, the only other senator who made
any attempt to stand up to him, fell foul of him, he treated
George Moore's amiable old brother with a sharpness which was

almost painful. I never knew a man with better voice control: he could assume any expression he wished at will and the sepulchral tone, with just a slight tremor of emotion in it, which he assumed when announcing anything at all tragic could not have been surpassed in apparent feeling by a Garrick or an Irving. His contempt for Gaelic Ireland was illustrated by his pronunciation of the words Saorstát Éireann which he invariably called *Sour State I ran.*

Not that better Irishmen than Glenavy were much superior to him in that respect. Even AE always called Naisi Naysy! AE was not a member of the Senate; but we had two poets in W. B. Yeats and Oliver Gogarty. Yeats's most memorable contribution to the debates of the Senate was his speech in June 1925 on the subject of divorce. He displayed an unexpected arrogance in his eulogy of the Protestant Anglo-Irish and in his castigation of the 'obscurantism' of the Catholic church. This affair had a legal and constitutional interest as well as a personal one. These aspects of it are discussed in Donal O'Sullivan's *The Irish Free State and its Senate* (pp. 164–171). Yeats could be constructive as well as obstructive. He was, for example, active on the Senate committee on Irish manuscripts, of which I was a member. Outside the Senate premises I recall him as a man with a large appetite. At least he had on the only night I dined with him: we were fellow guests of Sir Thomas Esmonde at the Stephen's Green Club. I was at a standstill when I had negotiated soup and a large sole; but the other two munched steadily through the menu. In that, no doubt, they were more normal than I was. Somehow I never got on friendly terms with him as I did with many others twice my age, though I had reason to be well disposed towards him: did he not, when we met in the lobby on the occasion of the Senate's first meeting, greet me – a mere flash-in-the-pan rhymer – as 'fellow poet in strange surroundings'. He did; but though flattered I did not take to him.

James Douglas was probably the ablest man in the assembly, that is as regards his grasp of political and constitutional questions, but in spite of that he was not a successful politician. His essential fair-mindedness was frequently misinterpreted as 'trimming' and his somewhat dry Quaker manner irritated some people unreasonably but effectively. His well expressed explanation of his attitude on the divorce question was, for example, widely misunderstood. Nevertheless he was the only one of the outstanding figures in the first Senate who was a member of the re-constituted body in 1938. This was intended to be constituted on vocational lines but in practice its membership proved to be more politically based than in the body it replaced.

I had a standing invitation to have my (midday) dinner with the Douglases any Sunday I was in Dublin. They lived in St Kevin's Park in the Dartry district. Their dinners were just the sort of good plain food I like and Jim's wife Ena was the soul of hospitality. Jim had a sense of humour of a sort, but only of a sort. He had books on humour, how to make amusing after-dinner speeches and so on, yet I am reminded by a diary entry in 1923 that apparently it had not occurred to him that one at least of the framed texts and aphorisms with which the house used to be decorated was highly diverting. After that solid midday meal I used to retire to a certain private apartment. As I sat therein I was faced by the words 'If you are going to do a good thing do it now; if you are going to do a bad thing, put it off till tomorrow.' Knowing Quaker Jim I do not believe he hung that card up with his tongue in cheek. Perhaps I should add that this jesting anecdote is not to be taken as detracting in any way from my high opinion of Jim as a man of sterling character or from my liking for him as a friend. Another diary entry will recall those days.

10 October, 1925

I have always had my dinner in the middle of the day so it is a tribute to the conversational powers of the men I meet in the gloomy basement of Bewley's in Grafton Street that I so often take a sketchy middle-day meal there. Jim Douglas is usually there. He belongs to the oracular type of talker: when we're alone and have no specific problem to discuss I choose my subject rather as I would choose a particular gramophone record and he does the rest – letting his scrambled eggs get cold the while – I just nod or make monosyllabic comments at sufficiently frequent intervals to keep the flood going. Jack O'Sheehan comes quite often. In spite of his very English accent and rather elephantine humour I find him pleasant company and his comments on current affairs shrewd. I doubt, however, if I would have broken away from my normal habits just for the pleasure of lunching with these two, especially as I see Jim often anyway. No, it is Jim Montgomery whom I find the real attraction. Apart from his wit he has a real charm of manner – he is Edwardian *pur sang*. He has, of course, a great reputation as a wit. Some people, rival wits I fancy like Oliver Gogarty, are wont to say that he thinks out his *bons mots* beforehand and so steers the conversation that he is able to bring them out with an appearance of spontaneity. Quite possibly some of his best known witty remarks, such as his dictum that Ireland is now suffering not from anglicization but from Los Angelesization, may well have occurred to him at some time other than the occasion of their utterance, but having lunched frequently with him during the past two years I have no doubt whatever that he really is extraordinarily witty and that most of his epigrams and repartees are entirely impromptu. I regret that I never had an opportunity of arranging a meeting between him and my father.

This prompts me to take this opportunity to recall an aspect of my father not referred to in my description of him in Chapter I, and I quote here part of a diary entry (10 Oct., 1925).

My father is a raconteur rather than a wit and he excels in the improvization of clever skits in rhyme: what an amusing collection his comic and satirical verses would make; but I feel sure he has not taken the trouble to preserve these fugitive pieces. Nevertheless, while not in quite the same category as Jim Montgomery, I have heard him say some very witty things quite on the spur of the moment. On one occasion, for example, I remember a rather gushing dame with a marked Australian accent coyly asking him did he notice any essential difference between 'An Austrylian lydy and an English lydy'. 'The main difference,' he replied like a flash, 'is that an Australian lady is more apt to call a spade a spyde.' She with no ear for sound, was delighted with what she took as a compliment to colonial forthrightness. Another time, also at a meal on a ship in which we were travelling together, he was irritated by the Lancashire accent of a rather consequential spinster from Wigan. When this good lady audibly asked the steward to give her some plum pudding (which she pronounced as if it rhymed with budding or flooding) he reproved her, saying: 'Miss X, you really shouldn't call it pud-ding.' 'And why not, pray?' she asked, bridling, and the rest of us felt that he had gone further than good manners would permit. 'Oh,' he replied, 'don't you know that at sea it is always known as plum-duff.' I might have known he would not be deliberately rude for, like Jim Montgomery, he belongs to a generation to whom discourtesy was anathema.

But to get back to the Senate after that digression, which was prompted by my memory of Senator Jim Douglas: it is more than doubtful whether the abolition of the Senate in 1936 and its reconstitution in a different form has effected any real improvement in its ability except that it now contains a larger number of men capable of carrying on business in the Irish language. The Senate has lost its distinctive character and the supposed attempt to make it vocational has merely resulted in it being a pale shadow of the Dáil and a convenient place to dump rejects from the lower house.

I took my duties as a senator seriously; that is to say, I did not, as a number of others did, constantly absent myself from the meetings of the Senate (though I was glad to escape as far as I could from the committees which, unnoticed by the public, constitute a considerable portion of the work of a T.D. or Senator). I also read all bills, amendments etc. conscientiously. But I was, I think, not a success. I am a poor speaker when I have not prepared my speech very carefully beforehand, except on the rare occasions when complete familiarity with my subject or sudden fury at the unfair remarks of some other speaker caused me to forget my natural diffidence. When, therefore, at the end of three years my term expired, I was half-hearted in my efforts to secure re-election and was not unduly disappointed when I just failed to do so.

A word on that extraordinary election would not perhaps be out of place. The whole country formed one large constituency, all citizens over thirty years of age being entitled to vote. There were seventeen vacancies to be filled in the Senate and seventy-two candidates. Every one of these names, with the necessary descriptions, appeared on the enormous ballot paper which must have been the despair of the ordinary half-educated voter. Some enthusiasts marked their papers right though, indicating even their 60th preference; and in fact so complicated was this election (which was conducted on the Proportional Representation system) that preferences very far down on the list did actually become effective.

The quota was something over 10,000 votes. The idea in the minds of the constitution makers who devised this cumbrous scheme was that by making the whole country one constituency the ordinary local influences of electioneering would be eliminated and that men who had rendered national service, being well known from Donegal to Wexford, would thus have a much better chance of being returned.

A man called Mr Thomas Toal, however, thought otherwise and proceeded to demonstrate that he was right. The quota required being not much more than 10,000, he calculated that by an intensive canvass of his own county, Monaghan, of whose council he was chairman, he could obtain enough first preference votes to make him virtually independent of the rest of the country. He did actually obtain in the area where he had local influence within a few hundred of the quota, and thus, though hardly known outside it, easily headed the poll on the first count. Yet so few preferences did he get elsewhere that he did not reach the required figure until many others had been elected before him.

The fact that Douglas Hyde, the popular father of the Gaelic League and later the unanimous choice as first President of Ireland, received only a few hundred first preference votes and was eliminated on an early count, while as I said the unknown Thomas Toal got nearly 10,000, shows how completely the theories of the constitution makers were nullified in practice.

Owing to the immense amount of counting and transferring of votes involved, the complete results were not known for more than a fortnight after the polling. Each day the papers recorded some elections and some eliminations. As for me, thanks to a generous number of second and third preferences, I went fairly close but eventually dropped out of the race when I was within four places of success.

I failed for two reasons: first and most important, I took very little trouble indeed to secure re-election – I did not make a single speech even in Co. Clare or Co. Cork or in the city of Limerick, in all of which places I had a number of willing supporters who deserved a more energetic candidate. I just depended on my record as a nationalist and on my reputation as a man of independent outlook. The second factor which militated against me was a positive one. Without grasping, as Toal did, that local support was all important, I had counted on a big percentage of Clare votes. I only received 2,000 odd in my own county. This I ascribed to a clever move on the part of a certain county councillor who had 'kept it in for me' because years earlier, before the Great War in fact, I offended him by refusing to take his side in a county council election. Well, what he did was this. He stated publicly that it was a scandal that our avenue at Raheen should have been steam-rolled at the public expense and he remarked later on that the 'Raheen road' had cost £10,000 to roll. This seemed to imply that the Raheen avenue cost that much. In fact, it was the public road between Tuamgraney and Killaloe, or rather the part of it commonly referred to as the Raheen road,

143

on which the £10,000 was expended, which by modern standards seems absurdly little for two miles. His statement appeared in the weekly Clare papers before the election. My answer appeared later but the many people in Clare who did not see it in time no doubt came to the conclusion that I was as corrupt and self-seeking as any old-fashioned party politician, and so I did not get their votes. It is a good illustration of what can be done by personal vindictiveness.

It all arose from the transference of the hospital to Raheen House, which I described in an earlier chapter. It is only fair to myself to explain my position in the matter. The Raheen avenue was steam-rolled by the County Council: that was the only benefit I received for giving my house for the use of the hospital for two years; and it was certainly done primarily for the benefit of the hospital. I think I should relate the sequel. Some twenty years later I was driving past Mountshannon one dark night on my way home from Dublin and intended to leave a message at a house of a man of whose whereabouts I was uncertain. I stopped at one which I thought might be it. Who opened the door in response to my knock but the very man who had misrepresented me – he had recently moved house unknown to me. 'I declare to God,' says he, ''tis Mr. McLysaght. You're welcome. Why, I didn't see you since the time long ago I helped you in that election.' Helped me! Well, in I went and we spent a couple of hours at his fireside engaged in a thoroughly friendly and interesting conversation (not of course once referring to the election).

I mentioned in Chapter VIII that I was a member of the Industrial Resources Commission under the first Dáil and while

Personalities

J. Birmingham (N.U.R.) E. MacLysaght Lord Justice O'Connor (President) W. Squ (A.S.

I was a Senator I served on three more formally constituted commissions. One of these was called upon to consider the question of education through Irish in the primary schools. We worked under the chairmanship of Fr. Lambert McKenna, S.J., to whom I subsequently was able to give some small assistance in the compilation of his English-Irish dictionary. I was not much use on that commission, though in a general way it dealt with a subject which interested me greatly.

To the second, the Railway Commission of 1922, I gave all my brains and attention. I found I had little skill as a questioner and I left that mostly to Judge O'Connor and Thomas Johnson. The other member of the Commission was Michael O'Dea. I realized very soon that he and I were unlikely to put our names to the same report. In the end, O'Connor, Johnson and I signed the majority report and O'Dea produced a minority one of his own. The judge subsequently admitted that his signature on our somewhat socialistic production, which was mainly the work of Tom Johnson, was due less to conviction than to the persuasive powers of Edward MacLysaght.

The Report of the Railway Commission resulted in (or, for Governments seldom pay any heed to the reports of the commissions they set up, should I say was followed by) the legislation which amalgamated nearly all the railways in the Free State and created the G.S.R., precursor of C.I.E. We showed a certain amount of intelligence in dealing with the situation as it then stood, but little vision: we simply failed to foresee the vast and inevitable increase in road traffic. I did show a glimmering of wisdom in an article I wrote in *Studies* on the railway problem

ilway Commission

M.P.Keogh
(M.G.W.R.)

G.E.Smyth
(G.S.W.R.)

H.W.
Ede

a little later on. One after the other the branch lines have since been closed down. The usual local protests were simply ignored because the very people who complained loudest were mostly those who never went near the railway station on their branch. The main lines will continue to provide, both in the way of fast passenger and heavy goods traffic, something which the roads cannot equal for a long time to come, for we are unlikely to construct autobahns in this country, while the challenge of the air seems unimportant when it is a question of conveying 500 people from say Dublin to Cork or a thousand tons of phosphates from Cork to Athlone.

The Report of the Railway Commission recommended a form of natinalization of the type later to be used in the Electricity Supply Board, but then as yet untried: something in fact very much like the plan which has been adopted, thirty years later. It is not in that respect that I believe our Commission to have been remarkable; but I do claim that it was unique because it *submitted* its report in both the official languages. When our draft in English was completed I set to work and translated the whole document into Irish myself – the other members did not, in fact, know Irish. I took a great deal of pains with my Irish version, which I aimed to express in the Irish of the people instead of the officialese which was already beginning to rear its ugly head, and when I had finished it I spent a weekend going over it with Brighid Ní Raogáin, having told her that the test was to be: would her father and mother, native speakers with very little English, understand my phraseology. And here again I met with another example of the tricks of memory: my recollection was that when it appeared in print I was annoyed to find my work, which had given me considerable satisfaction, corrected and mangled almost out of recognition; the truth, as I realized when I got a copy of the Report and looked it over today, is that my version was left as it stood except for some simplification of spelling and the elimination of a few of our more glaring Déisisms. I doubt if the archives of the State contain any more readable report in Irish than this.

I had almost forgotten the third Commission (that on Irish Manuscripts) of which I was an active member in 1924 and 1925. I was reminded of it by coming across the minutes of some of its meetings among a box of documents which I was sorting, a most interesting collection, chiefly letters of the 1916–21 period: I thought these had been seized during one of the raids by Auxiliaries but so well, it seems, were they cached that they escaped not only their attention but my own, too. They are now in the Manuscript Department of the National Library.

Actually the idea of establishing the Commission in question, oddly enough, came from the General Council of County Councils and its purpose was to enquire into the best means of preserving the folklore of the country and saving manuscript material likely to be lost or destroyed. I have little doubt that it was to the recommendation of that committee and of the Commission mentioned above that we owe the establishment of two valuable permanent institutions – the Irish Manuscripts Commission (of which I was chairman for seventeen years) and the Folklore Commission. The latter has now become part of University College, Dublin.

My only direct connexion with County Councils lay in the fact that I was the representative of the Clare County Council on the Governing Body of University College, Galway. I shall have more to say about this and the Governing Body of University College, Cork, on which I also served for a number of years, in the next chapter.

Many years later Telefís Éireann made a recording of my memories of the Senate. I felt I had made a good job of it. The following diary entry records its fate.

24 November, 1968

On looking back over this 'diary' I see that my part in the T.V. programme on the Senate was recorded on Feb. 22 last year and I was told it would be shown in the following April. Actually it was only shown quite recently. I was annoyed to see that my contribution to it was not included; only those of Ernest Blythe and Donal O'Sullivan were, neither of whom was a Senator. I was surprised too, because when I did my part at Montrose with Maurice McGonigal as interviewer he remarked when we'd finished that mine was the most interesting of the three and he added 'it put flesh on dry bones'. Well, I asked for an explanation from R.T.E. and the reply was a cheque for £15 with a letter to say that there was a technical fault in half of it and that the other half was more about the I.R.A. and pre-1922 affairs than the Senate. I have the notes I used and adhered to when interviewed and that is a mis-statement. The Feb. 22 entry shows that at one point McGonigal asked me a question about the Convention and possibly I may have made a passing reference to the I.R.A. in connexion with that. It only took a minute or two anyway. So if I did say something about

147

pre-1922 times that was his doing not mine. The director in his letter added that they hoped to make use of the extant part later. In my reply I said it would do for my obituary.

This is the last chapter in Part II which I have labelled 'Political'; so, though it will necessitate referring to events which occurred twenty-five and even forty years after I ceased to be a member of the Senate and had no further active participation in politics, as well as to issues which were controversial in my time, this seems to be the appropriate place to put anything I have to say about them. I shall make use of my diaries to denote my attitude to some questions of political interest.

29 October, 1975

On the 'Late Late' television programme ten days ago a Mr Freud, M.P., made a point against the Proportional Representation system we have in Ireland which I had not heard before, viz. that in a constituency which has three or more T.D.s the one who is most energetic and effective tends to get the bulk of the troublesome personal requests to pull strings in questions of local grievance or jobs. There may be something in that, though deputies with small majorities cannot afford to be unco-operative. Anyway that is no argument against the single seat constituency under P.R. That is now a purely academic matter though it was for a while a practical issue with Norton's proposed amendment to be considered before the Referendum in 1959. Personally I was in favour of that as I have mentioned elsewhere.

I am impressed by the figures produced recently by the Liberal Party in G.B. showing that under the straight vote system there they got twenty per cent of the votes but only four per cent of the seats.

In that 1959 Referendum the issue was confused, as a letter I wrote to Dick Mulcahy at the time shows.

> Raheen,
> Tuamgraney,
> Co. Clare.
> May 24, 1959

A Chara,

I don't know how far my political views represent those of the average voter, but as regards the questions to be decided on June 17th I find almost all those with whom I have discussed them take exactly the same views as I do.

As to P.R. I still think, as Mr de Valera (after nearly 20 years' experience of it) did in 1937, that it is a reasonably satisfactory system, and that the Constitution should not be altered unless some matter of vital importance arises to justify amending it. I also think that, notwithstanding the mistakes of his early political life, we should elect Mr de Valera as President.

Had he been unopposed I have little doubt that the Referendum would have decided for the retention of P.R. As it is, it is equally probable that the Referendum will decide against P.R.*, since what seems to be lack of political acumen on the part of Fine Gael has permitted the opponents of P.R. to link the two issues together.

I am asked by both parties to subscribe to an election fund: both appeals treat the two very distinct questions as if they were manifestly one. In these circumstances how can I, and all those who think as I do, subscribe to either side? We can't.

This letter leads me to quote an entry about another Presidential election.

30 May, 1973

For the first time – for how long?, at least sixty years – I have deliberately failed to cast my vote in an election or referendum. Today the voting is for the president to replace de Valera. Why? Childers is the son of an old friend of mine and a good honest man if a trifle pompous or starchy (what's the right word?) but to vote for him would be impossible for me whatever his party, but particularly as he is a member of one which has always ostentatiously proclaimed that the cause of the Irish language is, with the abolition of Partition, their first priority. Yet, while one must know Irish even to become a civil servant, they put up a man for the highest office in the land who hasn't a word of it. They proclaim, too, that his mother was Irish, which is nonsense – how well I remember that American dame – it was his grandmother (a Barton) who can be so classified. Then why not vote for O'Higgins? Certainly a vote for him would be equivalent to a pat on the back for the new Coalition government and I'm inclined to think they have started well enough to deserve that; but I am fed up with Fine Gael for having put up a party politician so hastily – thus

*My forecast was wrong: the electorate voted as I did.

rejecting the often expressed wish for an agreed non-politician man or woman – and so making this into a party contest. I wouldn't like to bet on the result. My guess is that Childers will win by a small majority.

The numerous references in my diaries to the affairs of Northern Ireland mainly date from 1969 when the present serious troubles arose. The problem of Ulster was prominent in the minds of all Irish people in 1912, in 1920, in 1925 and even in 1937, but somehow it seemed less urgent than it does now. Nevertheless to most of us in the Twenty-Six Counties it was an ever present cause of disquiet. The brief summary I made of this is as applicable to 1930 as it is to 1977 so I think it is pertinent to quote it here.

Ulster was the most fundamentally Irish part of Ireland until the beginning of the seventeenth century when its complete conquest took place and the greater part of that province was confiscated and the lands of the native owners were given to English and Scottish settlers, whose descendants now form the Protestant 'Loyalist' population there.

Re-unification not unification is the key word.

The solemn declaration made by the sovereign and parliament of Great Britain in the Reunification Act of 1782 is too often forgotten – that Ireland's right to be bound only by the laws of its own parliament was 'established and ascertained for ever and shall at no time be questioned or questionable'. The all-Ireland parliament of the eighteenth century was an ascendancy body with the Catholic majority excluded from membership. Ulster Protestants therefore had no thought of Partition then. It is they who were responsible for the partition of Ireland in 1920; and in order to be sure of firm control of 'Northern Ireland' they were obliged to secure the partition of Ulster. Few people outside Ireland seem to be aware of the fact that the most northerly point in the country is in the Republic of Ireland which is so often referred to as 'The South'.

The true practice, as distinct from the mere profession, of Christianity, would solve the Northern problem.

The loss of my seat in the Senate was a turning point in my career. My interest in and close connexion with agriculture and horticulture continued for a further thirty-five years but I dropped out of active politics and instead became involved in academic affairs.

CHAPTER XII

Schools and Universities*

After the Truce and before the Treaty was signed, I wrote the following letter to Professor James Hogan of University College Cork (who though from south Galway was a prominent member of the East Clare Brigade).

Raheen
3 August, 1921

A chara, I'm taking it for granted, now that the fighting is definitely over, that if we get a Dominion Home Rule compromise settlement we must take it because it gives us something to go on with, and if we didn't we'd lose the wonderful popular support we've had (as you know from your experience in this area) and we'd soon be beaten without it. Well I'm off shortly to France to join my family for a while – I sent them away when the raids on this place got so frequent and tough. Michael Brennan knows where to contact me if I should be needed.

My reason for writing to you now is that I am anxious to resume my university career and to get a degree in history at U.C.C. 'Resume' is an inapt word, as all I have done so far is to spend two terms at Corpus Christi College, Oxford, allegedly reading law; but at least I passed the matric, so am eligible to continue without an entrance exam. The hiatus is due first to working full time getting this place going for my father and then my involvement in our own war.

I have always been interested in history and this has been

*A word to the reader. This chapter is one I enjoyed writing, but having sought the opinion of several people I am in doubt as to its interest to the general reader. The point I wish to make is that the reader who is not much interested in the subject can conveniently skip that part because this book, as I said in Chapter I, is not an autobiography, which like a novel must be read consecutively and in full, but a commentary on the Ireland I have known for ninety years. Consequently any chapter after the introductory one can be read separately and its omission will only slightly detract from the overall picture I aim to present.

increased by the fact that my father got Tennyson Groves to extract every reference he found in the P.R.O. relating to our name from Macgillysacht to Lysaght, the result being specially interesting in the seventeenth century, e.g. the Irish Papist Cromwellian transplantation certificate which even tells me the colour of my ancestor's hair. I hope you can accept me as a student even though my existing commitments make it impossible for me to devote more than part time to historical research, so it will be a good while before I can present a thesis for M.A. if that idea commends itself to you. As my parents are now living near Mallow I will be able to visit you frequently in Cork.

No need to reply to this as I will get in touch with you when I go to Mallow early next week.

Yours sincerely,
E. MacLysaght

My proposal was accepted: some years later I submitted my thesis and in due course obtained my M.A. degree.

I became closely associated with University College, Cork in a different capacity as an extract from my diary will show.

9 October, 1929

I am probably the only man who has ever been a member of the Governing Bodies of both U.C.C. and U.C.G. at the same time. I had what amounted to a life seat at Galway, if I had not felt bound to resign it, for I was the representative of the Clare County Council on that body; and it is the rarest thing for such a representative to be changed except at the wish of the appointee. At Galway I was a fairly dutiful member: at any rate I can claim that I was not to be numbered among those county council nominees who seldom attended except when votes were required for the giving of jobs.

In 1926, perhaps as part of the effort then being made to de-anglicize University College, Cork, I was co-opted on to the Governing Body of that college. There I really did take an active part in college affairs, so much so that I felt I could not honestly retain a similar position at Galway, since I had not time to give proper attention to both; and in consequence I resigned my 'safe' seat there. In normal circumstances my seat at Cork would have been equally safe, because the same co-opted members were normally always chosen again if they so desired when their period of service expired. Then, however, circumstances in U.C.C. were far from normal. A very bitter internal war has been in progress among the members of the staff for some time. The *casus belli* doesn't matter, it is really a preliminary contest in the anticipated struggle for the succession to that most ineffective of presidents, Professor Merriman, who is a rather pleasant prevaricator, adept at turning a deaf ear to awkward questions (usually mine) and gifted with a sense of humour which he manifests at the most unexpected times. The protagonists at any rate are on the one hand that brilliant and acerbic (then) lay theologian, Alfred O'Rahilly, the Registrar, and on the other the Professor of Agriculture, Boyle by name, who with his slow and ponderous manner and bovine good humour is the very antithesis of the volatile 'Alfie'. I have taken no part whatsoever in this controversy: I have kept my feelings to myself and observed my neutrality so strictly that I have even dropped my regular habit of lunching with Boyle. Privately my view is that whoever is in the right as regards the actual dispute, O'Rahilly, for all his faults, is with his brilliant intellect an asset to the College in a way Boyle could never be, and I had decided that if and when it came to a showdown between them I would count myself on O'Rahilly's side. But he did not know this. While this was going on the prescribed date when the co-opted members were due for re-appointment approached. It never occurred to me to do any lobbying: I just did nothing, assuming that we would be chosen again as is usual in the case of co-opted members. To my surprise at the meeting new names were proposed, each having a patent party colour. Neither side put forward the apparently neutral MacLysaght, not knowing where he stood. Then on a sudden inspiration Boyle himself proposed me. That was the end as far as I was concerned because the O'Rahilly faction is in the majority and I had thus been labelled, without my consent of course, a 'Boylite'.

I kept up my connexion with U.C.C. in another way for some time, as a vice-president of the College Rugby Club. I am keen on rugby but, as a spectacle and because of its national standing and also as a test of skill I would unhesitatingly put hurling first among games. My inevitable digression on this subject will be found in Appendix C.

The big secondary schools all ignore hurling and play rugby. Blackrock probably has the best record of any of them at that game. I am, however, interested in Blackrock College more as a place of education than as a training ground for famous rugby players, having had three sons there.

5 October, 1955

I was annoyed three weeks ago because Brian, having been promoted from the preparatory school to the college proper, was with the rest of his class demoted again. Now I have the satisfactory news that with one other boy he has gone up to the college again.

The night I wrote that brief entry Brian had no home-work to do (I think they get far too much) so I was free of that chore and I spent half an hour or so writing an entry about Blackrock College. That I later extended to make one dealing with Irish schools in general. The result turned out to be more extensive than I intended and reads more like an essay than a normal uninhibited diary entry. The subject interest me very much. How far it would interest the reader of this book I cannot guess, but with some hesitation, having shortened it considerably, I include it here. (See footnote to p. 151.)

10 October, 1955

The big secondary schools such as Blackrock, Clongowes, Castleknock and Rockwell were modelled to a large extent on what are somewhat inaptly called public schools in England and even yet have not quite lost their Anglo-Irish atmosphere. What was lacking in Ireland, or at least in Catholic Ireland, was one which was founded as definitely Irish.

The book in which Pádraig Pearse's own description of St Enda's School appears (published by us – Maunsels – in 1917), is entitled *The Story of a Success*, and so to some extent it was, though it ceased to exist on the death of Pearse. That school, founded and run for the primary purpose of turning out patriots willing if necessary to be martyrs was, one may say, *sui generis* as also was that of Father Sweetman at Gorey, which may be described as the scapegrace offspring of the conventional Downside. It in turn failed. No institution will last which is essentially a one man show.

This fundamental defect was also the cause of the failure of the attempt to develop the flourishing preparatory school at St Gerard's, Bray, into a secondary school. I was one of the parents concerned in forming a governing body to ensure its permanence as such, but our plans to this end which the proprietor, Mr James – formerly an assistant master with Father Sweetman at Gorey – had at first accepted were eventually rejected by him: the two senior houses at Old Connaught and Walcot were closed and the whole school of boys from 8 to 18 concentrated at Thornhill.

This happened while I was away in South Africa.* When I returned I found my connexion with St Gerard's had abruptly terminated, our governing body abandoned and my son Fergus no longer there. He was one of a number of the senior boys removed by parents who disagreed with the abandonment of the three house arrangement – in his case the grandparent, for in my absence my father (who paid the piper and so called the tune) sent him to Downside at the unusual age of 16.

The defect I referred to does not exist in the cast of Glenstal. That extensive large mansion of the Barrington family was acquired by the Benedictine Order in 1927,† the boy's school there being started in 1932. In it we now have a first class secondary boarding school – Irish without being Gaelic-Irish or Anglo-Irish – which, being run by a religious order, is assured of continuity.

I remember a conversation I had one day with a young priest recently ordained and about to go on a foreign mission. He was lamenting the change which had taken place at Glenstal in the ten years since he was a boy there, when, he said, with only 25 or 30 pupils it was more a happy family than a public school; with a hundred he felt that it had lost that homely atmosphere. I argued in reply that it had also gained by the change: it could now compete with other schools in games and sports, and escaped the charge which had been made against it in its early days, that it had a tendency to produce oddities and 'cissies'. With his riposte that even if that were true (which he denied) it was better than moulding all to a conventional pattern, as the big English public schools normally do, I had to agree; but, as Glenstal is now, it does not turn out young men of that stereotyped character, nor is there any danger of this under the Benedictine system with comparatively small numbers and with Irish boys as the material to be worked on.

*I was engaged for some weeks in 1933 on a survey relating to the prospects for Irish exports to that country: my report to the Minister for Industry & Commerce is lengthy but is of no relevance here.

†The Priory became an Abbey in 1957.

During the years when [my son] William was at Glenstal I went there often and my very favourable impression of the place derives equally from his experience as a pupil and from my conversations with the priests in charge of the school.

Glenstal had, unlike many new schools, an existing tradition at its inception, that of the Benedictine Order. This element of tradition is not to be despised: Americans are conscious of the lack of it. I remember seeing in the rules of one American school 'the tradition of this college shall be' so and so! So far as it is created by antiquity in Ireland Protestant colleges alone can claim to possess it. King's Hospital (the Bluecoat School) and Kilkenny School date from the seventeenth century, as do Midleton and Drogheda grammar schools.

St Columba's, the leading Protestant boys' school, comparable to Alexandra College for girls, has given the lead to Ireland in one important respect. They have made the farm which is attached to the school an integral part of it, not merely a food-producing adjunct the boys are encouraged to participate in its operations and so, as part of their education, to get an intimate knowledge of what is the core of Ireland's national being, to use once more that illuminating expression of A.E.'s. I am glad to hear that Glenstal has taken the initiative among the big Catholic schools by following the example of St. Columba's.

The foregoing references to Protestant schools in the Republic – I see I had nothing to say in that diary entry about those in the Six Counties – inevitably bring me to consider the universities in that category. I know very little about Queen's University or the New University of Ulster but I have very definite views about Trinity College. Dublin University, to give it its more comprehensive name, is an Elizabethan foundation and dating from the sixteenth century can be classed as one of the long established ones: it has none of the characteristics of those which are often called 'red bricks'. If at the time of the dissolution of the Royal University and the establishment of the National, Archbishop Walsh and other Catholic leaders had had their way Dublin University would have been extended (as may have been the intention of its founders) by the addition of a second college so that it would have consisted of Trinity (mainly Protestant) and University College (mainly Catholic). There may have been some objection to this plan in Catholic circles on the grounds that the Protestant traditions of Dublin University would be too strong:

be that as it may the effective opposition came from the Protestant side and from Trinity itself. It is interesting to recall the ascendancy view of that time as it is expressed in an article in the *Dublin Evening Mail* quoted by Monsignor Patrick J. Walsh in his life of the Archbishop. Having vigorously denounced the idea of a second college in Dublin University it adds:

'Trinity College need not be ejected from the buildings of which it has made such good use. It will be time enough to throw sheeps' eyes at them when the Archbishop gets his Parnellite Parliament in College Green. When that goal is reached Trinity College and many other good things besides will have to go by the board.'

That was in 1885. Now, after more than fifty years of a far more independent parliament than Parnell envisaged, Trinity is in no danger of decline, though I think it would be in a stronger position had its authorities possessed greater vision when the university question was again tackled in 1908. They lost much by their decision; we lost more.

No doubt the university envisaged would have been constitutionally undenominational; so is the National University today, but that does not prevent it being, in spite of its sprinkling of non-Catholic students, essentially Catholic just as Trinity for all its large percentage of Catholic students still has to some extent a Protestant atmosphere. That, it must be admitted, has been due more to the Hierarchy's 'ban' than to the attitude of the present day authorities in Trinity. Now, thank God, this ban has been removed. When the controversy about the extension of the ancient University of Dublin by a 'merger' of Trinity College and University College in it became acute in 1966, after the death of Donagh O'Malley, the editor of the *Leader* asked me to give my view on this question as a university graduate having no connexion with either T.C.D. or U.C.D. My reply (21 March 1967) was as follows:

I agree with your leading article but would like to add that I have read all the letters which appeared in the *Irish Times*, *Hibernia* and elsewhere and I would say that with one or two regrettable exceptions none attacked the Archbishop personally.

My own feeling is that the worst result of the ban, as it is called, is that it is promoting a marked increase in anti-clericalism which as a Catholic I deplore since anti-clericalism, as is apparent in other countries, has led to indifference and a falling away from the Church.

No one can deny that Trinity College was essentially a Protestant institution formerly and even as late as 50 years ago was pro-British. But enough has since been done by them to show that they genuinely desire to be fully integrated into the Irish nation: the offer of a site for a Catholic chapel, repeated requests for the appointment of a Catholic chaplain and the recent election of a Catholic to the highest office of the University are to my mind proof of this.

As we know a considerable proportion of the staff are Catholics. As regards students the experience of people who were educated partly in England and partly at home is that being in a minority made them more consciously and keenly Catholic and Irish than during the period of education here. It seems to me that to give permission to some Catholics to enter T.C.D. (it is given in a good many cases) and at the same time to state that being there is a danger to faith and to deny them the safeguards supposedly provided in U.C.D. is quite illogical: and to ignore the many foreign Catholics in the College, to whom no ban applied, is equally lacking in logic and charity.

Personally I have always wanted to see Dublin University with its world-wide reputation extended to embrace two colleges, T.C.D. and U.C.D. In desiring this I am only following an illustrious Catholic Archbishop of Dublin, Dr Walsh.

The number of Protestant names among the prominent protagonists on the side of Ireland in her struggle against British domination has often been emphasized – Grattan, Wolfe Tone, Emmet, Lord Edward Fitzgerald, Burke, Parnell and the rest: nearly all of them were Trinity men and the lustre of their names, to say nothing of Ussher, Berkeley, Sheridan, Goldsmith, Dean Swift, Tom Moore, and many other great figures, famous in the literary rather than the political field, has made the absorption of Dublin University into the 'national being', as AE called it, a natural process.

I think the three following diary entries of comparatively recent date may suitably be placed here.

1 June, 1953
The first part of this entry being an account of a very full day's work at the National Library and a conversation during lunch at the Arts Club can be omitted. It continues:
Then at 4.15 R.I.A. Council meeting till 5.15 when Mgr

Boylan gave me a lift to Blackrock. We had as usual an interesting conversation, this time arising out of the death of Dr Walsh, the biographer of Archbishop Walsh. Mgr B. agrees with me that our present archbishop (who he calls a northern Catholic having the traits normally associated therewith) will never agree to trying to get back St Patrick's or Christ Church: he, B., has used every argument he could bring forward to persuade Dr McQ. without avail. Mgr B. agrees with my views as to the desirability of the merger of T.C.D. and U.C.D. in one Dublin University, and referred to Archbishop Walsh's efforts to that end. He thinks Dr Walsh's biography very good on the university question, but too prone to emphasize intrigue and not showing his subject in quite a fair light elsewhere.

17 January, 1968

John Charles is admittedly a northern bigot. I was shocked when I heard his statement on ecumenism read out at Mass on Sunday. Who would have believed a few years ago that we would be reading a public apology from responsible Catholics for the conduct of their archbishop – see letter in today's *Irish Times.* He is illogical too as I pointed out in my letter to the *Leader* two years ago. Nevertheless I always like to remind people of his many kind and generous actions behind the scenes which get no publicity. Here is a recent example. Theo Moody told me that in the course of organizing some non-sectarian fund he sent one of his subscription forms to John Charles. As it was addressed from Trinity College he didn't expect any response, but in fact, to his surprise, he received by return of post a cheque for – was it £1,000 he said? – something large anyway. I have personal experience too of Dr McQuaid's kind helpfulness in matters unconnected with money, as this diary testifies.

1 January, 1971

I chanced to meet Fr Raymond Kennedy (the Concern priest) my neighbour, and I think I may say my friend, today and we walked together to Blackrock. After a while I said 'I've often wanted to put a question to a priest and this is it. Is it not entirely foreign to the spirit of Christianity in the Creed to hold up to obloquy Pontius Pilate, at least by inference – the sole non-divine person mentioned in it?'. 'Not at all' he replied without the slightest hesitation, 'He's in it to mark the date'! (I put in the exclamation mark; as if Our Lord's death isn't date enough). 'Well', said I, 'I always omit those three words when saying the Creed and will go on doing so'. I even venture to think that Our Lord has forgiven Judas Iscariot. He repented immediately, didn't keep the money and killed himself in a fit of remorse. If he had lived he might even have become another Peter. Of course Peter did not betray Jesus but he repudiated Him; he lived on to become His greatest follower and advocate and died a martyr's death. Maybe Judas wouldn't have been accepted as Peter was because his crime was so much publicized.

I am critical of several other things in the new Mass in English. What is wrong with 'It is right and fitting' as we said formerly and still say in Irish; why change it? I liked 'under my roof' because it always reminded me of that centurion (my favourite character in the New Testament): 'to receive you' misses that, even if it is more applicable to receiving Communion. I could list quite a few instances of what seem to me to be unnecessary changes and at least one essential which I feel should have been made. The English '*Lead* us not into temptation' seems misleading to me where the Irish 'ná lig sinn . . .' gives the right sense. The most annoying of the new wordings in English does not occur in the Irish version, viz. in the Our Father: to start in the singular with 'who art' and 'Thy name' and end up the doxology (if that is the right word) with 'yours' not 'Thine' is just plain ignorance. There another thing occurs to me. The Protestant wording begins 'thine is the kingdom'; ours now begins 'The kingdom . . .' and ends 'is yours': can this switching be sub-conscious anti-ecumenism? I usually go to the Irish Mass where we. begin this 'is leatsa. . . '.

I am adding part of an entry (dated 12 September, 1977) on the same subject. It was written in Irish but I have translated it for insertion here.

Recently at Mass I noticed again another disturbing example of uncorrected mistranslation – or misrepresentation – viz. the use of the word 'hate' in the Gospel of St Luke (Ch. XIV, v. 26). I quote: 'If any man comes to me without hating his father and mother, his wife and children . . . he can be no disciple of mine'. The Irish version of the Four Gospels which I have (Ó Laoghaire & Ó Nualláin) does use the word 'fuath', the meaning of which unquestionably is hatred or loathing; but the editors appended a lengthy footnote pointing out that, taken literally, this is directly contrary to Our Lord's teaching and explaining what is really meant. Turning to the version in English no such footnote appears in Mgr Knox's translation (approved by the hierarchy of England, Scotland and Wales), though explanatory footnotes do appear frequently elsewhere in it. I may add that St Mathew in his Gospel (x, vs. 37) records the same saying in an acceptable way.

CHAPTER XIII

The Manuscripts Commission and
The Institute for Advanced Studies

Some time in 1936 I made up my mind to give up the calling of farmer and nurseryman, for I felt that anything I got out of the former was mainly due to a small allowance from my father for looking after his place in Co. Cork; and the nursery, while economically capable of paying me a modest living wage, involved unremitting attention to business, for the most part in the office. In short, I began to feel that I was to some extent wasting my time and earning less than I was worth, not to mention having little time for literary work. It soon became obvious to me that as long as I was on the spot, or even anywhere in Ireland, the partial withdrawal I had at first contemplated was not feasible. I can put a matter entirely out of my head if it has no longer anything whatever to do with me; but if the least responsibility rests with me I cannot half do a job: if I were to see the daily post at all I must see that every letter was answered and, moreover, answered competently. So the following year I decided to go right away for a year or two. This did not result in the closure of the nursery business which after a period in the doldrums, later on developed under my sons William and Brian into one of the largest in Ireland.

I did not have to think twice about my destination. Capetown was the obvious place. I had previously twice been to South Africa, partly on business connected with the Irish Linen House, which was my mother's property and was allowed to get into a bad way through mismanagement, as so often happens when a proprietor is an absentee and a manager is appointed through family pull and not because of any business qualifications. I had also toured a large part of the Union with the object of opening up a trade in Irish pedigree Shorthorn and Kerry cattle. This was of value to me in giving me a first-hand knowledge of the country, but of none financially as the prices ruling at home for pure-bred bulls and cows were considerably higher than South

African farmers were prepared to pay. Finally I had made many city contacts too, for in 1928 I carried out a semi-official survey of the export and import trade as between Ireland and South Africa. I remember little about the contents of the report which on my return I presented to Patrick McGilligan, then Minister for Industry and Commerce. It was certainly voluminous and much of it was typed upon enormous sheets of paper in order to fit in the quantities of statistics it contained. I do recall that I discovered that Irish shoe polish was used by natives to smooth out the crinkle in their hair. Another slightly amusing aspect of the matter was that McGilligan in thanking me made the more or less stereotyped remark: 'If there's anything I can do for you any time'; and a year or two later, instead of pulling the string thus offered to some advantageous purpose, I had to waste it in placating my indignant father by getting a line of E.S.B. pylons, which were going to pass too near his windows, deflected to a less unaesthetic course.

I recorded the impressions formed during the next two years which I spent in South Africa as a resident journalist, not a visitor, fairly fully at the time and summarized them later in a long entry I made in the ship on my voyage home. This would be out of place here, but as it is mainly about the Irish in South Africa I am including it in the Appendix C. In the unlikely event of anyone wanting to know my views on South Africa in general thirty years ago I may add that I gave them at length in a book entitled *An Aifric Theas* (1947).

When I returned to Ireland at the end of 1938, I had to face making a new start in life. I had a small income, just enough for a bachelor of simple tastes but quite inadequate to support a wife and young family. I had several reasons for not resuming my active life on the land; and my inclinations, whetted by the completion of my book *Irish Life in the Seventeenth Century* which was published a few months later as a follow-up to my *Short Study of a Transplanted Family* (1935) led me to seek some work in the historical field. This I was fortunate to find with the Irish Manuscripts Commission.

I began my work for that body by spending nearly a year at the British Museum. I was there when the War broke out, whereupon I returned to Dublin and was engaged for the next few months preparing a volume on the Orrery papers at the National Library. Had there been no Second World War I might have spent the best part of the rest of my life working in the British Museum. Robin Flower urged me to do this; he said I could do

no more useful work for Ireland, since the innumerable manuscripts of Irish interest there have never been systematically
examined and he estimated that it would take twenty years to
make an adequate detailed catalogue of this material. The
British Museum index of the Additional Manuscripts from 1864
does give some idea of the nature of this vast collection, though
the Irish material is not segregated in the annual indexes and
has to be laboriously picked out; the indexes prior to 1864 are
of less use for this purpose. Besides the Additional MSS there
are many other collections to be examined: the Gladstone Papers
alone might occupy a student of Irish history for years, though
being comparatively recent they are of less importance than the
earlier manuscripts to which I am referring. Anyway, fortunately for my personal happiness, this idea was not carried out,
for to be permanently exiled in London would be to me a dire
punishment, even if I could have arranged to rear my family in
Ireland.

In this connexion I should mention a subsequent development
in the field of manuscript reproduction which makes less necessary the preparation of a calendar such as Robin Flower
envisaged: that is the microfilm.

I was then appointed inspector for the Manuscripts Commission in Ireland and from that day on I had, thank God, constant
employment till I retired in September 1973.

The job was at first a temporary one. Although Charles
MacNeill had already been employed to report on some famous
manuscript collections for the Commission, the appointment of a
travelling inspector to search for and report on collections in
private hands represented a new departure in the activities of the
Irish Manuscripts Commission and was regarded as experimental.
It was up to me to make good. I did so.

The task of the new inspector was to discover and save from
oblivion as much as possible of what was still left in country
houses, estate offices and solicitors' deed boxes. A good deal of
publicity was given to this question. As a note in the *Journal of
the Cork Historical and Archaeological Society* pointed out at
the time 'the loss of historical material in manuscript form, which
may be regarded as normal from generation to generation, has
been accelerated to an alarming degree during the past twenty-
five years. Many country houses which were the repositories of
manuscript collections have been burned to the ground, old
estates have been broken up and family papers dispersed beyond
recovery where they have not been actually thrown away through

carelessness or ignorance.'

This warning was, and is, applicable to departmental and local government records as well as to those in private hands. Apropos of that I append a note made nearly thirty years later, when I was chairman:

15 November, 1967

Yesterday I led a deputation to Donagh O'Malley. I append the script of my intended introductory remarks (which I adhered to). He advised us to go further in our proposals and to link them up with former suggestions for greater independence of the Commission and also with the National Archives plans outlined in Jim Hayes' memorandum.

'We have asked you to receive this deputation as the Minister in charge of the Department to which the Irish Manuscripts Commission is attached and our purpose is to request that legislation be enacted to bring up to date the quite obsolete Act of 1867 which now governs the whole question of preservation and destruction of departmental and local government papers, or I might say to a large extent does not govern it in modern conditions. Owing to the absence of any definite procedure in this regard there has been an immense accumulation of material over the years for which the problem of storage is becoming more and more urgent, and therefore of course accessibility more difficult. Much of this is trivial and not worth keeping after its immediate purpose is accomplished, but much, on the other hand, has a potential as historical source material. There have been some cases of senseless destruction in the past, none worse than that of the four census returns of 1861 to 1891, which were deliberately destroyed during the first World War as not covered by the Act of 1867; and in regard to local government records we have only to read the comments of Mrs Woodham Smith, the author of *The Great Hunger*, on those of Co. Mayo.'

P.S. 24 January, 1969

O'Malley died a few months after we had met him. Brian Lenihan took his place but in fact no progress has since been made.

I have little to say here about my professional activities during this time because the results were published in four volumes by the Manuscripts Commission. Somewhat incongruously therefore my comments on those years will be devoted to the lighter side of this work.

During the years I was on the staff of the Manuscripts Commission about a third of my time was spent in Dublin writing my reports, etc., and a room in the National Library was put at my disposal as an office or workroom. It was then called the Exhibition Room, a fine and little used apartment over 40 ft. long having two large open fireplaces with carved overmantels and three large double windows facing due north and looking out on the bare walls of the adjacent building, the College of Physicians. It is now the Manuscripts Room, filled with rows of steel shelves for the thousands of manuscripts which it was my pleasant duty some years later, during my time as Keeper of Manuscripts, to classify and arrange. I was working there one morning in February 1943 when the telephone rang and the voice which spoke to me was none other than that of the Taoiseach, Mr De Valera. He asked me to go round to his office in Merrion Street and to see him there. I had no doubt that the subject of the coming interview would be the taking over by the Irish Government of the Office of Arms, which was the last of those miscellaneous public services not transferred after the Treaty in 1922. I knew that such a move was contemplated and had received a hint that I might be the person called upon to take it over.

When I arrived some twenty minutes later at Government Buildings I was shown almost immediately into the Taoiseach's room. I was surprised to find that the subject of our conversation was not to be the Office of Arms, which in fact was not mentioned at all, but the Institute for Advanced Studies.

This Institute was founded by Mr de Valera in 1940 and was one of his favourite brain-children. At the time of which I am now speaking, it consisted of two schools, Theoretical Physics and Celtic Studies. The former, under the guidance of a world famous mathematician in the person of Dr Schroedinger, an Austrian who found asylum in Ireland, has had a distinguished and comparatively untroubled history. The choice of a director for the other school was less happy. True, Dr Thomas O'Rahilly was a scholar of high repute; but the Director's duties are not confined to the production of brilliant work on his own part: they involve also, as the word implies, the direction of the work of his colleagues and students. For the performance of this function it would be hard to find a more unsuitable man. His personality and methods were such that no man of any standing could work with him and as a result the School lost (fortunately only temporarily) all its best scholars: Osborn Bergin retired at great personal financial loss to himself; Daniel Binchy accepted a fellowship at Corpus Christi College, Oxford; Michael O'Brien a chair at Queen's University, Belfast. At the time of the final disagreement the Government (which in this case, as in most others at the time may be taken to connote Mr de Valera) backed O'Rahilly. The event proved that such backing was ill-advised.

In the course of the conversation in the Taoiseach's room to which I have alluded, Mr de Valera, while being, as such men have to be, guarded in his remarks, said enough to let me see that he wanted some new blood in the Institute on the Governing Board of the School of Celtic Studies: the function of the new blood was obvious. I protested, when he asked me to be one of the new members, that I was no Irish scholar. 'My Irish' I said, is equivalent to the English of the ordinary postman or bus conductor'. However, he made it clear that in his view the principal qualification for a governor was not scholarship but a certain talent for administration plus a modicum of moral courage. I accepted then and served on the Board until I retired last year – not a very useful member I fear, but at least one who seldom missed a meeting. I should perhaps say incidentally that it is an unpaid position, and I may also add that after O'Rahilly ceased to be Director in 1949, both O'Brien and Binchy returned to the staff, the latter affording a very rare example of a man voluntarily giving up a fellowship in one of the leading Oxford colleges.

A controversy relating to the Institute for Advanced Studies of quite another kind from those precipitated by Thomas O'Rahilly, resulted in one of the major disappointments of my life. I was appointed, a few days after my conversation with the Taoiseach, to take charge of the Office of Arms and my experiences there will form the main subject of another chapter. But first, as this personal disappointment arose out of a matter of some general interest, I will relate how it came about.

Another 'live wire' in the literary life of Dublin was that disputatious but likeable professor, Dr Dudley Edwards. Edwards had the ear of Mr de Valera, and de Valera, almost alone of leading public men in Ireland at the time, was not only sympathetic but actively helpful in promoting cultural endeavours. (We might also so regard Seán MacBride.) Briefly the idea that Edwards put up to him was that another School be added to the Institute, a School of Irish Historical Research. The Taoiseach adopted the plan, the more readily no doubt because he also intended to create a second new School. The School of Cosmic Physics. In due course, the necessary statutory steps to establish these two new Schools as part of the Institute for Advanced Studies were taken. For two years the sum of £10,000 appeared in the official published Estimates to meet the cost of the proposed School of Historical Research.

Why then, it may as well be asked, did a School so authorized never function, though the School of Cosmic Physics set about its work without question. The answer is that the energy and enthusiasm of Dudley Edwards was negatived by his lack of subtlety; and that Father Aubrey Gwynn, S.J., is a very astute man.

The first of these two statements is easily enough explained. Any wise man who wishes successfully to launch a pet scheme considers who is likely to oppose it, and he should so approach a potential opponent as to make the latter feel that he is a joint author of it; Edwards evidently gave this ticklish matter little prior consideration. Consequently provincial jealousy and personal *amour propre*, coupled with a not altogether unjustified feeling that the plan involved the incursion by the Institute into the proper sphere of the Universities, produced opposition.

This opposition relied mainly on such futile arguments as that the establishment of the School meant concentrating research in Dublin and therefore the neglect of Cork and Galway, or that it would impair the work of the Manuscripts Commission which we envisaged as being part of the new School; alternatively the latter could have been taken over by the University as was done later in the case of the Folklore Commission. Such arguments were of little moment. Their supporters were given an opportunity of expression when Mr de Valera invited the Manuscripts Commission as a whole and the various members of it individually to give their views on the concrete proposals which had been put forward.

One man only, Father Aubrey Gwynn, made a really reasoned case against them. His case was based on the principle that the work envisaged should be done by the Universities and that the establishment of the School of Historical Research in the Institute would not only place that essentially independent activity under Government control but would also accelerate the already noticeable tendency of University College, Dublin, to become a technical college or professional training ground rather than a centre of culture. Personally, I think there was something in this viewpoint, except that I do not agree that the independence of historians was threatened any more than that of the mathematicians of the Institute, and I agree that it would have been better to have made the School part of the National University though that would have involved favouring U.C.D. and leaving T.C.D. out in the cold, a consideration which the impartial critic must regard as of some weight. However, as I pointed out to Father Gwynn in the course of a long conversation on the subject – we walked for an hour or more on the canal bank discussing the question one day – the essential point was that there was no chance of a University endowment whereas the plan actually adopted, and only held up on account of the opposition of individual historians, meant that a considerable annual sum would be available for historical research. 'It amounts to this', I said, 'You are deliberately spurning an offer of something like £100,000 over the next few years to be devoted solely to our own subject for reasons which appear to me to be academic. Let us be realists. The opportunity will probably never occur again.' 'Well,' he replied, falling back on his second line of defence, 'What it amounts to in practice is this; you are for accepting this £100,000, as you compute it, just for the sake of finding a job for a few professors there. What suitable people are there anyway?' I mentioned several names including Edward Lynam who was just about to retire from the British Museum, and Dr O'Doherty – here was a chance of rehabilitating an outstanding Maynooth professor who had been banished to the wilds of Donegal under a cloud – and finally some of the more promising young men like Tom O'Neill; and then I added 'I may also mention myself'. He said he had not thought of me in that connexion, imagining that I was quite content with my job at the Genealogical Office. I soon explained how comparatively uncongenial that work was to me.

This brings me again to the profound disappointment of which I spoke a few pages back. It was quite taken for granted at first that the establishment of the School was a *fait accompli*, and no one concerned seemed to have any doubt that I was to be one of the staff: so much so indeed that I was semi-officially consulted as to who should be my successor as head of the Genealogical Office. I did not aim high. I would have been quite satisfied with an assistant-professorship though I might have been given one of the higher posts. In brief, the effect of such an appointment would have been that I would be paid a good salary for doing the very work which I would choose to do as a labour of love had I sufficient independent means; moreover, I could hold my job till 75 (with a pension after that) instead of being retired at 65 or 70 at latest and, to crown its complete suitability, in place of 24 days leave – a mere nothing to a man who had to take it all in travelling at weekends to superintend a farm in Co. Clare – the Institute's vacations correspond with those of a University so that much of my historical work (not research, but writing) could have been done at Raheen.

This disappointment, though keen, came to me not as a sudden decision but through a gradual realization that there would be no decision.

I am inclined to think that if the General Election of February 1948 had not resulted in a change of government the School would have been established. When it became evident that some of the opposition to it was due to the alleged unsuitability of Dudley Edwards as Director, it was understood that other names were being considered, that of the Canadian professor J. J. Kenney, author of *Sources for the Early History of Ireland*, being regarded as the most likely.

It was quite clear to me that Fr Gwynn's motive in nullifying the plan (and he does not deny his major part in it) was not entirely altruistic. At the time we were discussing the matter Edwards had been warned by his doctor that he was killing himself by overwork. In practice there were two dedicated workers in the faculty of history in University College, Gwynn and Edwards. Remove Edwards and that left with the juniors one worker – Gwynn. It was too late for Father Aubrey Gwynn to take a different line, but if Mr de Valera had remained Taoiseach and the question had been raised again, he might perhaps have sung dumb.

I think it would have been reconsidered. In the first place, the plan had never been abandoned and was so much a reality that provision was made for it in the Estimates where it remained until the advent of an 'Economy' government. Mr de Valera was not a man to abandon any project initiated by himself. At a lunch given at External Affairs (now renamed Foreign Affairs) on the departure of the Spanish Ambassador, which I attended, I sat next to Seán Moynihan, the Secretary of the Government, a man with whom I had had no direct contact before. As a correspondent I had found him somewhat brusque, but I thought an hour and a half's contiguity might change this attitude and so it did. No one could have been pleasanter. *Inter alia* we discussed the proposed School of Historical Research and he gave me to understand that the Taoiseach had by no means given up the idea. Shortly after this luncheon I wrote a letter about the position to Mr de Valera who happened to be just starting on a trip in a naval ship to the Western Isles of Scotland. He returned to find himself faced with the first skirmishes of the coming General Election and quite naturally all minor controversial matters, such as the one which meant everything to me, were put on one side until after the election.

This long disquisition was prompted by the recollection of a telephone call. I have heard it said that digression is the soul of autobiography, but it is equally true that digression is tedious if the tangent is followed too far. I hope I have not done so in this case.

My expectation that I would be chosen to take charge of the Office of Arms in Dublin Castle was in fact realized shortly after that interview with Mr de Valera in February 1943. Paradoxically I had a number of sound reasons for being pleased to be transferred from a job I liked to one I was to find less congenial. As I had to earn my living the fact that the change meant an increase of almost a hundred per cent in my pay was an important consideration; moreover I became a permanent pensionable civil servant on the staff of the National Library instead of an extern worker paid according to the number of days worked each month. At the time this happened there was a special reason for finding my former job irksome: I am thinking of the appalling travel conditions which existed then.

Before I come to my years as an official in Dublin Castle, which will be the subject of my next chapter, I think it worth while recording some further recollections of the time I spent as inspector for the Manuscripts Commission.

The extra ration of petrol I had been allowed in connexion with my official work was withdrawn late in 1941 owing to shortages during the War; so that I had to depend on the railways and my bicycle. Even then I thought myself rather too old for long bicycle journeys hampered by my baggage and often by bad weather. Normally I count the train a pleasant way of travelling but just then the situation was almost at its worst. Such coal as was obtainable from England was incredibly bad; the remarkable skill subsequently attained by Irish locomotive men in overcoming the difficulty was yet to come and engines, when they did not break down entirely, were continually forced to stop en route while the firebox was raked out and the fire got going again. I have known as many as four different locomotives being employed to pull one train from Cork to Dublin. On one occasion, when I was working in Galway, my mother was to come and stay with me there. She was then living near Mallow and we decided that the most comfortable way for her to do the journey would be to go to Dublin, in normal times a run of about three hours in a fast train, stay the night there and to get the train to Galway with me next morning. I was waiting at Westland Row (now Pearse) Station, having with difficulty got two seats, expecting her to join me. As 10 o'clock approached, I became more and more impatient. Just as the train was due to start she arrived, tired and dishevelled, having spent the whole night in the Cork train in an overcrowded carriage, her neighbour a 15 stone commercial traveller who slept drunkenly more or less on her shoulder. We then took eight hours to reach Galway – 126 miles. That is a sample of travelling in 1941, the fact that my octogenarian mother was exploring the city of Galway at 12.00 o'clock next day is an example of her energy and resilience. Even when she died in 1952 at ninety-two, the only serious disability she suffered from was semi-blindness.

The cause of her coming to Galway was to get me out of a difficulty. I was at the time engaged on one of the most interesting jobs I had to do while I was employed as inspector by the Manuscripts Commission. It came about this way. Many years earlier, just before the first World War in fact, the Historical Manuscripts Commission in England had by arrangement with the then Bishop of Galway, Dr O'Dea, employed Dr Berry of the Public Record Office, Dublin, to make a calendar of the papers relating to the Wardenship of Galway, a peculiar ecclesiastical jurisdiction, the nature of which I explain in my report published by the Commission in 1944. First the 1914-18 War, and then presumably the establishment of the Irish Free State, held up the publication by the Historical Manuscripts Commission of Dr Berry's report, and when in due course the Irish Manuscripts Commission was established in 1928 the English body handed over that report to its new Irish counterpart. No progress was made for some time and when at last publication was contemplated, Dr Browne, not long consecrated Bishop of Galway, objected with some reason to the publication of Berry's report, principally and ostensibly because other documents had come to light since the report was made in 1912, and also I fancy because the Irish Manuscripts Commission, in this case represented by Professor James Hogan of Cork, had not approached him in a manner consonant with his episcopal dignity. It fell to me to go to see the bishop and to try to pour oil upon the troubled waters. Though I was supposed to be making a call *en passant* from my home in Co. Clare actually I made a special journey to Galway from Dublin. Somehow I managed to hit it off with the bishop whom I found very ready to be expansive, even on our first meeting when he discussed Mr de Valera with surprising candour. So far as the diocesan archives were concerned, he was skating on thin ice, because all he could actually do was to protest and to refuse access to the newer material: his predecessor having given permission to the Historical Manuscripts Commission to publish, *that* body could not be prevented from doing so. However, he invited me to come and prepare the whole collection for publication by the Irish Commission. I was authorized to do so and the work took several months. My estimation of the bishop's character and ability – subsequently slightly shaken by his high-handed action with Clement O'Flynn, the County Manager, over the site for the new city schools and more recently by his unecumenical outburst in connexion with Trinity College – rose considerably after I gave him the proofs: he not only read them so carefully that he was able to point out some minor errors, but also quite belied Hogan's confident expectation that he would eventually force me to omit much that might seem to the ecclesiastical mind to be unsuitable for publication; indeed Dr Browne told me at the outset that he relied on my discretion and in the upshot neither he nor I found it necessary to make any essential cuts at all.

I was somewhat in awe of him at first. Apart from Dr Fogarty of Killaloe, the only bishop with whom I had up to that time felt completely at home, was Dr O'Neill of Limerick. Dr Fogarty was a friend of the family and I met him much more often than any other bishop; twice at least under rather amusing circumstances. Once was in a railway carriage when a sycophantish person came in and cast himself on his knees before him imploring an episcopal blessing – 'Yerra, man, there's a time and a place for everything, have sense and get up out of that' was his reply. Another time was when my friend James P. O'Reilly (that product of Oxford and an Irish Catholic background, a type deserving a paragraph in himself), was at Raheen and Dr Fogarty happened to call. James aired his rubrical knowledge and paraded Cardinal Bourne to the annoyance of Dr Fogarty, to whom the cardinal was anything but a white-headed boy. The conversation or rather monologue was abruptly terminated by the bishop's turning to me and saying 'Come out now and show me your bull' and I thought I heard him mutter something at O'Reilly about Bulls and bulls.

It was in the summer of 1941 my mother made that 26 hour journey from Mallow to Galway. It was pleasant to have her there with me, but my primary motive in asking her to come was to enable me to do a day's work instead of a half-day's. Before she came I would go to the Bishop's House at 9.30 or 10 o'clock. By 1 o'clock, being as I am accustomed to an early dinner, I was ready to knock off. The bishop's household, to which I belonged for the purpose of dinner, had their meal at 2 o'clock. This, often gargantuan, repast lasted till 3.15. My work was hardly resumed, say at 3.30 when Father Jennings, the bishop's secretary, whose duty was apparently to see that I did not pinch any documents, began to get restless as his dinner was at 4 p.m. When my mother came I was able to go to my own dinner at 1 o'clock with her on the plea that she would be lonely. I should have left his collection of Wardenship papers in the same orderly fashion that I left the Kenmare Manuscripts after my time in Killarney; but Dr Browne impressed me (mistakenly I think now) as the kind of man who might be unreasonable and I therefore very stupidly decided to leave every single document exactly where I found it, no matter how chaotic their arrangement or lack of arrangement might be, so that it could not be said that I had misplaced anything. I wonder would he be horrified to learn that sooner than waste my days while in Galway I often carried away from the safe enough of his manuscript material to keep me occupied for that evening in my lodging; and would he breathe easier if he could be reassured, as he can, that every single item I so extracted was replaced without fail.

When examining and reporting on these manuscript collections – of the Bishop of Galway and of Lord Kenmare at Killarney – I remained long enough in the place to feel quite at home in it and to be untroubled by the not very serious but still real strain the social side of my work involved. Something more than three years constant occupation on that job brought me in contact with an almost uniformly pleasant type of people. Some carried their hospitality to the embarrassing extent of wanting to help and thereby interrupting and delaying me considerably: others left me to my own devices. I met the perfect hostess early in my career as inspector of manuscript collections in private hands in the person of Mrs Cameron of Bowenscourt, better known as the novelist Elizabeth Bowen. She took a keen interest in the work, yet never came near me while I was working. So sacrosanct indeed was the empty room which she put at my disposal that I could leave half finished bundles scattered around overnight without the least risk of their being tidied up: indeed I found my lost fountain pen when I called six months later in the exact spot I had left it in that room.

Even at Kenmare House, Killarney, I had one amusing and somewhat embarrassing experience. Lord Castlerosse was at home; he had been down to the estate office, where I was beginning the long and extremely interesting task which resulted in a book of 500 pages,* and in the course of conversation when I remarked that his agent had seemed somewhat nervous as to what I might find in the family papers, he replied 'Don't worry, the more scandals you unearth the better I'll like it'. Parenthetically, I may remark that it proved to be a horse of another colour for the Browne family have much to be proud of, particularly during the Penal times as I explain in the book referred to – and that tempts me to embark on a parenthesis within a parenthesis in order to mention that the Penal Laws did not prohibit the inheritance by a Catholic of landed property where there was only one son, as happened in the case of the huge Kenmare estate; in most cases the inheritance was frequently jeopardized or upset by compulsory division of lands and sometimes by the apostacy of a younger son. To get back to Castlerosse: he brought me up to the house that day and into a room well filled with Irish-Americans and such like (for the War was on and it was the day before the last regular ship was to sail from Galway with Americans from Europe). Inside the French window, he said in a loud voice to all and sundry: 'I want to introduce you boys to the eminent historian' – pause, and in a stage whisper to me 'By the way, what's your name?' I insert here two of the many diary entires I made about that time.

23 March, 1941

The *Cork Examiner* in yesterday's issue printed a very good account of the lecture I gave in Cork on the Kenmare Brownes. I didn't mention in it how I came on the La Cunha letters, which is worth remembering though not suitable in a historical lecture.

I had a long disused room in the yard to work in. The fireplace was blocked up with loose bricks. I casually noticed a small piece of paper peeping out between two of the bricks. Curiosity made me take them out. That piece of paper was the

The Kenmare Manuscripts – Dublin 1942.

edge of a letter. I removed all the bricks and found there a
number of letters written between 1716 and 1730 by Catherine
Browne, the wife of the Portuguese ambassador and these, with
others I found in an old bag, constitute a most interesting
collection which will fill many pages in my lengthy report. It
will be published later this year I hope. I guess it will be the
most valuable historical work I've done yet, apart from *Irish
Life in the Seventeenth Century*. I estimate that the volume
will run to five or six hundred pages.

In my three years I only covered a tithe of the country. As far
as possible I naturally concentrated first on such areas as could
be done conveniently from my two bases, my own home in Co.
Clare and my mother's in Co. Cork.

By a curious chance no difficulty was experienced in choosing
my successor. A week or so before I was appointed to the staff
of the National Library and transferred to the Office of Arms,
an individual of a type not common in Dublin was ushered into
my room at the Library. We afterwards became good friends,
but that morning as he came in he reminded me at first sight
of a Wodehouse character: spectacles, long jutting nose, Eton
accent and narrow brimmed hat turned up all round. He produced a letter of introduction from Terence Gray (of whom more
anon). It appeared that the British Army had found him as unsuitable for soldiering as he had found it uncongenial and he had
been invalided out. Having held the position of general editor,
British Records Association, in London, he sought work of a
similar kind in Ireland, where, though not technically an Irish
citizen (he became one later) he had close connexions, his father
being Sir Thomas Ainsworth and his mother Lady Holmpatrick.
I happened at the moment to be ploughing through a Latin document of the early seventeenth century, full of contractions and
written in a difficult script; and I was making heavy enough
weather of it. 'Read that', says I, without preamble, thinking it
was an easy way of getting rid of this stranger. To my astonishment he did so, quite easily. This is the man for me, I thought;
and I straight away made a proposition to him. I was most
anxious at the moment to pursue some historical research of
my own for which I had no time, and my proposal was that he
would spend two months with me as my unofficial assistant. I was
to devote half my time to my own work and half to that of the
Manuscripts Commission; he was to spend all his time at the
latter under my direction. I was to give him half my salary. Thus

all concerned would benefit. The Commission would get the work of $1\frac{1}{2}$ men while paying only one; John Ainsworth got a start; and I had half my time free for the work I wanted to do – or would have had, if it had turned out as I intended. However, after a fortnight, as I have said, I had to take up the Office of Arms job so could not do any private work. John Ainsworth on my recommendation fell in for my job as inspector. Eventually this inspectorship was transferred to the National Library as a result of the re-organization of the Manuscripts Department there.

The next entry was made shortly after I ceased to be inspector for the Manuscripts Commission.

24 March, 1943

I am sitting here in this panelled sanctum at the Office of Arms in the Castle and, strange experience for me after my years with the Manuscripts Commission, have nothing officially to do. I have now been about 3 weeks here doing little or nothing: Sadleir who is still in the next room – and will be till he clears out on 31st and finally hands over to me – has retained the keys of the strong-room and instead of coaching me or at least giving me *carte blanche* to poke around and make myself familiar with the place just hands me out a couple of manuscripts each morning presumably for me to peruse, which amounts to deliberate non-co-operation: the fact is he resents the present situation, though I understand he could have kept on the job as head of this Office, whatever it may be called in future, but he is such a dyed in the wool Unionist that he could not demean himself by working for the rebel Irish Free State! So I may as well spend an hour or so writing for my Diary some account of the more interesting experiences I have had when travelling around the country as inspector for the Manuscripts Commission.

I need hardly mention the two main jobs I did, which took months not days in each case, viz. Kenmare and the Wardenship of Galway, the results of which have been published by the Commission. No, I'm thinking rather of the lighter side of the job. I can't remember at the moment, having none of my diaries here, just when each of the incidents I hope to recall occurred – some of them indeed may be in them – anyway I'll make a note of them now as they occur to me.

It would be a pity for example not to record the affair of the Lane MSS. I was on my way back to Dublin after an inspection at Dromana (Villiers-Stuart) and as I drove along a road in Co. Kilkenny I happened to notice a farm cart plodding along and carrying a rather unusual load – a pile of paper. I stopped and having passed the time of day with the driver I asked him what he had in the cart. 'Tis a load of old papers the boss thrun out and told me to burn 'em or dump 'em out of sight' he replied. Not to make a long story of it, all I need say is that I gave him the odd £2 I had in my pocket and transferred the load to my station wagon. This 'waste paper' contained *inter alia* letters, some in cypher, from Charles II in exile to his supporter Sir George Lane in Ireland relating to his hopes and plans for Restoration, and that they are now in the National Library. Incidentally I may add that they came from an estate office and the agent was one of the people to whom we had sent our circular on the subject of waste paper in wartime.

The lucky chance of my being on that road in Co. Kilkenny that day saved what is among the more valuable of the smaller seventeenth century collections in Ireland. I should add that the bulk of the contents of that cart was of no value but what we salvaged out of it most decidedly was. No doubt many cases have occurred of useful material being wantonly destroyed. We quite often experienced the reverse after Hayes and I made a radio broadcast on the subject. We got a number of replies which necessitated my going to see the correspondents, only to be shown business letters of 1900 or even a Victorian bible. Well, we'd rather the likes of them than the Aunt Janes who decided 'only last week to burn those old papers' leaving us to wonder was there some treasure thus lost.

I could never trust the assertions of Aunt Janes or for that matter of Uncle Toms. One example of this is of special interest to myself. Knowing that Castlecrine had been sold and would probably be demolished I had to pay a visit there (most convenient for me being so near Raheen). As there was no one living in the house I called to the vicarage at Kilkishen to see the lady who was the representative of the Butlers. Yes, Butlers were prominent in Clare as well as Kilkenny. She assured me there was nothing in the nature of family papers in the house. I eventually persuaded her to come over to Castlecrine with me. When we got there she remarked that there might possibly be something in a certain press. In fact it contained a valuable collection now in the National Library and – this is where I have a special interest – among them a book in which is written a full account of a serious family row in the year 1680 between the Butler of Castlecrine and his neighbour my MacLysaght ancestor. We never knew the rights of it. I need hardly say that this document tells the story very much from the Butler angle.

25th March

I had a look at my diary last night and found that I made in it a list of more than ninety people I visited or met while on the Manuscripts Commission job: unfortunately the brief notes beside the names are mostly now unintelligible.

I don't care for writing on backs of sheets but I can't see any more of this paper in this room and I'm not going to ask Sadleir for some! I've found some – different size and shape: it will have to do. Now I seem to have lost the urge to continue on this theme at length. However, there are four incidents which I have in mind which I may as well set down while I'm at it and before I forget them. I remember that I did give some account of my long visits to Killarney (Kenmare MSS) and Galway (The Wardenship of Galway) a couple of years ago.

One of the earliest places I visited on behalf of the Manuscripts Commission was Derrynane. Miss O'Connell offered to give to the National Library, for a nominal sum, the whole collection of family papers, mainly of Daniel O'Connell and his father 'Hunting Cap', except for a few items of sentimental value to herself. On my return to Dublin, feeling that I had achieved something of importance, I reported this offer to the director, Dr Best. To my surprise he said he was not interested. Now Eoin MacNeill was then the chairman of the Commission but did not attend at the office at all regularly. He expected me as one of his staff to go to his house to consult him about the work I was doing and that evening I went there as usual. Michael Tierney was there at the time and on hearing my report to MacNeill he asked could I get the papers for University College, Dublin. I said I must give Best another chance first. However when I saw him again he still was not interested. So they went to U.C.D. where they are regarded as one of the treasures of the College Library and were on exhibition during the O'Connell bi-centenary commemoration in October 1975.

The second is my last visit to Doneraile Court. Lord Doneraile was in bed, dying actually. It was mid-August and there was a huge coal fire burning in the bedroom and the temperature must have been around 80°. He was almost inarticulate and I should never have been let up to see him, as it was a business not a social call. I kept saying 'I must go now' and each time a strange gobbling sound issued from his mouth which the accompanying gesture of his hand interpreted as 'Please stay'. After the longest twenty minutes I ever spent, Miss St Leger came in and hooshed me out of the room exclaiming, when we were outside the door, 'You've killed him, you've killed him'. And sure enough the poor man died shortly afterwards.

Hospitality may lead to odd situations. I had to go to Blarney Castle in the course of my inspections. Carefully avoiding an appointment which would involve lunch on a Friday I fixed a Wednesday, forgetting that it was one of those weeks, quarter-tense perhaps, when Wednesdays are, or rather were, also fast days. Máire [my daughter] was with me and we decided, having meanwhile remembered the fact, that we would eat whatever was put before us so as not to embarrass our host. When lunch was brought in it consisted of cheese and biscuits for our dyspeptic Protestant host, a special fish dish for the Catholic lady housekeeper, and a good solid meat meal for us.

And finally the incident of the Newbridge lady whom I had met a week before at the Public Records Office when she invited me to lunch. I arrived on the day arranged about 11 o'clock, planning to do some work on her papers before lunch. Evidently she expected her visitor about 1 o'clock, for on seeing me at the front door she scrutinized me through her aristocratic lorgnettes and said 'What can I do for you, my man'. That's what comes of having an old motor car and unfashionable clothes! The opportune arrival of her son restored normal relations. During lunch she informed me that she was descended from a Saxon king named Cynic.

CHAPTER XIV

The Genealogical Office

When in 1922 all branches of the civil service came under the control of the new Irish government the Office of Arms was for some reason an exception and for twenty years it continued to function under British control though situated in Dublin Castle.

On the death of Sir Neville Wilkinson, the last Ulster* King of Arms, in 1940, no successor to the office was appointed by the Crown and the Registrar, Mr T. U. Sadleir, carried on as best he could in his capacity of Deputy Ulster. Dr Hayes had put in a claim that if and when the Office of Arms was transferred it should be attached to the National Library under the Department of Education. No other department showed any interest in the matter, though it has always seemed to me that the legal nature of much of the work of the Office would have made Justice a more appropriate department to absorb it. However, Jim Hayes was a live wire and usually attained any object he aimed at. Unlike the general run of civil servants, he never hesitated to take on new responsibilities. I call him 'Jim' Hayes, advisedly for that is his name to his family and his intimates, though to the world he is known as Dr Richard J. Hayes, a cause of frequent confusion with his namesake Dr Richard Hayes, the historian (and for some years film censor).

I went over to the Office of Arms on the 1st March 1943, and I reflected as I made my way to the Upper Yard that the only occasion on which I had passed through the gates of Dublin Castle before was as a prisoner in the hands of the Auxiliaries twenty-two years earlier.

My first month there was quite futile, as the first few sentences of the diary entry quoted at the end of Chapter XIII (p. 177) have shown. The official transfer did not take place till

*The designation Ulster King of Arms does not imply that the functions of that dignitary related to the northern province rather than to the other three. The reason for its choice is not known. Possibly the fact that in 1552, when the Irish Office of Arms was established by Edward VI in Dublin, Ulster was not yet subdued by England, may have motivated it.

1st April (when it was renamed the Genealogical Office) so Mr Sadleir was still in charge.

As I sat somewhat helplessly for a part of each day at the desk in the room of Ulster King of Arms, which had not been occupied since the death of Neville Wilkinson, I wondered why Mr Sadleir had not moved into it, since his own room was dark and gloomy whereas the one I had is as charming an office as any man could wish to occupy. Its two windows look east and south, the latter facing the eighteenth century frontage of the State Apartments. Just outside is a covered balcony which gets the sun during almost the whole of the working day: there in the years that followed I did some of my work on fine summer days, whenever that work was of a kind which did not necessitate constant consultation of files or works of reference.

My friends thought that I had been given a job which was, if not a sinecure, at least one offering ample opportunities of engaging in congenial research. Perhaps it might have been if I had not allowed my exasperation at the slackness and inefficiency of my predecessor to goad me into a determination to put the Genealogical Office 'on the map' and to show that an Irish government service could be run in a business-like way.

I have had some experience in the course of my life of 'cleaning up messes' but never have I tackled anything as bad as was the Office of Arms in April 1943. I use the words slackness and inefficiency advisedly. Yet in a sense Tom Sadleir was neither slack nor inefficient, since he devoted nearly all his time to genealogical affairs (in his private capacity as well as his official, it should be added) and he was moreover an expert genealogist: that is to say he had the requisite talent and an immense store of knowledge. On the other hand he was completely 'through other'; imagine a man who seldom kept a copy of a letter, who had most of his official registers months in arrears, and possessed only the most rudimentary ideas of account-keeping.

It was obvious that while he was quite friendly to me personally he did feel a not unnatural resentment at finding an amateur in genealogy and an ignoramus in heraldry taking his place in the office in which he had spent a lifetime. It was equally obvious to anyone having access to the correspondence (incoming only, of course) and to the so-called accounts, that he was a prevaricator and careless about money matters; he was an unrepentant Unionist in politics, having nothing but ascendancy contempt for the new régime, and he had a pseudo-English accent delivered invariably in a raucous bark not unlike that of a sea-lion. In spite of these things, as I said, I rather liked the man and I had some sympathy with him, for the result of his refusal to work for the Irish government was employment in a very subordinate and ill-paid post in the library of the King's Inns. He had reason to believe that when he lost his job in Ulster's Office he would be given one of the herald's or pursuivant's posts in the College of Arms, London, but, owing to the unfortunate fact that the printers of 'Stubbs' were familiar with his name and that the then Garter King of Arms was particular on such matters, the appointment was never made. My sympathy with him for having to clear off the arrears up to 31 March, 1943, for the paltry sum of £250 in lieu of salary, was tempered by the feeling that he ought to have pointed out at the time that this was an impossibility (as it was – much of it was done by me eventually) and further that the said arrears were largely the result of having had to work with a skeleton staff for several years. He told me that he did not like to ask for any help lest the place should be closed down. His reluctance in this matter proved a great handicap to me as for a considerable time I was expected to carry on with the same office staff as he had; in effect a single clerk and a heraldic artist.

When the 1st April came I moved in effectively and as soon as the simple formalities of the transfer were completed by a formal visit from Mr de Valera, the Minister for Education (Mr Derrig) and Dr Hayes, I got to work.

I was fortunate in taking over at the height of the War because people had then less time to think of such inessentials as pedigrees and coats of arms. Even so I could hardly have found my feet so soon in my unfamiliar surroundings but for the assistance of a very capable former staff member, Miss Beryl Eustace, now Mrs Phair. When I started I found myself with no assistant but a typist who disliked my ideas of how an office should be run and whose nostalgia for the superseded British régime was patently obvious – she was well suited to a place which thirty years earlier had been an organizing centre for Carson's Covenanters. Because I wanted to make a success of the job and did not relish the idea of a breakdown through overwork, and at the same time had some small means of my own, I employed Miss Eustace and paid her out of my own pocket. My regret, or rather my grievance, in the matter is not that I thus made the State a present of a couple of hundred pounds but that the Revenue authorities refused to make me the appropriate allowance and I was obliged to pay income tax on the amount I paid her as if I had employed her for my own work. However, I suppose that is understandable for in no circumstances in the Civil Service must a new precedent be created. Anyway I got my officially appointed assistant before the end of the year in the person of Gerard Slevin (see Appendix B, p. 224).

After a few weeks with no very important new work coming in, one morning the post contained a request that our Office should make a Confirmation of Arms. This raised a fundamental question which showed that the transfer had been arranged without any definite decision as to what it involved: was our function in future to be solely genealogical research and the recording of information relating to Irish families or did the somewhat vague agreement provide that we should continue to perform all the functions of Ulster's Office including the granting and recording of armorial bearings, as well as such duties as carrying out the formalities required in changes of name by what had hitherto been called Royal Licence and so forth.

It was not for me to say. I referred the matter to the Government who attended to it with surprising promptitude. The decision was that the Chief Genealogical Officer, as I was termed at first, should perform all the functions formerly appertaining to Ulster King of Arms, except matters relating to the moribund Order of St Patrick. This decision was implemented by detailed regulations formulated by a conference consisting of the Attorney General, the Secretary of the Department of Justice and others at which I was present. It created a situation which resulted in our Office being at variance with the College of Arms in London. Its head, Garter King of Arms, after a lengthy correspondence came over to Dublin (a pleasanter place than blitzed London in 1944). Dr Hayes's knowledge of constitutional law, coupled with judiciously administered hospitality, convinced Sir Algar Howard that what he at first considered our presumptuous and unprecedented claims were not so outrageous after all, and eventually London agreed to recognize the validity of heraldic patents issued by the Chief Genealogical Officer of Ireland. The title was changed to Principal Herald the following year, on the advice of Lyon King of Arms, and finally to Chief Herald. There was never any question of retaining the title King of Arms.

Early days at the Genealogical Office were not without amusing incidents. The three diary entries which I am inserting here recall some of them.

The Genealogical Office

May 12, 1943

I made a faux pas today which it was quite impossible to explain away.

Sergeant O'Donoghue, who acts at once as guide in the Heraldic Museum and janitor for our office, seems the sort of man who will be successful in keeping undesirable callers at bay; but we are all new to each other's ways yet and today he let two typical touts up to my room who spun him some yarn about being neighbours of mine in Co. Clare. Such chancers always introduce themselves with some plausible excuse followed by a hard luck story: they end by asking the price of the fare to Ennis – they have probably never been in Co. Clare in their lives – without, of course, the least intention of leaving Dublin, and depart at length well enough satisfied with their morning's work if they succeed in pocketing the price of a couple of pints. Two in one morning, confrères no doubt though apparently unconnected, was enough to put me in a mood to give short shrift to any others of their type who might cross my path. Well, I went out at 1 o'clock to find a nondescript looking individual hanging about outside the door as if plucking up his courage to ring the bell and chance his luck with the new sucker inside. Seeing him I gave him no chance to speak first nor did I even enquire his business but I just went for him bald-headed. 'Clear out of this, you so-and-so', I barked, 'I've had enough of your sort around here' and so on, with, I fear, a string of Billingsgate. When I had finished he said quietly and rather plaintively that he was the archivist of the Dublin Corporation come to pay a courtesy call on his opposite number in the Castle. It was in fact the estimable Mr Patrick Meehan. What could I say? Shortsightedness, indigestion, worry – no excuse could palliate my unprovoked attack, which was aggravated by the inescapable implication or rather blunt statement that he looked like a down-at-heel confidence man. Being a decent man with a sense of humour, he took it extremely well. I should have asked him on the spot to come and have lunch with me but I was too much embarrassed to think of the right thing to do. I got to know him well later and had a high regard for him. He never seemed to hold my gaffe against me.

For many years I was regarded as fair game by Dublin street touts. My reputation as a soft mark arose from my spontaneous admiration for the slick work of a pair of these shortly after the end of the Civil War. I was walking up

185

Dawson Street and one of these fellows accosted me with the words, 'Will you help an old soldier, Major'. Much annoyed by the suggestion that I had the appearance of a British officer, I replied forcibly, 'Blast you, I'm not a major, I was in the I.R.A.' The tout apologized and faded away. I had scarcely reached the top of the street when another of his sort met me coming out of Stephen's Green. 'Please help an old I.R.A. man, sir, ' says he, touching his greasy cap. 'By Jay', says I, 'that's the smartest bit of work I saw for a long time' and with that I put my hand in my pocket and, having to choose between the sixpence and the half-crown which made up my loose change at the moment, handed him the latter. From that on I was a marked man until I went to South Africa and disappeared from their ken.

Apropos of all this I may perhaps recall one other incident. Soon after that I got Mary [McCarthy] to type out in black and red an imposing looking pseudo-legal document beginning 'Know all men by these presents . . .' in which I stated that no hard luck story, however moving, would thenceforward extract from me a single penny. I was working one day in the room at the National Library, where I did my Manuscript Commission work, when not travelling the country, and two men were shown in. I thought I foresaw another 'touch' so without ado I just handed one of them the said document. 'Waal' said he, 'that's the best thing I've seen since I came to Dublin.' He turned out to be the president of some major industrial company in the United States.

Whit Sunday, 13 June, 1943
    Writing the above date reminds me that this year we saw what must seldom have been seen before, viz. whitethorn in full bloom on Easter Sunday. . . .
    On Friday I gave – or rather John Ainsworth and I gave – a 'sherry party' at the Castle to the librarians (Kissane, Carty, Henchy, Greene, Bouch, Poulter, Miss Elmes also Miss Dunn – Hayes wasn't there) and to the G.O. staff in which the admirable Miss Beryl Eustace was included (she's only an extern member, unfortunately). She whispered that our Rawthmaynes specimen may shortly resign, which God grant, for to be stuck permanently with a northern, who worships the Union Jack and T.U.S. is a glum prospect. Yesterday her response to something I said was 'I hate Airish history'. [I refer, of course, to

the lady I mentioned above as a legacy from the British régime.]

To the point now. I brought to the party a bottle of S.R.'s carefully treasured 40 year old whiskey which was savoured sip by sip by all, except Bouch who dashed half a bottle of tonic water into his. Afterwards Kissane said my face was a perfect study for one of Bateman's cartoons on 'The Man Who Did So & So'. It did annoy me at the time but afterwards I reflected that while I would soon have forgotten the whole thing if Bouch had behaved in a civilized way I will now remember this incident with a grin till my dying day.

The third was written when I was in the National Library.

30 January, 1951

Eoin O'Mahony is one of the few remaining 'characters' we have in Dublin. He was with me twice today and instead of the loquacity one expects from him he was quiet and almost diffident. There is something very likeable and of late slightly pathetic about him. For sometime past he's barely scraping a living. I remember one day when I was at the G.O. he dropped his income tax form on the floor and went away without it. His total was minimal. That reminds me of something which is typical of him.

One day I had a caller who had been looking at the heraldic museum downstairs under the guidance of Sergt. O'Donoghue. He left half a crown with me to give to O'Donoghue who by that time had gone to lunch. When I saw him later to pass on the coin he said 'I don't take tips: I'm the secretary of a golf club'. I gathered from him that he refused quite a lot of them, so straight away I rang up a friend of mine connected with the St Vincent de Paul Society and suggested that he might instal a collecting box in the hall of our august building. He did so. That must be the only case of a charity box being located in a government office. It remained there for several years and St Vincent de Paul benefited quite considerably as a result. The first two people who contributed to it must be recorded. It was hardly in place when Dr Quane, an influential member of our Department, chanced to call and I happened to be crossing the hall when he entered. Taking the bull by the horns I said 'Will you hansel my box'. Without any official protest he inserted a coin. Shortly after that Eoin O'Mahony was going out and noticed the box. What did he do? Most unobtrusively be it noted, he slipped into the said box a ragged ten shilling note, probably the only one he had to buy his meals for the day.

Eoin was seeking to be taken on to the G.O. staff and both Hayes and I told him we would back him if the powers that be could be persuaded to create a new (and of course minor) post there. There I fear it will remain just as will be the case with Ned Keane whom we, and especially I, have backed for a duplication of John Ainsworth's job.

P.S. One of the amusing stories told about Eoin O'Mahony, not entirely hyperbole, is that having accepted an invitation at Henry Conner's (when the latter was living at Springfort – mem. Henry is surely worth an entry in his own right) Eoin remained on so long that at the end of a week Henry had to make out that he and his wife were due to go on holidays and close the house.

A further P.S. 1 June, 1975

Eoin, who did not get a G.O. job but later made good on RTE (his debt to me in that is worth another entry) is no longer with us, R.I.P. Ned Keane, former pub curate and entirely self-taught, has permanent work with the National Library, which reminds me of another self-taught expert, Kenneth Nicholls, whom I had working for the Manuscripts Commission for several years. He has now become a lecturer at University College, Cork, and is an acknowledged authority on mediaeval Irish sources.

Eoin O'Mahony wrote a review of the first volume of my *Irish Families* series in the *Irish Times,* in which he criticized *inter alia* the section devoted to the O'Connell family. In the course of the correspondence to which it gave rise in October-November 1957 Basil O'Connell pointed out that he read the proofs of the two pages I devoted to the O'Connell family and found nothing in them to justify adverse criticism. His final sentence reads 'Mr O'Mahony has done *immense* good in keeping alive and fostering an interest in family lore and pride of race, but one could wish that he did so by a more precise expression of the facts. The nine lines of his review which deal with O'Connells contain four phrases which could lead to confusion'. The letters include this one from Seán O'Casey: 'Kindly let my friend Eoin O'Mahony know that O'Casey was born O'Casey, lives O'Casey, and will die O'Casey. All good wishes to all the other families so finely set down and coloured in Dr MacLysaght's lovely-looking book.'

My books on the subject have sold satisfactorily. Publishers are often wrong in their estimate of the probable demand for a book offered to them. It would be hard to find one wider of the mark than that of another publisher who assured me that there would be no market for a work on families and surnames.

After a while the Genealogical Office undertook some new functions. I mentioned Terence Gray in the previous chapter. His arrival in Dublin made one of these feasible. Terence comes of a family long settled in Co. Down; he claims to be an Irishman and is a citizen – his blood he states is uncontaminated with that of the Saxon, being Scots-Irish plus French. His father was a well-known racehorse owner (Newmarket, England) a little scrap of an old boy who with his Britannia-like spouse would make a typical cartoonist's picture. Terence is big and strong, and French-bearded, aged at that time say fifty-five. By our standards he is very rich – to be able to smoke Corona cigars after every meal seems to me an infallible test. He belonged – perhaps still belongs – to the Kildare Street Club (he could belong to no other) yet had little, except remoteness from *hoi polloi*, in common with the other members, with whom he was frequently at odds.

8 September, 1950

Back too late last night to make an entry, having been with Mamie [my wife] and her mother to the Jimmy O'Dea show at the Gaiety; home 11.30. I had a couple of good laughs. Apart from Maureen Potter's impersonations and other normally amusing items there was a skit called the 'Kildour Street Club' based largely on the recent metamorphosis of Brigadier Eric Dorman Smith into Dorman O'Gowan who lately followed Sir Basil Brooke (Sir Babbling Brook in the skit) around America. O'Gowan got the change through at the G.O. shortly before I left it. It was an absolutely genuine case, plenty of evidence including a document we have at G.O. which describes his ancestor as O'Gowan alias Smith. Not long ago Terence (Gray) asked him to lunch at the Kildare Street Club but had uncomfortably to switch to Jammet's owing to anti-O'Gowan prejudice at the club. That may be due to his remarks about Winston Churchill rather than his supposed conversion to Nationalism. I don't know.

An unrepentant Republican, or rather Irish nationalist, for

Terence is a dyed-in-the-wool monarchist, with us he was an equally unrepentant partitionist.

Such a man, when not conducting an expedition of archaeological exploration in remotest Sudan or some such place, is sure to be an amateur of heraldry and genealogy. So it happened that when in 1940 the German military occupation of his French home drove him to become a landed gentleman in Ireland he gravitated to the Genealogical Office. For over three years he worked constantly with us there until the defeat of Germany enabled him to return to his vineyards at Tain l'Hermitage. The Germans, he told us, behaved very well at his place, paying for everything they used, and his Vichy sympathies made him *persona non grata* with the French Government after the liberation, but did not prevent his return. Though he worked with us regularly and assiduously, he remained an amateur, not only technically in as much as he was not paid, but also in the nature of his association with the office: we could never be sure that he would not go off on some business of his own at the critical point of an investigation or start some hare skimming on thin ice over which he did not feel inclined to follow. His unprecedented status, so hateful to the Civil Service mind, was regularized to some extent by making him a trustee of the Heraldic Museum, which gave me an excuse for allowing him a key of the building. He liked to work on Saturday afternoons and at other unofficial times and even that most unhidebound director, Dr Hayes, could not swallow the idea of an 'outsider' having the right of entry into premises for which he, Hayes, was ultimately responsible.

Having in Terence Gray what amounted to an additional assistant enabled me to tackle the vexed problem of the Irish 'Chiefs'. Ulster's Office had always ignored it with the result that anyone who chose could call himself 'The MacThis' or 'The O'That', and without much difficulty such people could get themselves included in the list which appeared annually in *Thom's Directory, Whitaker's Almanac* and elsewhere under the heading 'Ancient Irish Chieftains', and so acquire in the eyes of the world a certain *cachet* which simple assumption would not give. The situation verged on the ridiculous when a Mr Phelan became *motu proprio* 'O'Phelan Prince of the Decies', and half a dozen other persons were quasi-officially designated by titles to which they had no right, as fine sounding as that of the genuine O Conor Don. It was a whole-time job to sort them out and to this work Terence Gray devoted the greater part of his undoubted ability for several years. Eventually, the sheep were separated from the goats, and Thom's and Whitaker's agreed to get our office to supply them with the list (officially published in the *Gazette*) which they printed annually for some years.

We were sometimes criticized for taking action in this matter, particularly on the grounds that it involved recognizing the principle of primogeniture, for it is agreed that this principle is foreign to the laws of tanistry which under the Gaelic system governed the succession to chieftainries. Theoretically that is true, but it is a fact that by the beginning of the seventeenth century the Gaelic system was much weakened and three conquests within the century – Kinsale and the Plantation of Ulster, Cromwell and the Boyne – finally extinguished it. The only way we could check the growing tendency of impostors to assume the title – or rather the designation – of Chief of the Name was to accord courtesy recognition to those few men who could prove their descent by primogeniture from the last inaugurated or *de facto* chieftain. As a result of careful investigation, chiefly carried out by Terence Gray, who would spend as much as two months on a single case, we prepared an official statement for the issue of which I was careful to get Mr de Valera's personal approval as Taoiseach; this as I have said was published in *Iris Oifigiuil* and subsequently in *Thom's Directory* and in an abridged form in *Whitaker's Almanac*.

The opposition of such learned critics as Dr John Ryan, S.J. (then President of the Royal Society of Antiquaries, Ireland), was academic and friendly but we did not escape without some attacks from a very different type. Those *soi-disant* chiefs whom we demoted took it calmly enough. One of these, an English clergyman who called himself MacCarthy Reagh, had my sympathy as he had spent at least £40 on registering his pedigree in the Office of Arms in order to validate his claims and we found on examining it that it was an exact copy of that in O'Hart's *Irish Pedigrees*. How Mr Sadleir could have accepted this and the fee involved, knowing as he did that O'Hart is an entirely unreliable authority, is hard to understand: his excuse on being taxed with it was that he often had to accept rulings by Sir Neville Wilkinson with which he did not agree, an excuse on which no comment need be made. 'O'Phelan Prince of the Decies' favoured us with a dozen foolscap pages couched in the Irish of Keating's time, but our reply, composed very ably by Gerard Slevin in the same medium, elicited no further communication from him. The dispossessed, in fact, gave no trouble; but rejected new claimants were often difficult none more so than a certain Mr O'Brien whose extraordinary case is of sufficient interest to be recounted in some detail (see Appendix A, page ref. 211). One dame, whose name I forget – her mother was an O'Neill – came into my office one day and announced without preamble 'I am The O'Neill': my attempt at explanation was met by a fit of hysterics, though when it was over she was reasonable enough.

Such visits were but minor disturbances in our not very exciting routine. There was one name, apart from O'Brien, however, which we came to regard with some disquiet, whether it appeared at the foot of a letter – and their correspondence fills several bursting files – or was heard from the mouth of Sergt. Michael O'Donoghue announcing a personal call. That name is O'Malley. To this, by the way, Dr Conor O'Malley of Galway was emphatically an exception: his letters were neither dogmatic nor long-winded and his visits invariably left a pleasant impression.

On one occasion it happened quite by chance that two of the principal protagonists in the controversy which arose regarding the O'Malley chieftainship called at the Office the same morning. Sir Owen O'Malley was closeted with Terence Gray in his room when Major Harold and his wife arrived. After a quarter of an hour or so of suave but profitless conversation with the major I brought him in to Terence and left them to it while I entertained the lady, who turned out to be a daughter of the Edwardian producer George Edwards and reminded me of a comfortable London landlady, who referred to her husband as 'Daddy'. Having exhausted all our subjects of conversation I left her to see how the others were getting on. I found a silent Terence watching an irate major stamping up and down the room, metaphorically waving his shillelagh in the true Charles Lever style, while his rival, every inch the British diplomat, sat disdainfully eyeing him and, I guess, every now and then making a caustic observation in a cold Balliol voice. My entrance broke the tension and as it was by that time 1 o'clock. Terence took them all off to Jammet's for lunch in apparent amity.

My description of this incident must not be taken as implying that Sir Owen O'Malley was a difficult person. On the contrary I found him most helpful later on when I was keeper of manuscripts in the National Library; and I may add that I enjoyed his and his wife's warm hospitality (she was better known as the authoress Ann Bridge) when I stayed at their home in Co. Mayo on one of my periodical official visits to the west.

On another occasion I had some difficulty in deflecting the 'shillelagh' from my own head. That month *Dublin Opinion* had an amusing cartoon which depicted a negro in American uniform consulting an official of the Genealogical Office, the latter remarking that it must have been a considerable time since the client's ancestors emigrated from Ireland (see illustration). I am not sure that some of the family have ever quite satisfied themselves that the fortuitous choice of the name O'Malley by *Dublin Opinion* in this connexion was not inspired by me.

One of the cases we had to investigate was that of Col. O'Callaghan-Westropp (to whom I gave some prominence in Chapter V). A near neighbour of my own in Co. Clare, I had known him from my youth – it was at his place, Coolreagh, that I went to my first shooting party – and I was very reluctant to strike him off the roll. Actually it transpired that the O'Callaghan Chief was a man whose family was long settled in Spain and

98   *Dublin Opinion*

" I can't be sure about distant relatives, Mr. O'Malley, but I'm convinced that your branch of the family emigrated long ago—quite long ago."

the difficulty solved itself by the colonel's death and the sensible acceptance of the position by his son Conor, who is a fine type of progressive farmer and a man for whom I have a great respect. I would much rather such a man, resident and working in Ireland, could be registered than, as is so often the case, some exile who has no present connexion with Ireland at all. The O'Callaghan chieftaincy was not one of those which had been for years included in Thom's list: the old colonel was the first to style himself 'The O'Callaghan' in modern times. He did not, however, simply assume the designation. The procedure he adopted was unique. First he advertised that on a certain day at a certain hour he would be at the Royal Hotel, Mallow, which lies in the heart of the O'Callaghan country, and invited all and sundry of the name of O'Callaghan to meet him there for the purpose of solemnly electing him Chief of the Name, which he claimed to be by primogeniture, if they thought fit. My informant as to what happened at that gathering was Senator William O'Callaghan, who described the droll scene. According to him a couple of hundred people turned up; plenty of whiskey and porter was consumed and the brave colonel's speech was vociferously applauded and his election carried with acclamation; 'but of course' remarked Willie O'Callaghan, 'only about a dozen of the people present were O'Callaghans'! His next step was to execute in due legal form a deed-poll whereby he assumed the style of 'The O'Callaghan'.

There is much popular misconception about the efficacy of a deed-poll and indeed about the law relating to change of name generally. The legal position in Ireland is essentially the same as in Great Britain, the basic principle being that a man's legal name is determined by 'common repute'. There are several cases quoted in the law books of marriages being declared invalid as a result of the *true* name of one of the parties not being given when the banns were published, even though the name stated was actually that appearing on the person's birth or baptismal certificate, this having ceased to be his true name when superseded by another acquired by common repute.

A deed-poll itself has no legal force. The execution of a deed-poll whereby the signatory sought to assume the name 'God Almighty', 'Duke of Windsor' or at the other end of the scale, 'Bloody Fool' would be quite worthless, for the simple reason that the people with whom he had daily contact would not use it and so he would not acquire it by common repute. A deed-poll duly registered with the Registrar of the High Court is, however, the most effective means of creating common repute and is valuable as evidence thereof. It was first used for this purpose in Great Britain in 1865, and of late years has become increasingly popular.

The law as it stands is exceedingly unsatisfactory. There is nothing to prevent Mr Isaacstein from becoming Mr O'Connor and at a later date changing again to MacCarthy or O'Sullivan. Such a state of affairs seems quite incredible to a Frenchman or Swiss. Some years ago legislation was contemplated to regularize the use of the Gaelic forms of surnames and it was proposed that the Genealogical Office should be the authority in the matter. I took the opportunity of writing a very exhaustive memorandum on the whole subject of changes of name which was highly commended by the officials to whom it went: but in the end the matter was dropped and even the trivial measure first proposed was not proceeded with.

On my own initiative, however, I devised a new procedure to assist people who find themselves in a difficulty about their legal name. The Genealogical Office, having taken over the functions of Ulster's Office, was charged with the duty of carrying out the formalities connected with changes of name by what had been hitherto called Royal Licence – the only means whereby a name can be changed immediately and finally, as it were overnight. The fee for this was then £60. My action came about in this way. For some reason the newspapers have always regarded the activities of the Genealogical Office as good copy and we got a great deal of publicity which I did not welcome – the sales manager of a well-known Dublin business once asked me how it was done; he thought he might get some useful tips from me. One of the paragraphs dealing with us was headed: 'It costs £60 to change your name', which of course was a misleading half-truth. A few days later a poorly dressed woman, typical denizen of a Dublin back street, was ushered into my office. She said she had seen the paragraph in question and thought she could scrape up the necessary £60. She beat about the bush for a long time but at last, by assuring her that I did not look upon illegitimacy as very terrible, I elicited the facts. She called on behalf of her brother whom we will call John X. This man's wife had left him and gone to America nearly twenty years before and in due course a certain Bridget Y had a son by the said John X. The child, Michael, was born in hospital and duly registered as the illegitimate son of the unmarried Bridget Y, his surname being therefore Y. Subsequently, Bridget married

John and when the next child was born he was registered as, say, Peter X, John and Bridget being then properly married and so he had a perfectly presentable birth certificate. The same applied to the rest of the family which followed. As for Michael to the world he was Michael X. When, however, Michael reached the age of 16 or so he went up for some job to obtain which it was necessary to produce his birth certificate. This could not be done without all the unpleasantness which would obviously result if the boy hitherto known as Michael X had to go out into the world as Michael Y. The woman's surprise and gratitude when I told her that I could dispose of the major difficulty for the modest sum of £2, which was then the fee for a certificate issued by me, was quite touching. I proceeded thus: first I satisfied myself that the story was true by means of affidavits from the parents, a priest who had long known them and the boy's schoolmaster who knew him as Michael X; I then prepared and signed a certificate that his name was (by common repute) legally Michael X, and that Michael X was identical with the person called Michael Y in the attached and stamped birth certificate. This did not remove or hide the fact of his illegitimacy but it did confine that knowledge to such people as might have reason to see the certificate and it enabled him to retain the name of X and to avoid any publicity or scandal. I there and then instituted a register of changes of name in the Genealogical Office in which such certificates as well as the more formal changes by Government Licence were recorded. I think some 20 or 25 such changes were registered during my term of office. I did not presume to assume any powers in the matter; I merely applied the law of common repute and made use of an alternative to deed-poll and registration in the High Court to be available to persons who had in fact acquired their names but had no official evidence of such. Apparently my successor, who has no love for innovation discontinued this register when I left.

It is actually possible for a person to have two entirely different legal names. The late Brinsley Macnamara was a case in point. His other name was John Weldon. As such we knew him fifty years ago or more when, as I have already related, Maunsels launched him on his literary career by accepting his *Valley of the Squinting Windows* and his *nom de plume* Brinsley Macnamara. He became very well known as a novelist and playwright under that pseudonym: so much so that when he was made registrar of the National Gallery his letter of appointment was made out in the name of Macnamara not Weldon. I understand that he pointed this out to the authorities who, oddly enough – for the Civil Service mind is punctilious about the letter of the law – decided to let the matter rest as it was. So he was officially Brinsley Macnamara and had so to sign all official documents. He was known invariably as Mr Macnamara at the Gallery; yet he was still Mr Weldon in family life: he was so described, for example, when he attended the wedding of his son. Thus he had by common repute two distinct and valid names.

If my work at the Genealogical Office had consisted of directing the activities of an adequate staff there – say two assistants of my own grade, a clerical officer, a typist, a searcher and an artist as well as a man in charge of the heraldic museum, instead of only one assistant, one typist, one artist and no clerical officer – I would not have felt so much aggrieved at being myself graded as an assistant librarian, though the responsibilities and importance of the position with all its foreign contacts were those of at least a principal officer; for then I could have devoted most of my time to research when not engaged in carrying out the duties proper to an Ulster King of Arms. So far, however, from being able to undertake useful and interesting original work my whole time was taken up with endless and largely futile correspondence or with jobs such as making out receipts and keeping accounts and registers which should properly be done by a clerical officer.

No doubt the large amount of work to be done was to some extent of my own making. Nobody instructed me to take up the matter of the Chieftaincies or to assist people who were in difficulties about changes of name; it was my own doing that I took endless trouble to help emigrants to locate relatives in Ireland, that I made a point of answering every letter in a human and not a bureaucratic way – the only reward for which was an occasional note of thanks expressing surprise at such unprecedented consideration on the part of a government office; and I have only myself to blame for the days I spent, with little encouragement from higher authority, in combating the pretentions of preposterous impostors. At any rate, after six years, when the chaos of the former régime had been reduced to order, and I had arrived at the age of 60 with no prospect but ten more years as a hack too tired at night to do research or literary work of my own, I resolved to take a big risk and resign my position. On more than one occasion during my term of office my exasperation at the dilatoriness and soullessness of the Civil Service machine put me in danger if not of dismissal at least of severe censure, but my spirit of independence (which no doubt was due to my having the farm in Co. Clare to fall back on rather than to strength of character) usually got me through. On one occasion, for example, I was asked to prepare for the Taoiseach, Mr de Valera, a memorandum in connexion with the proposal to establish in Ireland an award comparable to the Order of Merit in Great Britain. As I understood there was some urgency about it I spent three nights overtime, examining *inter alia* the practice in other countries, and produced a lengthy report. I sent it, in accordance with the regulations, to the Department of Education for transmission to the Taoiseach. It did not reach him till more than a fortnight later. I swore that the next time I was asked by a V.I.P. to do a special job I would submit it to him direct. I may add that the project in question was dropped and Ireland still has no way, other than the conferring of honorary university degrees, of formally showing its appreciation of individual accomplishment or talent.

I am placing in Appendix B, page 226) a diary entry which deals with this aspect of the Civil Service.

I had in fact a good deal to do for other departments: with Industry and Commerce regarding mercantile marine flags; with the Attorney-General regarding impostors; with Defence on many matters relating to flags, medals and so forth; with the President's Department regarding *inter alia* the Presidential standard – our minute comparing Mr McDunphy's practice of flying two of these over Árus an Uachtaráin to his dressing the President in two tall hats was one of our best efforts but not designed to increase my popularity in certain quarters; with the Taoiseach's Department on many subjects ranging from the proposed Irish Order of Merit (not under that title, of course) to changes of name by Government Licence.

When I did actually decide to send in my resignation it resulted in a remarkable improvement in my way of life: a transfer to congenial work as Keeper of Manuscripts in the National Library instead of the wearying treadmill of the Genealogical Office, with a rise of salary of £300 a year and nine extra days leave. I owed this largely to Dr Michael Quane, then the administrative head of the National Museum. Had I not consulted him first I would simply have resigned, giving my reasons: overwork and underpay. He advised me to add that if I were promoted to the equivalent of the rank of 'Keeper' as in the Museum and got a second assistant I would willingly stay on. I took his advice. Dr Hayes then put in for me as Keeper of

Manuscripts; the Minister for Education interested himself personally in the matter and between them all they were kind enough to say that I was too good a man to let go. I should also mention that my action was responsible for an innovation, since prior to that there was no post of 'Keeper' in the National Library, though it existed in the National Museum. Failing that professorship in the Institute for Advanced Studies, I could ask for nothing better and was well content, the only fly in the ointment being my having to retain the titular position of Chief Herald and so the responsibility for the conduct of an office in the management of which I thenceforth took practically no part.

I have little to say about heraldry as such as it was the aspect of the work there which interested me least, though it does have a certain fascination. Its inclusion in the first volume of my *Irish Families* series was due to the fact that I was commissioned to produce a book on Irish coats of arms but I carried out the work in such a way that I made this a secondary element in it and concentrated mainly on the historical background of the families to which they appertain; and that led me on to do the same in two further volumes for the many families who have no arms. Apropos of that I frequently console people – Irish Americans for the most part – who express disappointment at being in that category by telling them that as a rule it was due to their ancestors being unaffected by Norman or English influence.

In any case heraldry as practised today is largely phoney. This does not of course apply to official Offices of Arms which are as correct as ever – that of Scotland even has some legal sanctions to enforce its decisions. I am referring to what I may call commercial heraldry. With some honourable exceptions firms carrying on this trade think nothing of giving a customer for whose name no arms are recorded an illustration of one which sounds something like it – Mr Brain gets O'Brien and so on; and when one of the required names is available they do not point out that correctly, apart from sept arms, it only belongs to the descendants of the person or persons named in the grant or confirmation. I have no inclination to pursue this subject here beyond adding one diary entry which is relevant.

16 August, 1969

Today I was searching through an old file and came across the correspondence I had in 1960 with an American named Murtagh regarding his appalling book entitled *Your Irish Coat of Arms.* No need to note any of his absurdities here as I showed him and his equals up adequately at the beginning of my introductory chapter in Vol. 1 of *Irish Families.* The trouble is that books like his are taken as gospel by many people, especially in America, and so they suffer disappointment if they later contact a heraldic authority.

This reminded me of an incident which illustrates the kind of thing I had in mind. John Synon has a brother who is an admiral or something in the U.S. navy. For some reason, I forget why (he was hardly returning from Vietnam via Shannon) he was at that airport. Seeing coats of arms displayed at the shop there he left an order for his to be mailed to him. In due course he received a beautifully executed blazon in colour. A fortnight later one of his officers found himself in the same place. 'Just the thing for the Admiral' he thought and forthwith ordered a picture of the Synon arms. On getting it John's brother noticed that the two blazons were quite different so they consulted me. One depicted Synot arms and the other those appertaining to some German name rather like Synon. They both got their money back and the quasi-experts in heraldry were duly rebuked. I understand that since then the people responsible have taken care that accuracy should take precedence over mere anxiety to effect sales.

Apropos of modern heraldry I don't think I recorded an incident worth remembering. Mr Pine the distinguished author and editor of many books on genealogy and heraldry, gave a lecture recently on the subject at Trinity College. I was asked to be the proposer of the vote of thanks. At dinner in Hall beforehand I asked how long his lecture would take and he said about forty minutes. In fact it took an hour and a quarter by which time the undergraduates in the audience were falling asleep. My contribution, which woke them up, consisted of one sentence: 'In thanking Mr Pine I should like to say that I was much interested in his lecture so far as it dealt with genealogy, and with heraldry as an exact science, but I must add that modern popular heraldry is, outside of Scotland, ninety per cent bogus'. Fortunately the seconder was Gerard Slevin who, needless to say, spoke at reasonable length, with his usual gentlemanly politeness and so minimized my rather discourteous gaffe.

CHAPTER XV

The National Library

I will finish by covering the last twenty years in one short chapter. I have ample interesting material in my experiences during that longish period but when I set about writing this valedictory chapter I found it well nigh impossible to treat the National Library and even to some extent the Manuscripts Commission (since I became its chairman) in the same way as the rest of the book, that is objectively and reminiscently. Describing institutions and their working has usually meant commenting on the people concerned, and I am not inclined to discuss the men and women with whom I have been in daily contact up to the present time, even though (as my diaries testify) I have found my colleagues there congenial – with perhaps one exception, and to him let *de mortuis nil nisi bonum* apply.

Of all the various jobs – or, if that is too colloquial a word, let me say professional and business activities – in which I have ever been engaged that of Keeper of Manuscripts in the National Library is the one I liked best. Early in 1949 I was presented with an untilled field and given a free hand. At that time there was to all intents and purposes no manuscripts department in the National Library.

Dr R. J. Hayes was the first director to regard the acquisition of manuscript material as one of the major functions of a national library. His predecessor, Dr Best, apparently did not regard it as even a minor function. His rejection of the O'Connell paper, recounted on page 179 exemplifies this.

Before Dr Hayes's time there was, it is true, a certain amount of manuscript material in the Library which had come there from time to time without much encouragement from former directors. The acquisition of some of this dates back to 1877 when the Royal Dublin Society's library was taken over to form the nucleus of the newly established National Library. For the next fifty years the number of manuscript accessions was small and these were mainly acquired by donation or bequest. Certainly a few purchases of importance were made between 1920 and

1945, notably a considerable portion of the famous Phillips Collection including some Irish language manuscripts and, worthy of special mention, the thirteenth century *Topographia Hiberniae* of Giraldus Cambrensis. Apart from these the collection of manuscripts in the National Library before the appointment of Dr Hayes as director was insignificant.

Dr Hayes was appointed director in 1940 but during the war years he was mainly engaged in some kind of censorship or secret service work (I believe he was a genius at breaking cipher codes) and so he was not at first able to devote the thought and energy to the development of the Library which he did when the war was over. This did not prevent him from at once taking the first steps towards the establishment of a proper department. He knew that I was then engaged on behalf of the Manuscripts Commission in locating and reporting on manuscript collections in private keeping and he instructed me to inform the owners of such collections that the National Library was anxious where possible to acquire them.

This could be done either by purchase, gift or occasionally in special circumstances on long loan. As I mentioned in an earlier chapter there was a grave danger at the time that the paper shortage due to war conditions might result in much valuable manuscript material being pulped. Hayes and I jointly made a Radio appeal pointing this out and we circularized many likely people such as estate agents and solicitors to the same effect. A considerable quantity of useful historical data was saved as a result and a good deal of this has found its way into the National Library since that time.

In 1948 the first major step towards the establishment of a manuscripts department worthy of the name was taken when the vast collection of Ormond papers and deeds was purchased by the government for £20,000 and transferred from Kilkenny Castle to the Library. This collection, dating from the twelfth century, is the most comprehensive and important in Ireland and is matched by few even in England, a country which has been free from destructive warfare within its own shores for three centuries. As there was a temporary legal hitch in the transaction the work of arranging and cataloguing it had to be postponed, and it was not until 1950 that we could deal with it. This presented a simple task compared with the work usually involved in arranging large manuscript collections since a great part of it was already in bound volumes, while the deeds, some 10,000 in number, had been sorted and listed by Prof. Edmund Curtis at Kilkenny when he was preparing the six volumes of the *Çalendar of Ormond Deeds* published by the Manuscripts Commission. These cover the period from 1171 to 1603. The remainder have still to be published.

My first task, with the aid of Gerry Nash, then an untrained but willing youth, was to reduce to some kind of order the manuscript material which had accumulated haphazardly over the years and had been more or less dumped. This involved sorting and classifying heaps of papers stored in large packing cases in the basement. I put in here a typical diary entry as the best way of showing how absorbing an apparently laborious and dreary job may be.

13 July, 1950

For the first time for several days today I had a chance to get on with listing and numbering mss, all sorts of distractions having prevented me from getting on with the job proper – people calling (some sensible, some aimless), meetings to be attended and so on; and also a trip to Castlerea where I collected a trunkful of O'Conor Don mss and an O'Conor in the person of Mrs Teeling, to whom I was able to give a lift to Dublin. Today after getting off some letters I continued the interesting occupation of delving into one of the packing cases containing papers dumped here during the war period. There was no Manuscripts Department in the Nat. Lib. then. I don't think I have actually mentioned in this diary that it was formally established last year and I was appointed to organize it. I enjoy work with mss anyway but the fascination of this particular job lies in the uncertainty as to what will turn up next in the almost chaotic mass of material it is my business to reduce to order. It will be even pleasanter when I get my qualified assistant if economy, not to say cheese-paring, on the part of the Government does not defer that day till I have the weight of it done by myself.

20th July

The 'bran-pie' today yielded a rich and varied harvest including a tenth century ms, admittedly only part of a missal but still a find of unusual antiquity. Of greater actual value are some early seventeenth century letters – no details here as the like of that find is of course recorded in my office files.

This preliminary stage took eighteen months or so by which time the large room formerly known as the Exhibition Room had been completely fitted out with rows of steel shelving. We then began cataloguing, numbering and arranging for binding and so on. Later I had the assistance of the efficient Alf MacLochlainn who in due course succeeded me as Keeper of Manuscripts and is now Director of the National Library. When Gerry Nash and I started on this work the number of manuscripts in the catalogue was a mere 894. When I retired it had reached well over the 9,000 mark, exclusive of deeds and Irish language mss both of which have separate numeration. It has now reached 16,000.

The Library was for many years officially treated as a sort of poor relation. A change in that attitude seemed likely when the late Donagh O'Malley, the minister responsible, shortly before his death in 1968, was interesting himself in the problems of the Library and the Manuscripts Commission, not only as regards space and accommodation but also in the proposals for legislation to create a National Library and Archives as one institution and to bring up to date the obsolete 1867 Act dealing with – or rather not dealing with – the preservation of government and local government records. Since then, though the latter would not involve any addition to departmental estimates, frequent reminders to successive Ministers for Education have fallen on deaf ears.

Lack of space in the Library is an ever-increasing problem. Until recently the entrance hall was piled high with valuable maps, etc. Owing to danger of fire and theft, the hall had to be cleared; the maps and a considerable amount of manuscripts have been removed to safety in another building, where they are not available to readers. It is anticipated that a way will be found to revoke this retrograde step in the very near future.

The necessity for a larger building was a live question thirty years ago. In 1941 a most attractive and up-to-date design for a new library was actually approved and the site selected. It was to be built on the grounds of the Fitzwilliam Tennis Club. All that remained to be settled was the amount of compensation to be paid to the club. This delay resulted in the abandonment of the whole project, because, before a final settlement was reached, the government went out of office and was replaced by the first coalition or inter-party administration whose policy was retrenchment. A few years later the three acres occupied by the Royal Hospital for Incurables at Morehampton Road, Donnybrook, was purchased for what was then a large sum – £40,000 I heard, but that may be wrong – as a site for the new library. That scheme seems to have died at birth. Following the assassination of President John F. Kennedy exciting plans were adumbrated for the erection of an extensive memorial building to comprise *inter alia* a concert hall and a new National Library (with Manuscripts Commission attached). The site provisionally chosen for this was the extensive premises at Beggar's Bush now occupied by the Stationery Office: but so many other suggestions have since been made and the cost of building is now so high that once again the idea became moribund. There is now the probability of a less ambitious plan being carried out: the optimists are hopeful, the cynics are still saying 'live horse and you'll get grass'. Anyway the former director, Dr Patrick Henchy, his successor Mr MacLochlainn and the trustees have fought their case with vigour and the prospects of an improvement are good.

Dr Hayes retired in 1967. His term of office is notable for several major innovations. Apart from the manuscripts department, specially important is the microfilming of manuscript material relating to Ireland from archives and libraries all over the world. Due to historical causes there is probably no other country for which there is such a wealth of information to be found in foreign sources.

There is also Dr Hayes's valuable work which has been published in eleven volumes entitled *Manuscript Sources for the History of Irish Civilization.*

Another important project, the organization of which was entrusted to me, was the microfilming of the Catholic parish registers. There must be few laymen who have kissed more bishops' rings than I have, for in each diocese it was essential first to get authority from the bishop to proceed with the scheme. I have a diary entry which, though it treats an important and serious undertaking rather lightheartedly, would seem to be worth including; but first I should mention that the Church of Ireland registers, being treated as official records, were kept at the public Record Office. All these were lost in the destruction of the Four Courts fire in 1922, except those which at the time happened to be in the custody of the local incumbent.

January 15, 1955

This is a very smooth running train and as I've more than an hour before we get near Dublin I'll occupy it in making a diary entry. I often did that on loose sheets of paper before,

I'm sorry my idea of carrying on the parish registers job for the National Library even though I've retired from the staff now, was not agreed to. I'd like to write a few lines about it while I have a chance. I may have mentioned some incidents of interest in the diary but I doubt it as my diary as far as I've written it at all of late has I think been mostly facts and figures.

I often thought of borrowing a Pioneer badge as a means of resisting the hospitality of the average parish priest. I was on the job for four years and only once during that time did I meet anything but the friendliest of receptions; that was at Murroe where the P.P. (a former cycling champion I was told) remarked that he would not let me over the doorstep only for the bishop or rather archbishop (who, like all the hierarchy, was co-operative with us). The only diocese in which I met any difficulty at all was our own – Killaloe. Indirectly that was because our old friend Dr Fogarty hasn't much control now in his old age. Actually he was against this micro-filming plan at first but eventually said he'd agree to anything recommended by Monsignor Quinn of Birr, whom I went to see with satisfactory results. However, there were some minor difficulties in practice. One or two cases occurred where the earliest registers were not handed to us with the others – Kilrush, etc. – and letters ignored. The only amusing one was the parish of Flagmount, Killanena. There Fr Dan O'Dea, in spite of my close friendship with the family, flatly refused to let me have the registers, quite obviously because for his own reasons he wanted to oppose the bishop where possible. We tried every approach, clerical and lay, without avail. Three months later one morning the Library postbag contained a parcel most insecurely packed, and of course not registered, which proved to contain the books he had refused to give me – no covering letter, just the parcel.

I spent one very harassing week in connexion with this undertaking. It was my usual practice when collecting registers to check them carefully with the appropriate diocesan official. When I was at Carlow I was just about to do this when I got a rather urgent message to go and see the bishop himself and the result was that for the first and last time I went to Dublin with a load of registers not properly checked. Of course I should have done it properly later but somehow one very slim item got overlooked. Three months or so later, long after the microfilming was done and the registers returned, one parish priest wrote and said that his earliest register had not been returned with the others. I was terribly worried because owing to my (I can truthfully say unusual) carelessness in that one case I was in a dilemma. What I did was first to make sure that the waste paper in the basement had not been removed during the previous 3 months; then a team of three of us (Gerry Nash and I and one of the boys) started to go carefully through several tons of paper. By Friday midday, after nearly a week at it, having lost all hope, we came to the last crate: believe it or not, in it was the missing register, a flimsy booklet covered in brown paper: buidheachas le Dia. For the record I may add that it went back to the eighteenth century which is unusual with Catholic registers: the majority begin about the time of Catholic Emancipation. I remember one (I think it was at Waterford I found it) which was very exceptional – somewhere about 1690; all such facts are in the files. Dublin is not done yet; I would not be surprised if my successor finds one or two equally old there.

I only saw the human side of bishops in a few cases. Dr Fogarty of course we knew well: he often visited us at Raheen but I did not see him personally in connexion with the registers job. Dr Kyne of Meath diocese, when I called for those which had been brought in to Mullingar, kindly insisted on helping me himself to carry them downstairs and load them into the van. Dr Walsh of Tuam did not resent a facetious remark I made about kissing his ring when he came into the room and found me on my knees examining a book on the floor; in fact he asked me to a tête à tête lunch and put me quite at my ease too. One bishop, thinking to do me a good turn no doubt, deprived me of an anticipated day of free tourism. I stayed the night at Ballina and had planned to go to Belmullet to collect the registers of that area there and was much looking forward to my first view of Blacksod Bay and all that north Mayo country. However just as I was about to leave the hotel his lordship arrived with the registers in his car. 'I thought I'd save you a journey' said he. So, as I had thus no excuse for spending public money on sight-seeing, I perforce had to steer eastwards not westwards that morning. I missed that run; but there's no doubt that the parish register job and all the travelling I did as inspector for the Manu-scripts Commission has given me a rare view of the countryside (not merely the beauty spots) that I would never otherwise have had, and indeed which few people ever have had.

The Cashel registers – but no, I must refrain from telling the tale of those even in this diary. The whole undertaking is a confidential assignment; the resultant microfilms are not available to the public without the permission of the bishop concerned.

I don't think of anything else of interest at the moment and anyway we have passed Sallins now.

I can travel to Dublin once a month free now as I mean to attend the monthly meetings of the MSS. Commission regularly. There's one tomorrow. I aim to be Chairman of it and if I get that I'll go back to Dublin most of the time and leave William to run Raheen with some guidance – he's hardly 18 yet but he has the makings of a sound man, he's already a hard worker.

In the four years during which I was in charge of the parish registers I completed about one-third of the dioceses of Ireland. With the exception of a section of the archdiocese of Dublin they are now all done, including those in the Six Counties. I stopped in November 1954 because having reached the age of 67 at which I had to retire I rather sadly cleared my desk at the National Library and said good-bye to Dublin for the next year, only going there for the monthly meeting of the Manuscripts Commission of which I had been appointed a member when I became Keeper of manuscripts at the Library.

Then in 1956 Dr Best resigned from the chairmanship of the Manuscripts Commission and I was appointed as his successor, which meant a return to Dublin and constant work there.

Within the past twenty years, over which in this valedictory chapter I am briefly glancing, one aspect of Irish life which I have not had occasion to mention before has become prominent: 'Festivals', from the Dublin Theatre Festival and the Cork Film Festival to smaller local affairs, have been established in many parts of the country, and in the same category we may include such institutions as the Yeats Summer School at Sligo. With one of these, the Merriman Summer School in Co. Clare, I have been closely connected. I would hardly count this worth mentioning here were it not for the remarkable *volte face* which has occurred in regard to it.

Here, with a few unnecessary sarcastic observations omitted, is what I wrote in my diary in 1949.

When many years ago, before the first world war, Pádraig O'Kiely, Ed. Curtis and I made an expedition around the shores of Lough Graney in search of traces or traditions of Brian Merriman, I little thought I would live to be ashamed of my connexion with the publication of an edition of *Cúirt an mheadhon-oidhche*. Yet so I am today: ashamed and disgusted. My shame is certainly not of the kind professed by those narrow-minded pharisaical hypocrites who have lately strangled the plan to put up a plaque in memory of Brian at Feakle. It was to have borne a simple inscription – in Irish – inviting the passer-by to pray for his soul: that surely is a Christian concept and a Catholic practice, and I never heard before that we should withhold our prayers for the dead because the subject of them is reputed to have been somewhat disreputable. Why I personally feel ashamed is that being treasurer of the fund collected for the plaque – it amounted to over £100 and came from people all over the country ranging from President Seán T. O'Kelly, Éamon de Valera and Douglas Hyde to parish priests and rural N.T.'s – I am willy nilly identified with the (what is the exact English equivalent of *suarach*, the adjective which springs to my mind in this connexion) the wretched substitute memorial we have allowed old Foley to foist on us, to wit a flimsy booklet containing his edition of the poem. This is marred not enhanced by the list of subscribers at the end which leaves out through sheer carelessness several of their names among them that of Denis MacMahon, (whose great-grandfather was a pupil of Merriman's) and arbitrarily gives some of them the tag M.A. while omitting other people's sometimes higher degrees altogether and so on. *Natus est ridiculus mus*, which makes us look fools; we have been bested by sheer obscurantism which makes us look chicken-hearted. I suppose it would hardly have been feasible to proceed in face of the local threats backed by one P.P. to demolish the plaque if it were erected. We should have simply returned the money when the object for which it was subscribed was frustrated. We offered to do so but no subscriber asked for his back. The self-righteous catchcriers (who I must say do not represent those parishes as a whole) have made East Clare a laughing-stock and that is my final reason for feeling ashamed.

Now twenty-five years later we have not only an annual commemoration of the poet lasting a fortnight, a plaque erected at Feakle in his memory and the Feakle people proud of it, the County Council backing the project instead of throwing cold water on it as it did twenty years ago, we even have a bishop taking the chair at one of the public sessions in Ennis (at which

I may mention I was the lecturer). *Tempora mutantur*: Ireland in fact has become less Victorian. This does not mean that we are heading for the Californian concept of life where apparently God has been replaced by Sex.

To return to the National Library, I still feel that I am so to speak an extern member of the Library staff, for both before and since I retired from the Manuscripts Commission my work has taken me there nearly every day, often to consult the collection of family history and surnames notes I have made over a period of more than forty years, amounting to more than 6,000 pages, which is now in the Manuscripts Department there. The day I retired from the Library (I find it hard to realize that it was more than twenty years ago) my colleagues made me a parting presentation and in doing so Dr Hayes remarked 'we also make you a life member of the Library', to which I replied 'I thank you and as a token of that I should retain my key'.

As I have said more than once in the course of this book it is not meant to be an autobiography except in so far as my experiences help to give a picture of Ireland during my long lifetime. And if I have at times strayed from this design no doubt it is in character: my father used often to say that my second name should be 'Tangent'.

During my long life, especially in the second half of it, I have given many lectures or talks mainly on historical, genealogical and literary topics. The latest of these – and I expect the last – was a few months ago when I had to make a short speech, not of course a talk or lecture, in reply to a presentation made to me by the Thomond Archaeological Society. More than a hundred people from Cos. Clare and Limerick attended a dinner at Bunratty to mark the ninetieth birthday of the oldest member of the society and the only one still alive who was a member of its predecessor the North Munster Archaeological Society, for such I am. I felt greatly honoured and count that a fitting termination to my career in public.

So I end my long life, as I have spent so much of it, commuting between Clare and Dublin. My final resting place will be in Clare, for I can rely on my wife Mamie to make sure that my remains will lie beside those of my dear son Pat in the graveyard at Tuamgraney.

Appendix A

Princes: A Serio-Comic Contest

During the course of my time at the Genealogical Office I had to deal officially with several gentlemen who claimed to be not only Chiefs of the Name but also Princes. One at least was genuine: MacDermot, Prince of Coolavin, will be found in our list of Chiefs in *Iris Oifigiuil*. Three were not. I have already referred in Chapter XIV to the Prince of the Decies. He left this country some thirty years ago and though at the time I heard some amusing stories of the contretemps arising from his insistence upon the use of his 'title' I will pass on to the other two. For one of these, 'Michael, Prince of the Saltees', as Mr Michael Neale called himself, I had a secret regard. I had to turn down the various propositions he made to the Genealogical Office with the object of getting some kind of official recognition of the title he assumed when he bought the Great Saltee Island and I was instrumental in preventing the Department of Posts and Telegraphs – another direct departmental contact I omitted to mention in the previous chapter – from giving him his 'title' in the Telephone Directory. Still he did possess a large island and if he chose to call himself prince of it it did not really do anybody any harm, though I would draw the line at allowing him· so to describe himself on his son's birth certificate and I would like to have seen the guards, or whoever was responsible, reprimanded for issuing a summons against him in that style which, if I am correctly informed, occurred about that time.

It is possible that in a small way he was adopting the technique of the soi-disant 'Prince of Thomond'. Here we had a man who for the greater part of his life devoted his undoubted talents to building up a façade of such verisimilitude that he had, for a time at least, an almost unprecedented success in imposing not only upon the ignorant and credulous but also upon many responsible people whose acceptance of his pretentious claims is almost incredible, or would have been had not the façade been so cleverly erected.

As the official concerned I had to deal with this situation over a period of five years and I only retired from what I may call my serio-comic contest with him when I became Keeper of Manuscripts.

The man's name was Raymond Moulton O'Brien to which he added the further Christian name of Seán after he came to Ireland at the beginning of the Second World War. His first appearance at the Genealogical Office was as plain Seán O'Brien – he purported that day to be the emissary of his distinguished cousin Raymond Moulton O'Brien, who, he said, had indisputable proofs that he was actually Earl of Thomond and entitled to the designation 'The O'Brien'. At the time we were about to investigate that case and while we fully expected that Donagh O'Brien, Baron Inchiquin, would prove to be Chief of the Name, we had no prejudice whatever against the new claimant and we approached the question judicially: whatever our personal predelictions in these cases may have been – and naturally we preferred registering a resident Irishman to, say, a Methodist minister in an English suburb or an obscure business man in some continental town – our task was to check evidence and certify facts not preferences.

The proofs that he put forward were quite unconvincing to anyone trained to examine genealogical evidence and in due course we accorded the usual courtesy recognition as Chief of the Name to Lord Inchiquin, in Co. Clare the historic county of his ancestors, whereupon our claimant threatened to take legal steps to upset this decision, though he did not implement the threat.

I forget how exactly Mr O'Brien started the building up of his façade. After some minor moves in America to create the impression that he was the Earl of Thomond he obtained in Mexico a court judgment that he did in fact hold that title. This judgement could have no validity in this country, especially as no evidence had been sought or obtained in Ireland or Great Britain, the only places where reliable facts could be found. He claimed to be descended directly from the last Earl of Thomond. According to official records, the last Earl of Thomond died in 1774 without issue when the title became extinct. Official records in the case of peers are most unlikely to be inaccurate but in any case Mr O'Brien's ancestor was by blood a Wyndham: he was the stepson of the eighth O'Brien Earl and had no drop of O'Brien blood in him and only took the name O'Brien on inheriting by will his step-father's estates. Thus even if Raymond

Moulton could have proved his right to the title – a matter for the House of Lords, not for us – he could not possibly be the chief of the O'Briens, which might conceivably carry with it the courtesy title of Prince of Thomond. That is the title he assumed, while still calling himself Earl of Thomond when it suited him, as soon as it became obvious that he had no hope of gaining official recognition for the latter. There is much less chance of legal steps being taken to refute it when the title assumed is a non-existent one rather than one which is on the records of the Peerage.

The apparent credibility of the Mexican judgement when presented to uncritical persons in the form he contrived was considerable. A 'deed' dated 5 March 1949 was submitted to and officially registered by the Registry of Deeds in Dublin. It is too long to quote here in full but the following extracts from it show how he was able to give the extraordinary Mexican ruling the apparent endorsement of a responsible government office in Ireland, and it also illustrates Mr O'Brien's grandiose assumption of his nobility which to the credulous enquirer unacquainted with the Irish legal system would appear to indicate official acceptance of his almost royal status.

> Memorial of deed 12 March 1949 'made between Colonel His Highness Raymond Moulton Seán, by the Sovereign Authority of the Roman Pontiff PRINCE O'BRIEN OF THOMOND also entitled THE O'BRIEN, PRINCE OF THE DALCASSIANS OF THOMOND, Earl and Count of Thomond and Baron of Ibrickan, Landowner, of Clare Castle (Co. Clare) Principality of Thomond (hereinafter called the Grantor) of the first part and His Highness Prince Turlough The Strong, Baron of Ibrickan of Clare Castle, Principality of Thomond aforesaid son and heir of the Grantor and Catholic Heir to the said Principality of Thomond'.

Details of the lands purporting to be transferred to his infant son aged one are not given, the assumption being that they comprise the whole barony of Ibrickan.

At great length the 'judgement decree' of a court in the jurisdiction of the City of Juarez, Mexico, obtained by Mr O'Brien in May 1936, is quoted, ruling that he is the sole person entitled to be called Earl of Thomond. Towards the end of the lengthy document it is declared that the said judgement was officially ratified by the German government in December 1936 and by Luxembourg and France in January 1937. Later it refers to New York and even 'His Majesty's High Court of Justice, Strand, London' as endorsing his claims.

I have said more than enough about this extraordinary document reference number to which in the Registry of Deeds is 146A.

Apropos of the reference to the Pope in the foregoing, the following notice, which appeared in the *Clare Champion* on October 23rd 1948, was inserted by Messrs Eugene F. Collins and Son, one of the most reputable and highly esteemed firms of solicitors in Dublin. A similar notice appeared also in the Dublin *Evening Mail.*

> O'Brien of Thomond, Col. His Highness Prince, has received from the Secretariat of State at the Vatican City through the usual Diplomatic Channels a grant of Letters Patent dated the 15th September 1948, confirming, inter alia, an Apostolic Blessing and a Plenary Indulgence (sub conditione) for His Highness and Family on the occasion of the recent birth of the Catholic heir to the Principality of Thomond (Clare) in the person of His Highness Prince Turlough the Strong, Seaghan, Baron of Ibrickan, whose sponsors are Her Supreme Highness Sonia, Duchess of Chateau-Thierry and Marchioness of Rais, and His Excellency Count Howard Horace d'Angerville KDO, FRSA, FRGS.

The relevant birth certificate is to be found at the Custom House. I do not have a copy of it to hand, but that of his daughter 'Her Highness Princess Grania Bebhinn', which I have in the file, is couched in much the same terms.

These can be added to the list of officially issued documents. It would, I think, be superfluous to quote the certificate in full: but to give an idea of its nature I will just cite one extract viz. Col. 5 '(name and address of father) Colonel His Highness Raymond Moulton Seaghan, Prince of Thomond, Earl and Count of Pogla (The O'Brien), Clare Castle, Principality of Thomond, 5 Charlemont St. Dublin'.

Reverting to the notice in the *Evening Mail* Mr O'Brien did not hesitate to describe it, quite erroneously, of course, as a certificate from the Vatican of the genuineness of his pretensions, and he had many facsimile copies of the document, complete with portrait of His Holiness, the Pope, and these were distributed far and wide. It is little wonder, therefore, that supported by his clever brain and suave manner, this document carried conviction with all but the most discriminating.

The letters K.D.O. after the godfather's name signify 'Knight of the Order of Dalcassians'. A reproduction of an item of their stationery is reproduced on the next page.

This Order of the Dalcassians, like his cognate Munster College of Arms, had, it need hardly be said, no existence except as a whim of its creator. Nevertheless, incredible as it may seem, he found a perfectly respectable solicitor (whom I had better not name) to append to the foregoing document as duly completed the following words, which he duly signed 'I XYZ an officer of the Supreme Court of Judicature of Éire, hereby certify and attest that the within grant of letters patent is authentic and entitled to full faith and credit before all tribunals in chivalry and consulates abroad'. Nevertheless I had their sympathy, especially that of the then Attorney General, Cecil Lavery, who, like myself, felt that a gross insult was being offered to the Catholic Church. I kept hammering away. Frequent enquiries came in: I answered these in a way which was a compromise between the reticence of the civil servant – Gerard Slevin was always beside me to counsel caution – and my own outspoken indignation: and these replies, together with warnings to responsible people here and there, hampered his plans somewhat.

The only time a responsible government official proved uncooperative was in connexion with the extraordinary document described on p. 213 supra. In that case, the head of the Registry of Deeds let me down badly. There was a man in that office who realized that O'Brien was proposing to make use of the Registry simply for the purpose of having in his possession further official looking documents which would impress the ordinary man. This officer let me know that deeds of a peculiar nature were being presented by O'Brien for registration and having been given an opportunity of perusing them I found them decidedly peculiar. These were indeed of such a kind that they should not have been accepted for registration and such was the view taken by the Registrar when I called to draw his attention to the matter. I was greatly surprised, therefore, to hear a few days later that he had withdrawn his veto. One of these documents was comic since it conveyed the Prince's castle at Clarecastle, a bare and roofless ruin to which he may or may not have had a legal title – if he had it was his only real property in Co. Clare – to the Order of Dalcassians with all the shooting rights (rats presumably) and forestry rights (all that was growing there

215

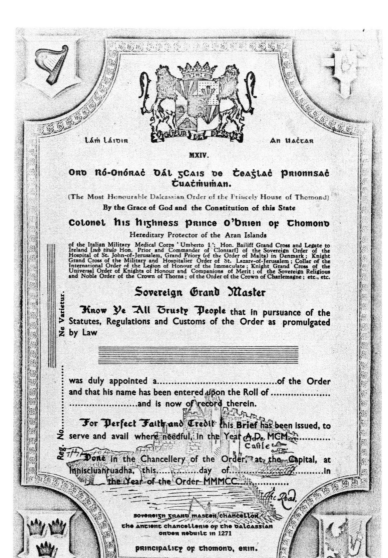

MXIV.

Ord Ró-Onórac Dál gCais de Ceaglac Prionnsac Cuacmuman.

(The Most Honourable Dalcassian Order of the Princely House of Thomond)

By the Grace of God and the Constitution of this State

Colonel his highness prince O'Brien of Thomond

Hereditary Protector of the Aran Islands

of the Italian Military Medical Corps 'Umberto 1'; Hon. Bailiff Grand Cross and Legate to Ireland [sub titulo Hon. Prior and Commander of Clontarf] of the Sovereign Order of the Hospital of St. John-of-Jerusalem, Grand Priory (of the Order of Malta) in Denmark; Knight Grand Cross of the Military and Hospitalier Order of St. Lazare-of-Jerusalem; Collar of the International Order of the Legion of Honour of the Immaculate; Knight Grand Cross of the Universal Order of Knights of Honour and Companions of Merit; of the Sovereign Religious and Noble Order of the Crown of Thorns; of the Order of the Crown of Charlemagne; etc., etc.

Sovereign Grand Master

Know Ye All Trusty People that in pursuance of the Statutes, Regulations and Customs of the Order as promulgated by Law

was duly appointed a..of the Order and that his name has been entered upon the Roll of ....and is now of record therein.

For Perfect Faith and Credit this Brief has been issued, to serve and avail where needful, in the Year A.D. MCM.............. Castle

Done in the Chancellery of the Order, at the Capital, at Inniscluanruadha, this...............day of................................In the Year of the Order MMMCC.......

sovereign grand master/chancellor
the ancient chancellerie of the Dalcassian order rebuilt in 1271

principality of Thomond, Erin.

216

was nettles). Another conveyed to his baby son vast properties in Co. Clare, which, of course, were not his to convey even if an infant could acquire property in his own name. These deeds, officially stamped and recorded at the Registry of Deeds, naturally give the impression of vast possessions and wealth to the uncritical enquirer.

The need for warning existed even among normally well-informed people. The College of Arms in London were never taken in by O'Brien either as an earl or a prince and their queries were little more than a request for confirmation of a view already formed. In all matters relating to heraldry and genealogy I always found Lyon King of Arms at the Scottish Office very satisfactory to deal with. In this case his interest was aroused by a long article in *Le Blason* which was O'Brien's next major move. This article appeared in No. 4 (1948) of that journal, a serious monthly published in Brussels and devoted to genealogy, heraldry and kindred subjects. The article which is entitled 'La Principauté Souveraine de Thomond' was, I am informed, written by O'Brien in English and translated into French by the editor who signed it as his own. It is plausibly documented with voluminous reference notes and, following on a newspaper article printed a month or so earlier in the daily *La Nation Belge*, which nobody troubled to contradict, it undoubtedly carried some weight. The newspaper article affected the judgement of the editor of *Le Blason* who, penitent though he was for so publicly falling a victim to an imposter's *supercherie*, was afraid to write a further article withdrawing the first lest he should lay himself open to a libel action: so long as O'Brien could produce documents of the quasi-official character I have mentioned in this chapter – the birth certificate particularly affected the editor – he hesitated to make any further move. If space allowed I would like to print that newspaper article and part of that in *Le Blason* here. For the moment it is enough to say that they described the principality of Thomond as an independent state within the Republic of Ireland. The newspaper article concentrated on the physical features of the territory, giving in that respect an accurate description of the County Clare, and in the sort of detail which appeals to the casual reader: it also mentioned, for example, that the prince, though he had his own currency (marks), permitted the circulation of both Irish and British money in Thomond! *Le Blason* has less about the territory and more about its ruler whom it treats with the respect due to a truly illustrious descendant of Brian Boru.

217

It contains many inaccuracies, from minor nuances to the un-equivocal and possibly actionable statement that his claim was endorsed by an award of the Irish High Court – but no useful purpose would have been served by taking any official action in the matter.

I have endeavoured to tell this story as briefly as possible up to this since I was myself only in the background, but I think I may recount more fully the one case in which I found I had to play a major part, especially as this too is not without its comic element.

It concerns his first major action in Ireland after he had been turned down by the Genealogical Office. In 1944 he took an action for slander against one Christy Byrne who, he alleged, stated in a certain public house that he, O'Brien, had no more right to call himself Prince of Thomond than he, Byrne, had to call himself King of Rumania. The case came on and his solicitor, no longer the firm which had dealt with us, announced that the parties had agreed to arbitration. In due course when the case was listed for hearing, the judge was informed that an arbitra-tor's award had been accepted by both sides and the not unusual request was made that the said award should be made an order of court. It so happened that this case came on at the very end of the Trinity term; the judge, so to speak, had his bags packed and his golf clubs in a taxi waiting outside the court: in normal circumstances he would have no need to make a close examina-tion of an agreed arbitration which was embodied in a formid-able looking document of several pages and included the provi-sion that Byrne should pay O'Brien the sum of £20 damages, which sum, it was stated, had already been handed over and generously passed on by the successful plaintiff as a subscription to some charity who duly acknowledged it. So the judge without question agreed to make the award an order of court.

And now O'Brien made his first mistake. He made sure that the case was prominently reported in the evening papers that day. I barely glance at evening papers myself and it was Beryl Eustace (now Mrs Phair) who saved the situation. She rang me up and drew my attention to the report in question. When I read it, I was astonished. Several paragraphs of the arbitrator's award were printed verbatim and I at once recognized that it could only have been composed by O'Brien himself since it con-tained whole sentences of pompous verbiage which were word for word the same as had appeared in some of the letters we received when he was attempting to make his case at the Genealogical

Office. Moreover, it conceded every one of his pretentions and bogus claims. There was need for immediate action.

The Registrar of the High Court, the late Con Curran, was an old friend of mine. I went at once to him and on hearing the facts he agreed with my point of view but explained his difficulty; judges do not like to have their instructions countermanded and the judge concerned had already gone away on holidays. However, Curran held over the formalities and the judge approved of his action when he came back, with the result that the case was listed for rehearing the following November in order that my evidence in the matter might be heard. That newspaper report of the case suggested to the uninitiated that the High Court had in fact endorsed his extravagant claims, so that O'Brien thus had another scrap of paper to add to his plausible collection. He almost succeded in getting a more useful document in this connexion for it was not without considerable trouble that I managed to stop the notice he proposed to insert in *Iris Oifigiuil*, and had already paid for, giving the 'arbitrator's award' in full with a statement that it had been made a rule of court.

These urgent moves made with some success, I had a breathing space in which to examine the position. The first thing I did was to ring up Denis MacMahon to ask him to go forthwith and enquire from Father Patrick O'Donoghue, C.C., of Clarecastle, what on earth he meant by putting his name to so outrageous an award; for the arbitrator's name was Rev. Patrick O'Donoghue and, as O'Brien claimed to have his property in Thomond at Clarecastle, the inference as to the arbitrator's identity was a natural one. Fr. O'Donoghue, however, was amazed at the question, for he had never even heard of the case, much less made an award in it. It thus became a matter for the Guards. The detectives were not long in discovering the alleged arbitrator: he had in fact signed the award and his name was Rev. Patrick O'Donoghue; but the reverend gentleman turned out to be a silenced priest from an English diocese whose address was some obscure lodging house in a squalid street in the Talbot Street area. Christy Byrne appeared to be non-existent and it became clear that O'Brien was in fact himself plaintiff, defendant and arbitrator. He very nearly pulled it off, but I can fairly say I won that round even though he did make some use subsequently of the newspaper report. When the case was called again in November he did not put in an appearance. He was at that date confined in the institution known as John of God's, and to conclude on another comic note the reader is reminded

219

that that institution is situated at Stillorgan Castle and our man was not slow in realizing that this address was well suited to his dignity.

Since the time I ceased to be actively concerned in his affairs I have not much to add. I might mention that one of his abortive moves – the issue of postage stamps by the Principality of Thomond, met with short shrift. He continued the pretence of maintaining an embassy in Dublin – no, he designated it a chancellery and a legation – at 5 Charlemont St. In the 1950 edition of *Thom's Directory* the occupier of these dismal premises formerly entered as 'tenements' is given as 'His Highness, Prince of Thomond' but only for that one year: evidently Thoms smelt a rat and thereafter it was amended to 'R.M.S. O'Brien'.

As I have said my file contains many other items which add to the picture. His later efforts, however, were comparatively feeble, like for example his widely distributed exhortation to the Catholics of Clare to combine to defeat the sinister schemes hatched by the arch-Communists of the Kremlin and their dupes at the Genealogical Office, Dublin Castle.

Mr O'Brien died in Dublin on March 31st of this year (1977). In the notice which appeared in the *Irish Times*, the *Irish Independent* and the London *Times* he is described as Raymond Moulton-O'Brien (hyphenated), Earl of Thomond; the funeral 'service' to take place at Messrs Fanagan's funeral chapel in Aungier St. on April 5th prior to the burial in England (Birmingham) the next day.

As a final word I would like to say Requiescat in Pace.

Appendix B

Some aspects of the Civil Service

1 August, 1952

Though the leave of the Irish civil servant is short compared with that enjoyed by our predecessors under the British régime in the old leisurely days, I have reached a status which carries with it the maximum now allowed – 33 working days, plus the two privilege days allowed at Christmas and Easter, to which we may add six bank holidays. These 41 days judiciously combined with as many as possible of the 52 weekends* and a few more days when, as at present, official business frequently brings me to Limerick or some place near Raheen, enable me to spend quite an appreciable portion of each year at home, provided of course that I am willing to take no holidays in the usual sense but to be satisfied merely with a frequent change of scene. It often happens that my leave is anything but a rest or a relaxation. A few weeks ago, for example, I came down from Dublin by the evening train, arriving at Raheen about 9.15 p.m. I spent that night from 10.15 p.m. till 1 a.m. holding an electric torch in a cold and draughty byre while an exceedingly painstaking vet manipulated and stitched the udder of a recently calved Kerry heifer, whose presence in the herd must have been resented by some old stager of a cow, with the result that she was pushed into a barbed wire fence and the most valuable part of her severely torn. This heifer was giving 4½ gallons of milk per day, a fine performance for a three year old Kerry. I merely mention the incident as a reminder of the difference between leave spent on one's own farm and that of the man who takes three weeks playing golf at Lahinch or cruising in the Mediterranean. I don't think I would trouble to do it if I had not a family to follow me, please God, in the place.

I am still a farmer in Clare as well as a civil servant but I find myself more and more attracted by the fascination of

*At the time this was written the five day week was not yet in operation.

forestry. It is the sense of continuity which makes silviculture so satisfying an occupation. I feel as I see trees taking root and thriving, that even if the exigences of the uncertain world we live in should decree that I should not be followed here by my own descendants, someone at any rate will benefit in the future by what I am doing. A man establishes a pedigree herd or a specialized library and how often does it happen that on his death his life work is dispersed at an auction sale; so too the ruins of the once apparently everlasting landlords' houses of the nineteenth century, to be seen all over the face of the country, are ocular evidence of the futility of imagining that one can leave a mark on the future. But a well-established wood will remain until it is mature; and if the trees planted are hardwoods, with a fair proportion of oaks in their composition, the chances are that it will be there several hundred years hence. I do not seem to mind the fact that the name of the planter of a wood is seldom if ever preserved, so well expressed in the Irish proverb, 'maireann an tor ar an gelaidhe ach ní mhaireann an lámh do chuir', for there is a definite satisfaction in saying to oneself, 'here is something which will last'.

Following the establishment of a Department of Agriculture as a prelude to Home Rule a Forestry Division was added. A. C. Forbes*, an Englishman, was the first Forestry Director. He was followed by one Crozier, a typical Scot of pawky humour and very inelastic ideas on forestry. When his term of office expired, the British régime, under which one expected men of his type to be appointed, was a thing of the past and under the new system his successor had to be chosen by a selection board. In this case the board consisted of an official of the Department of Finance as chairman – it was J. J. MacElligott – my friend, Michael Deegan, the secretary of the Department of Lands (of which Forestry is a branch), another official whose name and personality I forget, and two laymen – Robert Barton and myself. The applications for the job were numerous, some 65 if I recollect aright. Each of us was furnished with a complete copy of the credentials of all of these, perusal of which made it obvious that 40 or 50 of them were quite unsuitable while the other 20 or so had qualifications worthy of careful consideration. The first meeting of the selection board was called for 3 p.m. on a day when there happened to be a Davis Cup match taking

*See Chapter II, pp. 37-38.

place at the Fitzwilliam Club. We have only limited opportunities of seeing first class tennis in Dublin and I bought a ticket thinking that, as I expected play to continue till nearly 6 p.m., I would be able to watch it for an hour or two: I argued that all we had to do that first day was to pick out the more likely candidates and arrange for the more lengthy work of interviewing them on a subsequent occasion. How wrong I was! At 6 p.m. we were still ploughing conscientiously through the list, obvious duds being scrupulously considered, whose claims I personally having read their applications would have dismissed in thirty seconds. Eventually at any rate a preliminary selection was decided on. The dozen or so chosen for further consideration included several from various continental countries – in one case we paid the fare of a Norwegian to come to Dublin by air for interview.

The man who impressed me most favourably was the only Irishman on the list: a genuine Irishman at that with an O name, hailing from Co. Limerick. In voting for him, I was in a minority of one. I may have been wrong because so far from blowing his own trumpet, he was of the self-depreciating type and may have been lacking in the drive necessary in a director whose main function was to be the reorganization and vitalizing of a service which up to then had been somewhat stagnant; but with the arguments used by the other selectors against him, I still do not agree. Most of this man's forestry career had been in India: consequently, they argued, he could know nothing of Irish forestry requirements. My answer was that he was therefore in no danger of starting with preconceived ideas – he would hardly be likely to advocate the growing of mahogany or teak in Ireland – whereas a man with experience in a country not altogether unlike Ireland might tend to favour practices unsuitable to our usually damp summers and mild winters. Moreover, I urged, Mr O'F. knows the Irish people, as well as the Irish climate, and this appears to me to be a prime essential in a Director of Forestry, since so much of the success of an ambitious afforestation programme depends on the acquisition of land from landowners who are far from forestry-minded and on creating enthusiasm in a staff hitherto accustomed to indifference almost amounting to defeatism. As I say, I was in a minority of one so there was no more to be said. I then concentrated on pushing my second choice, one Reinhardt, a German. Barton agreed with me in this; the others were undecided. As usually happens in a committee, when two or three members have decided views and the rest have not, the former carry the day. The result was that Reinhardt was appointed. He was, in fact, only a moderate success and when the War broke out in 1939, he returned to Germany and the senior permanent official, a dour Scot called Dr Anderson, was automatically promoted to the directorship. After a while he resigned, only to be succeeded by another official, again a Scot but not a dour one, an able after-dinner speaker who potters along awaiting his approaching civil service pension. I have hopes that the next director will be the young and energetic Irishman who now occupies the position of chief inspector.

I have been on several of these selection boards and say emphatically that those critics who allege that strings be pulled at them are wrong. The first time I sat on one (in 1944) we spent a whole week interviewing some forty candidates for three positions, two as assistants in the Public Record Office and one, nominally as an assistant librarian in the National Library but actually as my assistant at the Genealogical Office, which is a branch of the National Library. Having sized them all up, I came to the conclusion that a young graduate of University College, Cork, called Gerard Slevin, was the man for me. I did all I could to increase the number of his marks but the system is too rigid to allow of weighting of the scales in any candidate's favour. He got sixth place, but luckily for me three of those above him dropped out for various reasons, so that Gerard ended up third; the first two elected to go to the P.R.O. with the result that I did actually get the man I wanted.

Some remarkable candidates presented themselves for examination. Of these I remember two particularly. There was one abnormally truculent neo-Gael who demanded with marked lack of courtesy that all questions be put to him in Irish. Four of us, Leon O'Broin, Gerard Murphy, Louis Roche and I, did this, somewhat reluctantly on account of his tone, as we had already done willingly when decently requested by a less belligerent Gael. Diarmuid Coffey said he was not proficient enough to conduct a *viva voce* exam. on legal matters in Irish – I forget how that was got over. The culmination came when Prof. Semple, who was the Latin examiner, bluntly stated that he knew next to no Irish and this produced an impasse calculated to invalidate the whole business. If the matter had been carried to its logical conclusion – the constitutional rights and so on – a reconstructed selection board would have had to be set up. The prospect of another three or four months delay was so disturbing that I hastened to propose a compromise which was somewhat reluctantly agreed to. The candidate was allowed to write out in Irish his translation of the Latin passage, which the others had to translate *viva voce* and so he gained thereby a decided advantage. In the event he came out quite low in the markings so no harm was done. The second man startled us on being presented with a page of St Thomas à Kempis to translate by exclaiming 'Oh Janey, take it away'. When asked what he meant by coming before us when he apparently did not know a word of Latin he replied with an engaging grin 'Well now, men, 'tis like this, I'm in for a job under the Tourist Board and I thought it was worth two quid to find out what a selection board is like: I have to face a real one in a few days time'. How he managed to qualify in a competition like ours where a University degree was a *sine qua non* I cannot imagine.

Another incident in that week-long sittings which I recall with a chuckle relates to the only girl who applied. She was Éilís Clune, one of the Quin family and a close relation of Conor's, and let me add, extremely good-looking. Should anyone but myself ever read this page I must explain that each member of the board, as well as awarding marks in his own subject, has to give marks for 'general suitability' and when the chairman asked me for Miss Clune's marking I replied 'Nought'. 'What do you mean, nought' said the chairman. 'Well', I replied 'how could I do any work with that lovely girl in the room?' Of course I did give her quite high marks in fact. Shortly after I chanced to meet Éilís and I said 'I'm after paying you a compliment' and told her what had occurred. She did not get the job but from subsequent experience of her work I think she would have been a good choice.

The system now in vogue for making appointments to the Civil Service undoubtedly to a great extent eliminates wire-pulling and jobbery and it probably is the best method of recruitment, though like all systems which are governed by hard and fast rules, it does not always result in the best man being chosen.

As a result of the immense extension of public services resulting from the socialistic legislation of the past forty years coupled with government participation or interference in industry, transport and even in cultural affairs, the Civil Service has grown into a vast and unwieldy machine which works in a way which would spell bankruptcy to any ordinary commercial concern. How to eliminate some of the red tape which clogs that machine and how to vitalize the personnel which composes it is a problem for which no one has ever propounded a solution, though Capt. Peadar Cowan did, in his election address in 1948, make a few suggestions of a practical nature.

The root of the trouble is that there is little or no incentive to enthusiasm or initiative: a civil servant gets on best if he shirks responsibility and so avoids making mistakes, the tendency below the highest grades being to let someone else make decisions, with the result that the public, who are more and more under the necessity of obtaining official permission to engage in all sorts of activities, have to submit to inexcusable and maddening delays. The only reason things are not worse than is actually the case is that the majority of civil servants are in fact conscientious workers in their easy going and humdrum way. From my own inside experience, I would say that sixty per cent of them do a fair if not very hard day's work; twenty per cent do more than is expected of them and are often overworked; and the other twenty per cent are incorrigible slackers who should be sacked on the spot.

I have had some experience of these maddening delays both inside the Civil Service and as an ordinary member of the public. One such occasion has already been mentioned (see Chapter XIV, page 197). I had another row, or misunderstanding perhaps, with officialdom which is worth recording. In October, 1944, after an interview with Mr O'Kelly, the principal officer in the Department of Finance who attends to such matters, a Scale of Fees for the Genealogical Office was drawn up, and, where such fees involved the employment of artists or searchers not on the regular staff, the proportion of such fees to be paid as remuneration to these external workers was determined, with the understanding that these decisions would be reviewed after two years. When that probationary period had elapsed, I put forward a revised scale increasing the fees in cases where extern workers were employed solely for the purpose of enabling a somewhat higher rate of pay to be allowed to them, since the provisional figures did not give them a living wage. Finance approved the increased fees but did not sanction the increased remuneration pending further details as to why it was proposed. The intermediary, one of our own departmental mandarins, told me to go ahead and put the new Scale in force while reluctant to submit my reasons for increased remuneration to Finance. I said point blank that in that case I would leave the old Scale of Fees as it was. He was horrified at the idea of flouting a Finance instruction, which to his mind was tantamount to *lèse-majesté* and said I must obey. The conversation took place on the telephone and I replied: 'I'm damned if I will' and banged down the receiver. Even Jim Hayes, who is by no means a dyed in the wool conventional civil servant, thought when I reported this to him that I had gone too far, and for several days I lived in a state of suspense, not knowing what would be the consequences of my insubordination. In the event, the upshot was a complete victory for me, for within a week of my rebellion, a minute came from Finance (who were perfectly reasonable throughout) authorizing everything I recommended. There was no delay in that case when I had taken a firm stand.

What the public have to put up with is well illustrated by another personal experience. One of my sons was born while we were living temporarily in South Africa and when he was about ten years old it occurred to me that, in order to ensure his being without question an Irish citizen, I ought to have registered him as such within a year of his birth. It seemed ridiculous that he might technically not be of the same nationality as his brothers who were born in Ireland. I got my solicitor to write to the Department of Justice giving the facts, but without names, and asking for a ruling as to whether the boy was an Irish citizen or not. No reply was received. Just a month later the solicitor wrote again, enclosing a copy of his first letter. No reply! Again a month later he wrote, giving copies of both his previous letters. This communication received a printed acknowledgement and no more. By chance I was consulting my friend (and we like to say distant relative) Michael Lysaght Rynne, legal adviser to the Department of External Affairs, about the egregious 'Prince of Thomond' and, since that person's dubious citizenship was under discussion, it occurred to me to tell Michael of my experience in the matter of the citizenship of my own son. He took up the telephone and had a talk to someone high up in Justice who said he thought the boy was an Irish citizen all right and promised to have the matter dealt with forthwith. In a day or two my solicitor received a detailed reply with an apology for the delay which was due, it was coolly stated, to the correspondence having been mislaid! The not-so-high official whose duty it was to deal with it had received the query three times and he still had the hardihood to plead that most transparent excuse. This is not an isolated or exceptional case. Most people who have to deal with Government departments could give similar if not always such flagrant examples. It is only right to add that in this respect the Department of Agriculture is an exception. As a rule, they answer letters and deal with questions submitted to them expeditiously and efficiently.

Our Civil Service, like that of any democratic country, is on the whole slow and not very efficient but it can definitely be stated that it is not corrupt. Very few indeed of its members can be bought; in fact I have never myself met first-hand evidence of such a thing. Personal pull, however, can of course accomplish much, particularly in expediting something which would normally take a long time to put through. Even without the exercise of any influence the personal interview is worth a dozen letters: the ordinary civil servant whose pen is wrapped in red tape and steeped in stiff and forbidding phraseology is human and obliging if once you get talking to him.

I think I should add here, without going into detail, a brief account of the most noteworthy case of the kind within my personal experience. In May 1972 the Manuscripts Commission unanimously passed a resolution proposing an urgent and essential change in the procedure regarding the production of their publications. On receipt of this the Department of Education arranged that a meeting would be held at which representatives of other interested bodies, notably the Department of Finance, would be present. The date of this was fixed for July 30th. On July 28th we received a message to say that for some reason one of these could not attend on that day and that consequently there must be a postponement. In spite of frequent reminders as to a new date the meeting was actually not held till March 1973 – nearly eight months delay. Accompanied by two other members of the Commission I went on the appointed day to Marlborough Street. On entering the conference room we were met by a junior official who informed us that the man from Finance was not coming and that the senior civil servant in the Department of Education who was officially in charge of the matter was 'busy at another conference'. The said young man knew very little about the case: our visit was a waste of time and inevitably nothing was done as a result of it. I retired from the chairmanship of the Commission soon after that. It is certain that problems which did not exist in 1972 and had nothing to do with the initial procrastination did arise subsequently, but it is remarkable that six years have since passed without a single volume being published by the Manuscripts Commissions whose average publication since its establishment in 1928 had been approximately three books per annum.

Appendix B; Some Aspects of the Civil Service

To end on a more cheerful note I am glad to be able to add that the difficulties have at last been got over and a full publication programme is to be resumed forthwith.

Appendix C

Hurling and rugby

6 September, 1932

I never thought I could feel so dejected at the result of a game as I still do after last Sunday's All Ireland hurling final at Croke Park where I went with other Clare supporters. The last time we won an All Ireland was nearly twenty years ago (1914). Clare led by 3 pts to 2 at half time. Coming up to the final whistle Kilkenny led by 2 points but Clare were attacking and it looked odds on that Tull Considine's puck would find the net and leave us winners, but it went inches wide and so we lost.

Even so I rejoice at the very real revival of hurling in Clare and I wonder will this near triumph result in the game spreading over the whole county – at present it is hardly played at all in west Clare where Gaelic football, that foul a minute game (due to no sensible rules about tackling) takes its place.

This revival has had its reward at last: in 1976 Clare (still however essentially east Clare) reached the final of the National Hurling League and in a replay after a draw were beaten by Kilkenny; in 1977 and 1978 Clare finished winners having defeated their old rivals Kilkenny in the finals of those years.

As well as being a real test of courage and fitness rugby possesses the glamour of the international campaign which arouses an enthusiasm that even the excitement of an All Ireland Final at Croke Park, with its purely local patriotism, can hardly rival.

Ireland has been champion country several times and only narrowly missed being the first country to gain the mythical Triple Crown for three years in succession: but oddly enough it is not the victories but the near-victories which remain most vividly in my mind. Those tantalizing and infuriating 'ifs'! If only Mick Lane (who otherwise played a fine game) had not dropped a pass with the line at his mercy in the last minutes of that drawn Triple Crown game with Wales; if only that ball which struck an upright had fallen to the right instead of to the left of the posts in one match; if only the too corpulent referee had been up to see that vital forward pass in another; and so on. I could write a whole chapter describing famous and thrilling games but this is not the place to indulge in that form of self-entertainment and I will turn to another aspect of the subject.

Rugby has further claims to our adherence: like the G.A.A. the Rugby Union is strictly amateur. There is nothing comparable to the great defect of soccer: the buying and selling of players and the transference of stars from one club to another in the middle of a season. Ugly incidents where players lose their tempers or excited spectators invade the field are not absolutely unknown, but nothing like the rowdy scenes, which occur sometimes at Gaelic games and more frequently at soccer, even necessitating strong barriers and forces of police at the latter, happen when rugby is being played. It also has the great merit of being a unifying influence. Belfast Protestants scrum down with Catholics in green jerseys at Lansdowne Road and find no difficulty in standing to attention there while the Irish national anthem is being played before an international match begins. There are no bans in rugby.

I was delighted when the G.A.A. ban was abolished. If conditions were the same today as they were when the G.A.A. ban was first imposed I would find no fault with it. We were then an occupied country and rugby, though played generally at the large Catholic schools in Ireland, was nevertheless more or less identified with anti-national forces, notwithstanding the existence of the famous Garryowen team in Limerick and the presence of such stalwart Irishmen as the Ryan brothers of that club on the first Irish team to win the Triple Crown nearly seventy years ago. Then the G.A.A. was in its infancy: it was struggling to establish national games in the face of tacit if not overt opposition and to revive the Irish spirit in a community sunk in anglicized apathy. Now, apart from the ecclesiastical sphere, it is the most widespread, the most numerous and most virile institution in the country, and surely needed no artificial prop for self-preservation. Almost every third year at the annual congress a motion for relaxing the ban was proposed (and I may say always supported by the Clare delegates) only to be rejected by a majority. Seldom do I meet a G.A.A. follower who believed in it : it was an example of the truism that the sentiments of a crowd are not necessarily the same as those of its individual components, or, to put it in another way, a determined and narrow-minded but vociferous minority can usually sway the easy-going majority with slogans of a pseudo-patriotic nature. The ban had in fact become a manifestation of inferiority complex mainly on the part of the older members who control the policy of the Association.

When speaking on television in September 1975 Mr Seán Ó Síocháin, the popular and influential secretary of the Gaelic Athletic Association, expressed the opinion that while soccer actively assists the anglicization of Ireland, rugby on the other hand has not that effect. With that view I think most people in this country would concur.

Personally I would like to see hurling substituted for cricket as the summer game at schools, tennis being retained in its secondary position: it would not be practicable to make tennis the sole summer game in a large school without incurring a very large expense in making hard courts; and in any case the team factor, so valuable in school games, is wanting in tennis.

Appendix D

An Irish view of South Africa

Written on board ship in 1938

On my former visit to South Africa, in the course of my abortive semi-official campaign for the furtherance of Irish exports I met several cabinet ministers – they must be the most easily accessible in the world for I at any rate found no official obstacles placed in the way of interviews. During the two years I have actually lived in South Africa, however, I have had no contact whatever with politicians.

Politics, nevertheless, cannot be ignored, they are too much a part of everyday life in the Union. The work I have been doing is not calculated to draw me into the maelstrom: in fact it assisted the detached role I desired to play, for my earned income was derived solely from writing and as a journalist – chiefly free-lance but with a steady part-time job on the Literary page of the *Cape Argus* – my wares were more in demand on any subject in the world other than Union politics. I was commissioned by the *Rand Daily Mail* and other leading dailies and weeklies to write leaders and features on Irish affairs whenever Ireland got into the news, as for example at a general election or the passing of the 1937 Constitution. Between all that and some private literary work of my own, I was kept busy enough without any excursions into politics. On the one occasion I ventured near this field of journalism I was told 'where I got off' in no uncertain manner. Encouraged perhaps by my success as a leader writer on Irish subjects I thought I would compose a short sub-leader on the Eucharistic Congress, which was held in Capetown in 1938. Knowing the editor and his readers I merely welcomed the delegates to the city with the same detached attitude one would have adopted towards the delegates to, let us say, an international conference on polar exploration. There was nothing pro-Catholic about that sub-leader, just common courtesy to visitors, but it found its way into the editor's wastepaper basket just as surely as it would have done had it been obviously written by an enthusiastic Catholic. Thus not even by guile can a Catholic as such get any hearing in South Africa, except through the medium of the Catholic press. The *Southern Cross* is a lively and formidable opponent of all anti-Catholic bigots, exposing their activities most effectively. Now that it has lost its able editor Mgr. Colgan – who died in the pulpit of his Cathedral in the very middle of one of his most impressive sermons – I do not know how far his successors have been able to keep up his high standard.

The ignorant intolerance of this great body of Afrikanerdom is a fact which cannot be denied or explained away; and it is only emphasized by the liberal broadmindedness of a number of the more intellectual Afrikaners – such men, for example, as are to be found among the professors of the Afrikaans-speaking universities of Stellenbosch and Pretoria.

It is possible that the more liberal outlook will eventually prevail, but taking things as they are, and not as they may be at some problematical time in the future, the detached onlooker must come to the conclusion that intolerance is the chief blot on the Afrikaans character. Under modern conditions the need of that ruthless courage and indomitable perseverance which marked the Afrikaners' ancestors is no longer urgent; but their forbears were little inclined to be a tolerant race and the survival of the voortreker spirit is now more evident in their bigotry. This is seen in its more virulent form in their religious outlook, and, as might be expected on the part of a sect professing a puritanical form of Protestantism, their animosity is directed chiefly against Roman Catholics, and to a lesser degree Anglicans.

The hatred of the Dutch Reformed Church for Catholicism leads its members into excesses of abusive language. If these were merely the extempore expressions of heated feelings indulged in by the rank and file, or even by their leaders in moments of excitement, they could be ignored; but so far from that being the case it is not the ordinary man who gives vent to these boorish outbursts of ill-feeling but persons holding responsible positions in the national church.

Die Kerkbode, the official organ of the Dutch Reformed Church, envinces a mentality which is supposed to have died out in the eighteenth century. Its militant Calvinism is indicated by the cant phrases it uses in referring to the Catholic Church, which is described as 'the scarlet woman', 'a national menace' and so on, and its beliefs as 'accursed idolatry'. The abuses which admittedly disgraced the Catholic Church in the early sixteenth century are raked up and paraded for the *Kerkbode*'s simple readers as if they were the commonplaces of today, and its poor dupes have really come to believe that Catholics buy remission of sins for cash, that they worship saints and even that Jesus Christ has no place in the Catholic's creed. There is evidence, however, that the intemperate language of *Die Kerkbode* and its satellites has to some extent defeated its own object, since all its readers are not quite so credulous as to swallow its extravagant charges and some occasionally take the trouble to investigate for themselves with results rather disconcerting to their predikants. Occasionally even the predikants themselves revolt against an official policy which is merely negative and destructive.

Die Kerkbode excelled itself in its attempt to bring about the failure of the Eucharistic Congress which was held in Cape Town in January 1938.

Whatever his personal attitude towards that church may be every fair-minded spectator must have rejoiced that the Congress was a complete success if only because of the nature of the opposition it encountered. The English Protestants, Anglican and Nonconformist alike, refused to participate in the sectarian strife which the Dutch Reformed leaders tried to stir up, while the Mayor and Corporation of Cape Town – a wholly Protestant body – did not hesitate to hold a civic reception to welcome the distinguished prelates and clergy who had come to the Peninsula for the occasion. I personally got a great kick out of seeing the said Mayor, Mr Foster, a Belfast Orangeman by origin, sitting in the front seat of the Cathedral at the High Mass which concluded the week's ceremonies. The very impressive procession on that final Sunday was the largest of a non-military nature ever witnessed in South Africa and fully 20,000 people assembled to listen to the sermon of Mgr Colgan before the steps of St Mary's Cathedral in the square called Stal Plein, where the equestrian statue of the most tolerant of Afrikaners stands, with its simple bilingual inscription: 'Louis Botha: Boer, Krygsman, Staatsman – Farmer, Soldier, Statesman'.

The English papers, by which I mean those published in the English language, were guarded in their references to this Congress and they treated it as of less news value than the wedding of a Jewish stockbroker or the arrival of a liner on her maiden voyage. *The Cape Times* in my time was always inclined to hedge if it was a question of offending some powerful interest and I did not expect the leopard to change its spots. The *Argus* showed more courage: it ignored the actual Congress as far as editorial comment is concerned, but it did have the pluck to rebuke *Die Kerkbode* beforehand, and its outspoken comment on the bad taste and unchristian spirit shown by that journal in choosing its Christmas number to launch a particularly violent attack on a sister faith embracing some 150,000 souls in the Union, and many millions of British subjects elsewhere, must have pierced the thickest hide. The *Rand Daily Mail* of Johannesburg is another paper which consistently showed an independent outlook in dealing with this question. If this hostility were manifested only on certain special occasions it would scarcely be worth more than passing mention, but it is inveterate: examples of it occurred to my knowledge repeatedly in everyday life. To take one instance, when the local council at Mossel Bay appointed (on her professional merits) a district nurse, who happened to be a Catholic, the Dutch Reformed minister of the place announced that the financial support of the members of his church would be withdrawn from the fund which provides for the nurse's upkeep, and this openly on the grounds of the successful applicant's religion. Similarly a movement which aims at practically boycotting Jewish doctors has been set on foot in some Nationalist districts.

The English South African stands aloof from this contest, the protagonists being the Afrikaans-speaking predikants on the one side and on the other principally men of Irish stock with some Germans and a few Hollanders, who, by the way, may be sharply distinguished from Dutch Afrikaners. The Church of England in its native land covers so to speak a multitude of sinners – not that its percentage of criminals is high: it is probably lower than in most denominations, for it is the church of the well-to-do and the respectable. What I mean is that it allows a great latitude of beliefs, and indeed, judging from the Lambeth Conference, of unbelief too: it embraces at once very High Church Anglicans, evangelicals and rationalists of the Dean Inge type. In South Africa it definitely inclines towards ritualism: its members are officially described as Catholics or Anglo-Catholics and many of its clergy encourage the use of the title 'Father'. This predominantly High Church, the Church of the Province, as it is called, is independent of Canterbury, its relation to the parent church being that of daughter to mother. At the same time there is a small but very articulate section of S.A. Anglicans who call themselves the Church of England. Since the death of the first Anglican bishop, the only one consecrated at Canterbury, these people have refused to recognize the 'Metropolitan of the Province' (i.e. the subsequent Archbishops of Cape Town): they still look to Canterbury as their spiritual head. Thus a peculiar situation exists in South Africa, where the spirit of compromise which is the essence of the very existence of the Church of England seems to be wanting.

Even the normally easy-going Anglicans have had experiences of the intolerance of the Dutch Reformed Church at times. When, for example, the Bishop of Bloemfontein suggested the holding of a joint Good Friday service fourteen Dutch Reformed predikants published a letter justifying their refusal on the grounds that the Anglican Church is the Church of the English conqueror. In the same way the Orange Free State synod of the Dutch Reformed Church refused to participate in the World Sunday School Convention describing that body's opposition to discrimination on the score of colour as a challenge to their traditions. Yet from the Dutch Reformed Church conference at Bloemfontein (the capital of the Orange Free State) went forth an appeal for greater tolerance in the political life of the country, an appeal which is endorsed by *Die Burger* and recommended by that influential Afrikaans paper to all Afrikaners. Tolerance, however, in the eyes of these people should, it seems, be restricted to politics. Even in politics, the appeal seems to have fallen on deaf ears, for only a short time after it was made the Congress of the Purified Nationalists in the Cape Province passed a resolution barring Jews from membership of the party; and Dr Malan himself, against the advice of *Die Burger* (his most powerful supporter in the press), refused point blank to acquiesce in the invitation to Gen. Hertzog to lay the foundation of the Voortreker memorial – which was to be extended to him, not, be it understood, in his capacity of Prime Minister, but as an outstanding Afrikaner with a long and distinguished national record.

There is quite a considerable Irish colony permanently resident in and around Cape Town, but never before has it been so much in evidence or so closely drawn together as during that week in January, 1938, when the Eucharistic Congress was held at Cape Town.

From first to last there was a distinctively Irish atmosphere about this Congress. In itself it commemorated the centenary of the coming of an Irishman to that country – Dr Patrick Griffith, the first resident Bishop of South Africa. Most of the priests in the Cape Province and many throughout the Union are Irishmen, if not themselves out from home the sons of Irishmen who emigrated a generation or two ago. O's and Macs, or at least names from which these prefixes have at one time been dropped, are very plentiful among the clergy. No one who heard him speak could have any doubt as to the nationality of Mgr John Colgan, the principal organizer of the Congress. It is not surprising, there-fore, that the men chosen to fill most of the responsible positions in connexion with the Congress itself and whose careful organiza-tion resulted in such smooth working throughout should be Irish by birth or blood.

No doubt there was something unfamiliar to Afrikaner eyes in the procession of the Blessed Sacrament to St Mary's Cathedral and, as it wound its way through the principal streets of the city, its 'idolatrous pageantry' (as they term it) may have been re-pugnant to the feelings of some of the onlookers, if we can judge by the sentiments of hostility which were publicly expressed in most abusive language by men in responsible positions, men who thereby not only showed extremely bad taste and worse manners to distinguished visitors to the Union capital but revived a spirit of intolerance which can only be paralleled in Belfast. The majority, however, of those who witnessed the procession cannot fail to have been impressed by its dignity and reverence.

The opening ceremony, Pontifical High Mass, was held under the shade of the oaks in the grounds of St Joseph's College, Rondebosch. It was a memorable scene: not to be compared, of course, in immpressive grandeur with that wonderful morning when, in Phoenix Park in company with a million people I heard, though faintly*, with a joy that was at once religious and patriotic, the tinkle of St Patrick's bell and was thrilled by the voice of John McCormack as he sang the Ave Maria, but it was none the less remarkable. For in Dublin the great Eucharistic Congress of 1932, like the Emancipation Centenary three years earlier, was an expression of the faith of the great majority of the people of the country, while in Cape Town we were in the midst of a population alien in race and creed. Our very surroundings that day emphasized this. Through the trees we could see, brilliant in the midday sun, the fine buildings of Cape Town University – an essentially non-Catholic institution – looking down on us from the slopes of Table Mountain; in the valley below us the shriek and rattle of electric trains, bearing innumerable citizens, unaware of our existence, to the seaside, punctuated the voice of the preacher; and on the outskirts of the congregation itself here and there men were to be seen – chauffeurs, St John's Ambulance men and the like – who were so little in harmony with the pro-ceedings that they did not remove their hats even at the most solemn moments of the Mass. It was a mixed throng, principally white, with a good many coloured people and a sprinkling of pure

*In my entry of June 27, 1932, I said I did not actually hear it.

African native; and, though they probably understood little of what the Irish preacher was saying and less of the lengthy ceremonial, none was more attentive and devout than two woolly-headed Kaffirs who stood or knelt beside me. Two naval detachments were conspicuous: the one from the British squadron at Simonstown, the other from a German battleship which had been paying an official visit to Cape Town.

If any reminder were needed that we were not in Ireland it would be provided by the prominence given to the British flag. On all occasions where flags are officially flown or draped the Union Jack has been given equality with the South African tricolor, this being the custom in that country at all public events, such as football matches, race meetings, flower shows, and so on. In this connexion it should be remembered that the Catholics of South Africa have no reason to complain of British administration, so far as religious toleration is concerned, and it is of interest to recall the fact that Bishop Griffith was actually supported by a stipend provided by the government, who indeed contributed to the upkeep of clergy of all denominations until about thirty years ago. Previous to the British occupation at the beginning of the nineteenth century, if we except the occasional visits of Catholic mariners from Portugal and Spain before the Dutch settled at the Cape in 1652, it is true to say that the Catholic Church was not permitted to exist in the country. This hostility on the part of the Dutch authorities was carried by the Voortrekkers into their new territory and it was not until the year 1870 that the law of the Transvaal Republic, allowing no other religion within its borders but the Dutch Reformed Church, was repealed as the result of the joint efforts of a French priest, the Portuguese consul and an Irish resident of the name of O'Donoghue.

The national flag flies proudly over the public buildings, but it is the Union Jack which one usually sees ostentatiously displayed by private persons. There is something rather truculent and self-assertive about the demonstrativeness of imperialist sentiment. I well remember the impression made on my mind by the appearance of the town of Port Elizabeth, where I happened to be during my visit in 1928 on the 'appointed day' for the hoisting of the new Union tricolour flag. Port Elizabeth is of course one of the towns where English colonists are strongest. Everywhere the Union Jack was flaunted in your face; wherever you looked you could not escape it: small ones adorned motor cars and buttonholes, middle-sized ones were draped from windows, and some enthusiasts had even taken the trouble to wind enormous stretches of red, white and blue material around their very chimneys. When some weeks earlier mutual agreement in Parliament terminated the long and embittered flag dispute I had listened a little cynically to the somewhat hysterical sentiments of brotherhood expressed on both sides. To an outsider like myself, not yet well acquainted with the peculiarities of South African life, the apparently unanimous manifestation of pro-British feeling which I saw in Port Elizabeth was a revelation of the gulf dividing the two European races in the Union; while to an Afrikaner it must have seemed a mere exhibition of provocative jingoism, a breach of the spirit of the agreement and an incentive to overbearing tactics on his own part when and where he was in the majority.

Appendix E

Two opinions of the author

9 August, 1978

I really must write an account of Charles' [Charles Lysaght] remarkable and controversial career (I might even use the word amazing); however it's not to do that I'm scribbling a diary entry tonight, but to record something he told me the other day: viz. that George O'Brien once summed me up by saying that most people are caterpillars trying to make themselves butterflies but that Ned McL is a butterfly anxious to be taken for a caterpillar.

This reminds me of another reference to myself – I forget who told me of it: talking of the first Senate Ernest Blythe said he had expected MacLysaght to be one of the most useful members of it but in fact he had turned out to be just a crank.

Far from being offended at these comments I recall them both with a chuckle.

Index of Persons

MacDermot, The, 211
McDonnell, Lord, 73, 77
McDowell, Sir Anthony, 79
McDunphy, Thomas, 198
McElligott, J. J., 222
McGilligan, Patrick, 163
McGonigal, Maurice, 147
McGrath, J., 128
McGuinness, Joseph, 65
McKee, Dick, 90, 128n
McKeon, Seán, 129
McKenna, Fr Lambert, 145
MacKenna, Stephen, 54
MacLochlainn, Alf, 204, 205
MacLysaght, Brian, 154, 162
McLysaght, F. P. *see* Lysaght
McLysaght, Katherine, *see* Lysaght
MacLysaght, Máire, 180
MacLysaght, Mary Frances, 16 189, 210
MacLysaght, Patrick (of Kilfenora), 15
MacLysaght, Patrick R., 16
MacLysaght, William (of Ballymarkahan), 8
MacLysaght, William (of Doon), 9n
MacLysaght, William X., 21, 25, 48, 156, 162,
MacMahon, Denis, 22n, 51, 60, 62, 69, 70, 80, 81, 96, 98, 103n, 108, 109, 119, 126, 209, 219
MacMahon, Sir James, 108
MacMahon, Michael, 119
MacMahon, Siobháin, 103n
Macnamara, Brinsley, *see* Weldon, J.
MacNamara, Francis, 29
MacNamara, Henry, 51
MacNamara, Nicolette, 29
MacNamara, Val, 28, 29
MacNeill, Charles, 164
MacNeill, Eoin (John), 64-66, 74, 83, 92, 129, 179
MacNeill, James, 57, 74
McPherson, Ian, 108

McQuaid, Most Rev J. C., 157, 159
MacRory, Most Rev Joseph, 79, 81
MacSwiney, Mary, 132
MacSwiney, Terence, 117
Magee, W. K., 55
Mahaffy, J. P., 73, 79, 83
Malan, Dr, 237
Markievicz, Countess, 79
Martyn, Edward, 52, 58, 80
Maxwell, General, 64
Maunsels, publishers, 59-63
Meehan, Patrick, 185
Merriman, Brian, 208
Merriman, Prof P. J., 153
Midleton, Lord, 84
Moloney, J. D., 98
Moloney, 27
Monteagle, Lord, 56-58
Montgomery, Jim, 140, 141
Moody, T. W., 159
Moore, George, 52, 53, 59, 61, 138
Moore, Maurice, 52, 53, 57-59, 138
Moran, D. P., 33
Moreland, Mr, 20
Morrissey, Paddy, 28
Morrissey, William, 24-28, 42
Moseley, Sir Oswald, 107
Moynihan, Seán, 170
Mulcahy, Richard, 92, 128, 147
Mullins, John, 38
Murphy, Gerard, 224
Murphy, William Martin, 73, 77, 79, 84
Murtagh, Paul, 199

Nailor, Miss, 60
Nash, Gerry, 203, 204, 211
Neale, Michael, 211
Neill-Watson, C., 61-63
Nevinson, H. W., 96
Nicholls, Kenneth, 188
Norton, William, 147
Nugent, 97

As Mac and Mc and formerly M') are usually interchangeable, the form given in this index is that normally used by the person indexed. Where there are several persons under one surname, their usage of course, may be different.